© Copyright 2017 – All rights reserved

In no way it is legal to reproduce, duplicate or transmit any part of this document in either electronic means or in printed format

Recording of this publication is strictly prohibited and any storage of this document is not allowed unless with written permission from the publisher or the author. All rights reserved

Respective authors own all copyrights not held by the publisher.

http://ashleylhunt.com/

Albaterra Invasion

Sci-Fi Alien Romance

Table of Contents

Table of Contents

CLICK & FOLLOW US HERE: 9

FREE STARTER LIBRARY 11

PROLOGUE 13

THE FINDING 17

CHAPTER 1 18

CHAPTER 2 42

CHAPTER 3 62

CHAPTER 4 83

CHAPTER 5 104

CHAPTER 6...125

CHAPTER 7...149

CHAPTER 8...171

CHAPTER 9...191

CHAPTER 10...209

CHAPTER 11...230

CHAPTER 12...248

THE UNFOLDING 270

CHAPTER 1...271

CHAPTER 2...298

CHAPTER 3...319

CHAPTER 4...339

CHAPTER 5 363

CHAPTER 6 387

CHAPTER 7 407

CHAPTER 8 431

CHAPTER 9 453

CHAPTER 10 473

CHAPTER 11 492

CHAPTER 12 513

THE RELEASING 530

CHAPTER 1 531

CHAPTER 2 559

CHAPTER 3 585

CHAPTER 4 611

CHAPTER 5 636

CHAPTER 6 658

CHAPTER 7 684

CHAPTER 8 711

CHAPTER 9 736

CHAPTER 10 760

CHAPTER 11 785

CHAPTER 12 808

Click & Follow us here:

 ashleylhunt.com

 facebook.com/authorashleylhunt

 twitter.com/ashley_lhunt

 pinterest.com/ashley_lhunt

 instagram.com/ashley_lhunt

Free Starter Library

Dear Reader

Before you start traveling to another planet I would like to inform you that I have some Free Books which I am giving them ONLY to my loyal readers!

If you are interested in receiving those books and be informed every time about my new releases just Copy and Paste this link into your browser

http://ashleylhunt.com/tgp5

Fill in the blanks and I will send you your First Free Book!

Thank you again for downloading my Book!

I am sure you will love it!

Kind Reads

Ashley L. Hunt

Prologue

A roar filled the air, and I recognized the voice at once as Rex's. I was struck by two bolts instantly; one of lust and love, and the other of terror he would put himself in danger to save me. I wanted to call out to him, but, before I could, Powell wrenched me from his shoulder and set me on the ground. He spun me around until I was facing the army of A'li-uud, the Elders, and Rex, who were near enough to make out their faces but far enough I would have to sprint to reach them before Powell could catch up. I felt a cool, sharp something against my throat, and Powell tipped my face upward by the chin so I could only see the heads of the A'li-uud rather than their entire bodies. I realized he was holding me at knifepoint.

"We are not here to fight," Powell called out. His voice seemed to disintegrate into the open expanse of prairie lands, but I knew that the A'li-uud had heard him by the distant sounds of clacking and clicking that was their native tongue. Then, quietly to me, he asked, "Do these things speak English?"

"Yes," I muttered back in a voice strained by the fear of accidentally slitting myself with the blade.

"I am Captain Powell of the Epitome," he continued loudly. I saw the eyes of the other Elders staring at him, but Rex's eyes were fixed solely on me, unmoving and intense. "We are here to retrieve the survivors of the Paragon."

The tall, slender form of Vi'den stepped forward, and Powell tightened the knife against my neck. Rex made a move to leap forward, but Vi'den threw out an arm to stop him. They both stood still in their places and looked at Powell, Rex with fury on his face and Vi'den with tolerance.

"I'll kill her if you come any closer," Powell threatened. "I'll slit her throat, and her blood can water the soil of your godforsaken planet."

"I will rip your head off with my bare hands," Rex barked suddenly.

The Finding

Chapter 1

Rex

I didn't think; I just shot.

The herd of hicorn—wild, free-roaming goats with four large, spiral horns—meandered lazily around the vigibrach tree without the slightest sign of unease. Despite their skittish nature and tendency to run at the slightest noise, hicorn were notoriously easy targets for hunting tribesmen, and they were useful from horn to hoof. In fact, most hicorn were killed with a weapon made of a brother goat's horn.

The goats were safe from me today, though. I wasn't hunting for prey. I wanted the predator.

On the opposite side of the herd, its golden eyes fixated on a particularly large hicorn, crept a broad-shouldered sabrecat with teeth as long as my forearm. Its fur was nearly as golden as its eyes, and it blended into the tall plains grass without a problem. The moment I spotted it, I aimed and released my arrow. A fraction of a breath later, the sabrecat screamed coarsely, sending the hicorn into a panicked frenzy, and crumpled into invisibility amidst the grass. I let the goats scatter away before wading through the waist-high plains flora to claim my prize.

It was still breathing when I reached it, but barely so. The arrow had slid cleanly between two ribs and successfully punctured its heart. It was the ideal kill for harvesting meat and pelt. I would, of course, bring the beast back to the village, but I was interested in its sabres. They were the ideal close-range weapon. The curvature fit perfectly into my hand, and the pointed ends were so sharp they drew blood with the merest graze.

I preferred hand-to-hand combat. Most of my warriors were skilled marksmen and dangerous sharpshooters, but I reveled in the beauty of a kill up close. I was renowned across Albaterra for my lethal melee; it had been that trait to tip the scales in my favor for Tribe Elder after the civil war had left the Campestria Kingdom without one. Some of the other Elders had been wary of appointing me due to my youth, but the youngest tribe Elder in A'li-uud history had been one hundred and seventeen, so it was overlooked.

The sabrecat let out its last breath and finally became motionless. I crouched down beside it and ran my fingers through its fur. It had a thick coat, beautifully intact with no mange to be seen. *It would make a lovely blanket.* I wrapped my fingers around the arrow's shaft, eased it off the body, and wiped it clean of blood once it was extracted.

There was something magnificent about death. It commanded respect and care, but, more than that, it served as a reminder of the Grand Circle. I lowered myself further to the ground until one knee pressed into the soil, and I dropped my gaze to the creature's open, lifeless eyes to silently thank it for its sacrifice. To have foregone this action would have been egregious blasphemy. It was A'li-uud law to revere our planet for all of its gifts. To treat the cat's end without entitlement would have been to spit on the laurels of the Grand Circle. It was a crime punishable by death.

My ears pricked as I heard the sound of footsteps coming up from behind me, but I didn't move from my position. The steps ceased when they drew just a few strides nearer.

"I don't mean to interrupt, Wise One." The voice was that of Ca-es'a. He was an unshakably loyal warrior who had joined the ranks as a child when his parents became casualties of the civil war. *He was perhaps the warrior I trusted most.*

I got to my feet and turned around to look at him. Were it anyone else, I would have continued with the preliminary cleaning of the sabrecat, but I had great respect for Ca-es'a and demonstrated it.

"I was finished," I said. "What happened?"

"We just received word that the Tribal Elders have called for an emergency Forum. I was sent to fetch you at once." He stood stiff and straight-backed as he spoke. I normally would have given him permission to relax, but the news of the Forum had me distracted.

"Thanks, Ca-es'a," I said. He nodded once in acknowledgment, and I motioned to the fallen cat. "Take this back to the village. Have it cleaned and gutted, but make sure the sabres are kept for me."

"Yes, Wise One," Ca-es'a replied. Before the last syllable fell from his lips, however, I had already departed.

The Forum was held inside the gates of P'otes-tat Ulti, which marked the single point where all eleven Kingdoms of Albaterra met. To reach P'otes-tat Ulti on foot was a sixteen-day journey from my village, and flying was still nearly two days away. Tribe Elders, however, were granted the power to travel with the winds, a ritual in which our souls gripped the aether of Albaterra, and it moved us through space and time. It was no harder to do than blinking, but it was a sacred practice and one never to be abused.

Moments later, I stood outside of the intricate gates of P'otes-tat Ulti. A breeze brushed across my cheek, and I saw another Elder beside me.

"Rex," he said acknowledging my presence with a nod of greeting.

"Nice to see you, Duke," I replied. "Do you know what this is about?"

"No idea." He stepped forward to the gates, and then his body passed through the thick bars as though they weren't there at all. I followed suit and kept pace with him as we walked to the massive doors that would admit us to P'otes-tat Ulti.

The doors were exquisite in their perfection and intimidating in their guard. Upon their appointment, all tribe Elders were told of P'otes-tat Ulti's secrets, starting with the doors. They were constructed of each kingdom's finest and strongest materials. I could see hicorn horns and the teeth of sabrecats in their eye-bending designs, meshed amongst the sparkling purple aspex minerals of the mountainous Montemba Kingdom and the Altisuam wood from the Truncata rainforests. Duke pressed his fingertips to a section of aspex just as the doors opened and granted us entry.

As usual for the Forum, the chamber was dimly lit by firelight and smelled of Albaterran musk. Duke and I were the last to arrive, but the room was silent despite the other nine Elders' presence. We took our seats—mine to the left of Duke—and waited for the Forum to begin.

Vi'den, the Elder for the Kingdom of rolling hills known as Finiba, stood. He was a very tall, very thin A'li-uud of great age and renowned wisdom. In his calm, clear voice, he said, "we shall take presence. Elder Vi'den Et'Solum Fini'tribus of Finiba."

The others around the circle of firelight stood one-by-one, just as Vi'den had, and announced their names and kingdoms.

When it was Duke's turn, he got to his feet and said loudly, "Elder Du'ciact Et'Petrum Montem'tribus of Montemba."

I allowed the proper moment of silence to pass before mirroring the action. I rose from my seat, looking through the smoke rising from the fire, and spoke. "Elder Rexstrenu'us Et'Herba Cam-pes'tribus of Campestria."

"Forum shall commence," Vi'den announced.

We all took our seats again, save for Vi'den, who started to explain the topic of the Forum.

"It has come to our attention that our galaxy has been penetrated. At least four human ships have breached the borders of Andromeda, and one, in particular, is very near to Albaterra." Suddenly, there were several sounds of fury and unhappy surprise at this news, but I remained quiet to find out what we already knew about this.

"The course of action is at the discretion of the Tribe Elders."

"Blast'em all!" Shouted the burly Elder of the cave Kingdom.

"Take them hostage!" Another one said.

"Detonate Earth!" Another one shouted.

The outcries of rage layered over one another until the chamber was filled with the din of angry voices. I looked at Duke, and he, too, looked irate.

"What do you think?" I asked, my voice low.

"I don't know," he muttered sourly, "but they certainly need to be stopped."

I nodded in quiet agreement. Vi'den waved a commanding hand through the air to silence the yelling Elders.

"We will discuss this peacefully and rationally," he said, his tone firm. "This is not a matter to be handled with rash impulse."

"Peace be cursed!" Barked back the cave Elder. He slammed his fist on the arm of his chair. "They're pests, the lot of them. Exterminate them now before they infest Albaterra."

"I agree," I said suddenly. All eyes turned to me. Some of the Elders seemed surprised by my input, but the expression on some of the others' faces made it clear they didn't care to hear my opinion. I was used to such a response; my young age tended to impair my credibility, as far as some of the Elders were concerned. "We can't wait for the A'li-uud race to be at risk, or, worse, injured, before we take action."

There was a smattering of agreement, and Duke gave me one hearty nod of approval.

"We need to find out what they want," said Ma'ris, Elder of Albaterra's only underwater Kingdom. His voice was garbled and gravelly, almost as though he spoke with bubbles in his mouth. I had to strain to understand what he was saying. "We need to question them."

"As honorable as I find your amicable intentions, Ma'ris, humans are not known for their honesty," Vi'den replied.

"There are ways of making them talk," Duke snarled with surprising viciousness. The cave Elder grunted his agreement.

"They don't know about us, though," I interjected. "What is the great danger?"

The response I received was as if I had suggested we turn Albaterra over to the humans immediately. Everyone began talking, some yelling, and a few Elders jumped to their feet. Duke stared at me with a visceral expression of disbelief and disgust.

"You don't know what you're saying, boy," Ma'ris rumbled.

"Traitor," spat the cave Elder.

"Quiet," Vi'den intoned loudly. The chamber fell silent again, but I could still feel glaring eyes on me. He looked around as he spoke. "Rex is new to Elderhood and speaks out of ignorance. If he is to learn, then we need to teach him."

"With all due respect, Vi'den," I interrupted, "I'm very comfortable in my Elderhood. My point was that we have an advantage. Humans are self-destructive by nature. Blend that with their utter lack of knowledge about the existence of A'li-uud, and there is nothing to fear."

"You're naive," the cave Elder growled.

"And you're bloodthirsty," I shot back.

He grinned toothily at me. "I say we put a hole through their planet and call it a day."

"You're willing to kill an entire species of intelligent beings to prevent an undetermined level of risk to our people?" I asked, appalled.

He leaned forward in his chair and stared directly into my eyes. "You're not?"

I said nothing. Soundless tension expanded within the confines of the chamber, prompting Vi'den to speak.

"Let us address this in pieces," he said. "First, and most importantly, the ships in the galaxy. Andromeda has already been compromised, but a ship is making its way to Albaterra at an alarming speed. We need to come to a decision about this now."

"They need to be destroyed," Duke said. He turned to look at me. "Even you can't disagree with the level of risk those ships pose."

I sighed and shook my head. "No, I can't."

"Anyone else?" Vi'den asked, looking around the circle of Elders. Heads shook, and Vi'den nodded once. "So be it. All human ships inside the borders of the Andromeda galaxy will be eliminated, beginning with the ship closest to Albaterra."

"So it shall be," everyone said in unison.

"Now we must decide on what to do regarding the general human population," Vi'den continued. "Perhaps there is no decision to be made. Perhaps there is a dreadful one to be made. Let us open the floor."

"I've said my piece," the cave Elder said loudly.

Ma'ris looked sagely to Vi'den. "I believe they should be questioned. We do not know if they have any information about us. Our spies know only what they learn through the masses. It stands to reason they could know just as much about us as we do them."

"What reason?" Duke asked. "Humans are about as smart as hicorns."

"They are intelligent beings," Vi'den said wisely. "They are capable of growth and expansion both as individuals and a species. That, Duke, is to be acknowledged and respected."

"And feared," Ma'ris added.

"It seems," Vi'den went on, "that we have two very different opinions to consider. Are there any others someone would like to add?"

He looked around again as everyone shook their heads one more time.

"Very well. We shall vote then. Those in favor of destroying Earth and the extinction of the human race?"

The cave Elder shot his hand in the air with such vehemence he almost toppled off his chair. Several other hands, including Duke's, joined his. I tried to count how many there were, but the hands were retracted before I could see through the smoke properly.

"Those in favor of journeying to Earth to question the humans?"

I raised my hand, as did Ma'ris and Vi'den himself. Again, I tried to count how many hands were in the air, but the smoke was too thick to see through to the other side of the circle.

"It has been ruled, then. After eliminating all intruding ships in Andromeda, A'li-uud shall be sent to Earth to question human officials." The cave Elder pounded his chair again, but Vi'den ignored him and continued to speak. "We will meet again in two days to begin devising our plan."

He dismissed us, and everyone clambered to their feet. Being the nearest to the door, I exited first with Duke following close behind me. We stood aside to allow the others to pass so we could talk.

"That was interesting," I said when we were finally alone.

"My biggest concern is the ships," he said, looking up at the sky. "We don't know what their intentions are or what kind of weapons they have onboard."

"No, we don't," I murmured, following his gaze upward. The sky was clear, disturbed only by the pale purple flourishes of daytime. I shook my head. "Well, we—"

My words dropped into nothingness as I looked back down and realized Duke had already gone. I was alone.

Chapter 2

Tabitha

"Do you ever wonder if it's all pointless?"

I looked over at Leanne. She was reclining on her bed, hands clasped together across her chest and a faraway expression on her face.

"What's all pointless?" I asked.

"This mission," she answered, but she didn't look at me as she spoke. "Do you ever wonder whether there's anything to find? Like, what if we were sent out here for no reason?"

"You mean intentionally?"

"Not necessarily," she said, finally turning to face me. "Although that's a possibility as well."

I shrugged. "Not really. We would be pretty naïve to think we are the only creatures in the universe."

"It's never even crossed your mind?" She probed.

"I guess it has once or twice," I admitted. "I just don't dwell on it."

She sighed and resumed staring at the ceiling. "You're such an optimist, Tabitha."

"No, I'm not. I'm just realistic."

Leanne smiled with veiled amusement, and then said idly, "I'm so hungry."

I glanced at my watch and got to my feet. "Speaking of that, I should get to the kitchen."

"Don't you ever get tired of serving people?" She asked, also getting to her feet. She moved to the mirror to pluck her stray hairs into place.

"No more than you get of taking their measurements," I replied with a snarky grin.

Leanne turned around to face me, with her hands on her hips. She was the seamstress aboard the *Paragon*, and it showed. Even on a spaceship hurdling through an unknown galaxy at impossible speed, Leanne was the very image of fashion. She was the only crew member who insisted on wearing Armani and Chanel when she wasn't in uniform.

"When are you going to let me make you that dress?" She demanded.

I rolled my eyes. "What do I need a dress for? The *Paragon* prom?"

"You're so frustrating." She walked over to me and smoothed the hem of my shirt down. "You'd be a total knockout. You have such a nice shape, not like those stick-figure supermodels I was making clothes for in Milan."

I batted her hands away and said, "aren't supermodels supposed to be the measuring stick for beauty?"

"Please," she scoffed. "You know why supermodels have to be so skinny? It's because a body with no shape allows the designer to create whatever shape they want out of the garment. It's a blank canvas. You're not a blank canvas. You're a masterpiece."

I couldn't help but blush a little. I was by no means self-conscious about my appearance, despite being aware of having a few extra pounds. I received plenty of attention from men, but

Leanne's compliments were so genuine and heartfelt that I felt embarrassingly adored.

We exchanged goodbyes, and I headed for the kitchen. I had been hired on the *Paragon* crew as the chef when I had unknowingly served my perfected Beef Wellington to a NASA recruiter. Space travel had never been on my bucket list, but the prospect of literally getting off the planet had been extraordinarily appealing at the time. I had accepted the offer without much thought. Leanne and I had met during orientation when she'd eyed my blouse and insisted on—in her words—bringing me out of the past and into the present.

I continued thinking about my conversation with Leanne as I prepared tonight's dinner - Salisbury steak. *I hadn't been entirely truthful with her;* it had crossed my mind more than once that we would return to Earth with nothing to show for our time in space. It just wasn't as big of concern for me as it appeared to be for her. My decision to join the *Paragon* crew had much less to do with being a part of something huge. *Instead, it had almost everything to do with escaping my past.*

Even as I sautéed the massive pan of green beans, I could still see his face in my mind, bloodied and blank. His lips were parted as if he was about to speak, and he stared at me so intently I wasn't able to look away. His fingers were wrapped around my wrist so tightly I could feel my veins pulsing in an effort to circulate through my hand. I hadn't realized I was screaming until I choked on my own voice.

    It had all started in college. His name was Patrick and was the ultimate all-American guy. He was a football player, part of a fraternity, and he was majoring in Business Management. He came from money, which I'd realized the first time I'd seen him driving his Porsche. He'd been the kind of handsome that physically stopped women in their tracks. I wasn't immune to his structured jawline, the aristocratic nose, and the suggestive blue eyes. His charm and wit had only served to draw me under until I was drowning with heart-wrenching, gut-rolling, mind-numbing love for him.

Like all things, it had been good for a while. I'd go so far as to say it had been amazing. It had been thrilling for me to be chosen by such a man, not because I didn't have self-confidence but because I'd idolized him so desperately. Little had I known. Patrick was drinking in my adoration and reciprocating with a poisonous cocktail of shameless devotion and unyielding dominance.

He'd done his job well. The first time he laid a hand on me, I didn't even question it.

Two years and countless bruises later, I was finally free of him.

I shook my head violently, trying to shake the images off my brain, and turned my focus to the food. Cooking was the one thing in the entire world—*no, the entire universe*—that kept me sane. It was cathartic, therapeutic in its methods and manipulations. It gave me the creative freedom to explore different flavor combinations and plate arrangements, but it was also regimented in its instruction and execution. *I felt balanced when I cooked.*

Of course, it was just a bonus to hear how wonderful my food was.

As usual, I served dinner to the crew instead of eating with them, despite having a sous chef and a handful of kitchen staff. I plated each meal myself and handed it off with a smile. While the *Paragon* was a huge ship, the crew itself was small: ninety-seven people. In truth, I didn't know everyone, but I'd learned everybody's name and learned the rest from Leanne. She was an unabashed gossip. Having her on board was like having an outer space edition of *TMZ*.

"Hey, beautiful."

Trey Jones stepped up in front of me and winked. I had to restrain myself from rolling my eyes. He was a mechanic onboard who was persistently trying to date me—or sleep with me, most likely. I had turned him down at least six times already. He was actually rather attractive with his sandy blonde hair and well-toned form, but his overt and explicit personality repulsed me.

"Hello, Trey," I said, trying to inject as much ice into my tone as I could.

"What has the chef prepared for me tonight?" He asked, looking at the food hungrily. I silently wished it was the only thing he would look at hungrily.

"Salisbury steak," I said. Pointedly, I added, "It's Walt Clark's favorite."

Trey turned to look around the dining hall for Walt, who was several tables away. His mouth was full of steak, and each of his hands was holding a hunk of bread. He was a portly guy with exceptional knowledge of computers. I didn't consider myself friends with Walt, but I found him a very nice guy; *I felt a little bad for using him to dig at Trey.*

"Well, every dog has his day," Trey said sarcastically before turning back to me. "Why don't you join me for dinner, beautiful?"

"I have to finish serving, Trey," I replied absently. "And you're holding up the line."

He stepped aside to allow the person behind him forward, but he didn't walk away. Instead, he reached to me and brushed his fingers through my ponytail. I lurched backward in surprise.

"I love curly hair," he said. "They're so sexy."

I didn't respond as I handed a plate to another diner.

"I bet it looks even sexier down," he purred, leaning closer to me. "Like those chocolate curls, you put on your cheesecake."

At my wit's end, I slammed my gravy ladle down onto the table top and turned to him with the meanest glare I could muster. "Trey, I am trying to work. These people are hungry, and it's my job to feed them, so either throw on an apron and get scooping or sit down and shut up."

Several of the crew members waiting in line for their food whooped and clapped. One of them even barked out, "Yeah!"

Trey's cheeks reddened slightly, though not nearly as much as I would have liked. His ego, however, was too swollen to allow much room for proper shame. He yanked the plate I'd just finished making from my hand and stalked across the dining hall to the opposite side. He sat down and jammed his fork into the steak as though it had personally offended him.

I reached for my ladle again, but, before my fingers made contact, I was suddenly thrown to the ground. My ears exploded with the gritty, deafening sound of a blast, and my stomach lurched as the very floor beneath me rocked violently from side to side. Before the roar from the blast could leave my ears completely, I was assaulted with the screeching wail of alarms.

We'd been hit.

The realization hit me in the face like a mallet, and my stomach lurched again, this time in terror rather than in response to the haphazard motion. I instantly felt like I wanted to vomit from fear, *but I knew I had to get myself together, and I had to do it quickly.* I reached for the lip of the table and pulled myself up. The sight that met my eyes was just as frightening as the initial hit had been.

The food had gone everywhere. Slabs of Salisbury steak had been flung across the floor, drenched in puddles and smears of gravy. Green beans were scattered across tabletops like beads from a broken necklace. Gobs of mashed potatoes were piled randomly all over the ground, creating a miniature mountain range of starch. Torn and tattered slices of bread rolled from one end of the room to the other with each heave of the ship.

 Amidst the culinary havoc, crew members were running clumsily to the doors, fighting against the ship's aggressive movements. I watched Walt Clark slip in a pool of gravy and land on his chin. Trey had already gone, probably to the engine room to help. Leanne was nowhere to be found, but I hadn't seen her come into the dining hall at all that evening. It was almost like watching ants race to the entrance of their anthill, sprinting in droves to safety. Crew member after crew member ducked out of the doors, presumably to go to their emergency zones. At that time I remembered I had a zone to report to as well. Every member of the *Paragon* had received training outside of their field, including basic medical training and emergency maneuvers.

I pulled myself all the way to my feet and joined the chaotic crowd flooding the dining hall exit. Even through the shrieks and yells and commands, I could make out a few words here and there.

"Move! I'm with the command center!"

"We're not going to make it! We're not going to make it!"

"GET TO YOUR ZONES!"

I closed my eyes briefly as I was jostled from all sides, and, once again, the image of Patrick's bloody face flashed behind my eyelids. It had never occurred to me when I'd accepted my place on the *Paragon* that I might never make it back to Earth, but I steeled myself against the idea. *I was going to do everything I could to make sure everyone returned home safely.*

And, if I never made it back alive, I sure as hell wasn't going to spend my last minutes thinking about him.

Chapter 3

Rex

The smell of hicorn meat filled the house and had my mouth watering as if I hadn't eaten for days. I loved my mother's cooking, so much that I came by my parents' house several times a week for a meal. My father always commented on the irony that I was Tribe Elder with anything I wanted at my beck and call, but still depended on my mom to make my dinner. Of course, I knew he enjoyed having me visit so frequently. At the very least, it offered them some relief from taking care of my little brother and sister, who had been surprise twins.

"You look tired, my *parva'li*," mother said sympathetically, stroking my cheek with love.

"Beni," my father interjected. He sounded exasperated, as he often did when Mother doted on me. "He's an Elder, not a baby."

"He'll always be my baby," mother crooned, stroking my cheek again.

I smiled back at her. I certainly wouldn't have allowed my mom to behave in such a way with me in front of other tribesmen, and definitely not in front of other Elders. However, I didn't mind her doing so in the confines of the home. *I knew it made her happy.*

"The hicorn smells great," I commented with a hearty sniff. "Did you do something different?"

Before she could answer, Igno—my little brother—shrieked. "Who! Who!"

Mother, father, and I all looked around to see where he was pointing. Through the window, I could see the approaching figure of a woman. I recognized her instantly. My parents did as well, and they shot looks back and forth between each other. *They thought I couldn't see it.* I ignored them and got to my feet.

"I'll be right back," I told them.

I had stepped out of the house before she drew near enough to announce her presence, and we met on the walkway. Her name was Pugna'ta, a beautiful tribeswoman with exquisite cheekbones and a figure that made A'li-uud men quiver. Her skin was as azure as a clear-day sky, which was a rare trait in our race, but it appeared lighter than it actually was in contrast with her long, braided, silvery-white locks.

"I knew you'd be here," she purred.

I offered her a small, unemotional smile. "Hello, Pugna'ta."

There was no bad blood between us, but Pugna'ta and I had a history; one I was insistent on never repeating again. We had engaged in a very brief, very intimate relationship many years ago. It had ended with mutual disinterest and a vivid knowledge of one another's bodies. Pugna'ta was a warrior of my kingdom, widely regarded as merciless and lethal in battle. I considered her indispensable to my militia, but my desire to have her around no longer went beyond those lines. Prior to my being made Tribe Elder, she had reciprocated those feelings. Since my crowning, however, she had taken to showing up at my parents' house, as well as mine, on a fairly regular basis with an excuse flimsy enough to see through but legitimate enough not to question.

I wasn't foolish. I knew her interest in me was power-deep.

"It's been a while," she said smoothly. "How is the Honorable Rexstrenu'us?"

"I'm well, thanks. What can I do for you?" I asked crisply.

She tossed her braid over her shoulder, and I could clearly see slight irritation marring her otherwise perfect features. *I didn't care.* If I gave her even the slightest hint of possible interest, she would jump on the opportunity to sink her claws in.

"I've heard some things," she replied. "Disturbing things."

"About what?" I asked abruptly growing a little annoyed. I knew Pugna'ta and her games, and I knew she would draw out the conversation as long as she could in hopes of being invited inside. *I wasn't interested in playing her games tonight; I wanted to eat mother's hicorn.*

Her eyes narrowed, and I realized she was actually serious. "Humans."

"What about humans?"

"Look," she said suddenly, sounding snappish and short-tempered. "I know you were at the Forum and you know what I'm talking about. This is serious."

I maintained my calm as I said, "I know this is serious. What I don't know is how you know anything about what was said at Forum, being you're not an Elder and surely not present."

"I have my ways," she said dismissively.

It took a lot of effort on my part not to interject my own comments to that. Pugna'ta certainly did have her ways, and she was less than moral. It wasn't surprising to me at all that she would stoop to such a level, but I couldn't help wondering which Elder had been the one to bend to her will.

"The point is that we're at risk. Albaterra is at risk," she continued. "Never in our history have humans gotten so close to our planet. Our great advantage was knowing about their existence while they knew nothing of ours. That might have been compromised now."

"I am aware of this, Pugna'ta," I said exasperatedly. "What's your point?"

"My point is that we need to do something," she hissed, stepping closer to me.

"We are doing something. And, by 'we,' I mean the Elders."

She scoffed, rolling her head back with cynical amusement. "As long as that peace-monger Vi'den is running the forum, we're not doing *anything*."

My movement was swift and aggressive. I slammed my forearm into her throat, sending her flying backward. She landed off the path in the waist-high grass on her back. I heard bustling from inside the house and knew my family was watching everything that was happening, but I didn't restrain myself. Walking to where she lay, I looked down at Pugna'ta with daggers in my eyes.

"I ought to have you locked away for that," I said icily.

She scrambled to her feet, looking disheveled and furious. "How dare you," she seethed.

"You've got that backward," I said. "It's a crime to disrespect an Elder, you know."

For a moment, I thought she was going to attack me. Then, her face mellowed, and she looked at me with wide eyes.

"I'm sorry, Rex," she murmured. Her tone was layered in false innocence, and she kept her gaze trained on mine. "I was out of line."

I didn't reply. In truth, had she spoken ill of any other Elder, I probably wouldn't have even addressed it. Vi'den was my mentor, though, and an exceptionally kind soul. I was unyieldingly defensive of him, and I wasn't going to let anyone—much less the haughty Pugna'ta—dishonor him.

"Really," she said, closing the space between us and tracing a finger along the muscles of my chest. "I'm truly sorry, Rex."

I grabbed her wrist and eased it back to her side. "What do you want, Pugna'ta?"

She pouted slightly with my rejection but said, "I want to help."

"What do you mean?" I asked. "How?"

"However you need me to," she replied silkily. Again, she lifted her finger to my chest and dragged it along my pectorals, but I didn't stop her this time. She looked at me with earnest, suggestive eyes and added, "I want to offer myself to you in any way I can."

The offer was double-edged, and there was no good way for me to answer. If it became necessary for us to go to war with the humans, Pugna'ta would be a vital resource. Her sword skills alone could slay an army. She also, however, was implying something much more personal, and to accept or turn down one offer would be to accept or turn down the other. Of course, as Tribe Elder, she would go to war if I commanded her, but Pugna'ta was the stubborn type of individual who was at her best when she wanted to be.

Finally, I settled on a response. "Thank you, Pugna'ta. I'm glad to have your support."

"Always," she murmured.

"Let me walk you to the post," I said pointedly.

She shook her head. "No need, My Liege. Why don't you just"—she brushed the tip of her finger over my lips—"get back to your family?"

I waited outside until she reached the post that marked my parents' property anyway, mainly to make sure she wasn't going to turn around and come back. She threw a coy look to me over her shoulder before taking off at a sprint, and I knew I could finally go back inside.

"Is everything okay?" My father asked once I closed the door behind me.

I quickly ran through my options in my mind. I could tell them everything was fine and pretend the nature of Pugna'ta's calling was purely social, or I could tell them something was going on. If I opted for the latter, I would have to decide how much information to share. Had it been anyone else, I would have shared very little, but, since they were my parents, I chose full disclosure.

"Pugna'ta visited to offer her help with a recent crisis," I said slowly. My mother and father exchanged looks immediately, but I continued to speak. "The Elders were called to Forum today—"

"What's going on?" Father interrupted. His tone was sharp and brusque, and I knew it was because he was worried.

I sighed and leaned in close to them so that my siblings wouldn't hear. "I'm going to tell you, but you cannot tell anyone. I mean it. This could be a life-or-death matter."

"Son," my father said, putting a hand on my shoulder, "just tell us what's happening."

I looked at him. He stared back at me with a hard, concerned gaze. I turned my eyes to my mother, and she gave me a small nod of reassurance.

"Humans have entered our galaxy," I said. I tried to keep my voice calm and level to prevent them from panicking, but my mother's eyes opened wide immediately, and my father stiffened. "We have knowledge of at least four ships within Andromeda, and there is one ship approaching Albaterra."

"Oh," Mother said softly, placing a hand to her mouth.

"A vote was taken and passed to destroy the known ships within Andromeda's borders, starting with the one nearest Albaterra, of course. Another vote was taken as to our next move after destroying the immediate threat. It was agreed that A'li-uud would go to Earth to question human leaders." I inhaled a brief, slightly shaky breath and added, "we don't know if they are aware of our existence or not."

"I thought that was known," father said loudly. He sounded angry. "We've been told they didn't know of us."

I nodded. "That was what we honestly believed. Now that they're so near, we can't be sure. It's possible they just happened to be across our galaxy and Albaterra and have no idea we're here. However, it's equally as possible that they're here for a reason."

Mother's eyes were as wide as saucers, and she looked over at my little brother and sister. I knew she was frightened, but I had nothing to say to reassure her.

"Does Vi'den believe they know about us?" Father asked. My father and Vi'den had known each other for many years, and much of my father's concerns for the well-being of the A'li-uud race were alleviated in knowing Vi'den ran the Forum.

"He didn't say, but I don't think he believes—"

My words were cut off by a sudden, ground-shaking boom, and my father and I both jumped to our feet. Mother raced to my siblings and tugged them into her arms, but Igno tried to disentangle himself from her as he yelled, "Oh no! Oh no!"

"Quiet, Igno!" I barked, and he silenced immediately. There was another boom, smaller this time, and I turned to my father. "Stay here. Protect them."

"You can't go alone!" He said.

"They need you more than I do right now," I told him. "Stay."

Had I still been a child, he never would have listened to me. As his Tribe Elder, however, I had authority over him, and he knew it. He inclined his head in a show of obedient respect, and I darted out of the door.

I scanned the horizon for any sign of trouble or disturbance, and I found what I sought almost at once. Sooty smoke rose in billows across the plains, and I could see the flickering glow of flames within the curls. The source was too far away to see from my parents' walk, so I took off at a run toward the smoke. I reached down as I sprinted to ensure I was armed, and, as I drew nearer, I was glad I did.

In the eye of the smoke cloud, there was a ship.

Chapter 4

Tabitha

I woke up to blindness and a strange, high-pitched buzzing in my ears. It felt like my eyes were open, but I couldn't see a thing. My muscles tensed as I started to panic, and I didn't even notice how sore I was until I moved my legs to kick at whatever was on top of me. I realized with horror that the *Paragon* had crashed, and I was trapped under the wreckage.

The stink of acrid, burnt rubber and thick smoke filled my nose and forced me to choke back vomit. All I could hear was that buzzing, and I didn't know if it was from the sudden pressure change which had occurred when the ship careened into the atmosphere or something else. I gritted my teeth and forced my legs upward in an attempt to shove the object above me away. I felt it give slightly, but not nearly enough to move it. *My panic increased as I wondered if would die of starvation trapped here.* I tried again, and it gave a little more. On the third try, it separated from its other parts with a loud whine of protest, and I was instantly dazzled with weird, white sunlight.

I righted myself and started to awkwardly maneuver through the warped metal of the destroyed ship. I was certain I was going to throw up at any moment now, and my vision was blurry in such a way that everything I saw seemed to have a disconcerting ripple effect. After what felt like hours, I was free, and I collapsed onto the ground like a dropped puppet.

The grass beneath me was bizarre. It was tan in color, but it was brighter and more vibrant than the kind of grass I was used to. It felt as soft as gray dandelion fuzz. Through the tall blades, I made out the forms of several bodies gathered around the ruins of the ship, and my stomach rolled violently as I realized they weren't moving. The buzzing was finally fading away into a soft hum, and I pricked my ears for any noise inside the *Paragon*, hoping against hope that those inside were still alive. I didn't hear a thing except for the crackling of flames.

    I realized that, if there were any survivors, I might be their only chance. I inhaled deeply and was instantly struck by what I breathed. The air was different, cleaner, almost sharp in its purity. It seemed to take less effort to fill my lungs and satisfy my need for oxygen. I let out the breath slowly and methodically, counting each second as a measuring stick. Then, I shakily got to my feet again.

My eyes had finally adjusted to the white light, and I was instantly paralyzed with awe as I saw my surroundings. The peculiar grass seemed to stretch for miles on flat, limitless land until it met with an ethereal sky of turquoise and lavender swirls. Despite the sunlight, I could clearly make out the pricked pattern of winking stars between each elegant flourish. Punctuating the landscape, there were several trees, widespread and alone in their roots. They each boasted at least eight long, gnarled branches which extended in all directions and were adorned with queer tendrils of leafy flora. Everything seemed to be in Technicolor, brilliant and utterly brazen in each hue, almost as if from a painting. I couldn't stop myself from repeatedly blinking just to make sure that the crash hadn't injured my eyesight—*or my brain, for that matter.*

I turned back around to look at the *Paragon*. The ship was utterly decimated and looked like nothing more than a pile of rubble from a junkyard. Thick flames licked the creases between bent and broken metal, and I noticed immediately that the flames were unusual in their color: a rather salmon-like hue. Dark gray smoke poured continuously from every inch of the spacecraft in bursts so thick they looked more like cement than smoke. I wanted to cry. *There were almost certainly others inside, still alive and frightened, but to attempt to rescue them would basically be a suicide mission.*

There had to be something around that could help me. I scanned the visible perimeter of the ship before glancing around the foreign terrain, searching for anything I could use to clear a path or push the burning debris aside. Before I located anything, however, movement caught my attention. In the distance, I saw the form of somebody who seemed very human approaching. I felt panic swell in my chest, and I wondered if I should hide. *It was possible that, on this strange planet, whoever that was would not be friendly to me.*

Before I could decide if I wanted to hide or to ask for help, though, I saw the humanoid reach to its side and unsheathe a weapon. It looked like a scimitar, but it glowed a bright fuchsia color and seemed to pulsate. I knew that thing had seen me and hiding would do no good now, so I stood with my feet planted firmly in place, waiting for whatever was to come.

As he drew nearer, I wondered if my eyes were deceiving me. He was very human in form; tall with two arms and two legs, and a head, of course. His face looked like any other human's face as well, but his skin was blue. It wasn't the shade of sickly blue caused by suffocation, either; it was a beautiful, hydrangea kind of blue, and it seemed almost translucent. I realized that what I interpreted as translucence was actually a pale shimmer practically indiscernible if not for the white light of the alien sun dancing off of it.

His eyes were trained on me, unmoving and focused; *I lost myself in them for the briefest of moments*. They were small, but they were intense in both their color and their expression. He clearly had an iris and a pupil as human eyes did, but his iris was ghostly white. His eyes were set beneath a stern brow and above a pair of exquisitely-sculpted cheekbones.

I was so captivated by his eyes I almost didn't notice his body. When I did, I was just as enthralled. As sculpted and angular as his cheekbones were, his abdomen put them to shame. I could clearly see each and every muscle, so defined that the indents between them looked like marker-drawn lines; as he walked, they flexed and rippled. His arms were equally as toned, but he wasn't beefy as I would have expected by looking at his stomach. They were lithe and athletic with evident but gentle curves where his biceps and triceps were. I couldn't see his legs, for he was wearing a pair of pants made from some kind of leather I had never seen before, but I imagined they were just as impressive.

He stopped walking when he was about ten feet away from me, and we just stared at each other. I didn't want to speak. I wasn't sure what he was going to do, and I couldn't help noticing the way he alertly gripped his weapon. He looked back at me with the same kind of wariness I felt, and then he opened his mouth.

What came out was a series of clacks and clicks and snaps, and it sounded strangely similar to the crackling of the flames behind me. They were staccato sounds which only lasted for a second, but so unusual were they that I was rendered speechless for a second. He stood there, looking at me with his weapon brandished, and I realized he was waiting for a response.

"I-I don't understand," I said.

My voice sounded extraordinarily weird to me. *It was like I hadn't heard myself speak in years and I'd finally broken the silence.* The unsettlingly clear air made my words sound almost melodic, rather like a song. I tried to remain stock-still to avoid appearing threatening to him as I waited for some sort of conversational reciprocation.

He opened his mouth again, and I expected some more clacks. What I heard, instead, stunned me.

"Who are you?"

He had a low, growling voice which seemed predatory in its nature. His words had the same kind of staccato delivery as his clacking had. *I was able to understand him, though, and it surprised me so much that I almost couldn't answer.*

"You...speak English?" I asked.

"I speak whatever language is spoken to me," he said. He jerked his scimitar forward and repeated, "Who are you?"

"Tabitha," I answered at once, my eyes on the sword. "Bartel."

"You are human, Tabitha Bartel?" His eyes were unnaturally still as they stared at my face.

I started to nod before remembering I meant not to move. "Yes."

"You are from Earth?"

"Yes," I said again.

He stared at me a moment more before slowly-*painstakingly slowly* turned his gaze to the *Paragon*'s wreckage behind me. In the same growl, he asked, "What happened?"

"I-I don't know," I said. I started to turn to look at the ship as well, but the movement startled him, and he leaped forward with the scimitar extended toward me. I shrieked, my hands shooting up involuntarily to both protect myself and show him I was not a threat. He placed the tip of the weapon below my chin and used it to tilt my face up to his.

"You will not move," he intoned.

"Okay," I whispered. I didn't realize I was shaking until I felt the sword jiggling slightly against my neck.

He didn't speak as he looked back at the ship, keeping the glowing scimitar in place beneath my chin. I watched his eyes glide slowly over the broken structure, lingering on something unknown for a second or two before moving on to something else. I kept my hands up by my ears and tried not to swallow for fear of the sword puncturing my throat. There was silence between us for a long time as he just looked, and, finally, I spoke.

"Where am I?" I asked.

My words jarred him, and his ivory irises darted back to me. For a moment, I thought he wasn't going to answer me—*or, worse, that he was going to kill me*—but then he responded.

"You are on the planet Albaterra," he said.

"And…what are you?"

He studied me for a second. "I am A'li-uud."

"Are there more of you?" For some reason, I couldn't stop the questions. They offered me some reassurance, though I didn't know of what nature.

Again, he studied me before replying. "Yes. We are to Albaterra what humans are to Earth."

I wanted to nod, but I refrained. The tip of the scimitar was still resting against my throat, serving as a reminder that this creature, this A'li-uud, could kill me at any moment.

"Do you have a name?" I murmured hopefully.

This time, he didn't answer me at all. Instead, he lunged forward unexpectedly, and I yelped. His fingers closed around my upper arm and yanked me to him with such a powerful grip I had no chance of getting away without tearing my own arm off in the process. Trembling violently, I started to whimper, and tears flooded my eyes. I was certain I was experiencing my last moments of life.

"You are to come with me," he said.

"What?" My voice sounded high-pitched and gravelly with fright. "Where?"

"You will come to my village to be questioned." He shoved me forward with such strength I nearly fell on my face, and, when I straightened up, I felt him press the tip of the sword against my spine. "You will lead."

I nodded as the tears finally started to dribble down my cheeks and took a step forward. Then, I remembered the other crew members and stopped dead in my tracks, not even thinking I should warn him in case he continued to walk and ended up spearing me clean through.

"The others," I said loudly. "There might be others. There were ninety-seven of us. Some may have survived the crash."

"They are not your concern," he growled.

"I can't just leave them to die!" I cried tearfully, now weeping freely.

I anticipated being told to shut up, to keep walking, to do as I was told, but he said none of those things. Instead, he was quiet for a beat, and then he spoke.

"If there are any survivors, my warriors will find them."

"Will they kill them?" I asked.

"They will be ordered to bring them back safely to the village," he told me. His voice was calm and steady, and it sounded so genuine I felt relief flood through me.

"Thank you," I whispered. I was sure he wouldn't be able to hear me, as my words were quiet and he was standing behind me, but he replied at once, and I realized his hearing was exponentially better than a human's.

"You are welcome, Tabitha Bartel. Now, walk."

Chapter 5

Rex

I had seen humans in Elder recollections and surveillance logs, but I had never met one in person. *She was different than I had expected.* From what I knew of humans, they were self-destructive creatures with a paralyzing fear of the unknown and self-serving morals. They invented reasons for the things they couldn't explain and dismissed the things they could. Abuse of their land, their race, and their existence was instinctual for them, and self-preservation took precedence over the greater good.

Tabitha Bartel skewered those notions.

It was possible, of course, she'd wanted to save her fellow humans to ensure herself allies. It was also possible she'd desired to be lauded for her heroism. I had heard her words in the wind, though, and they had whispered of the honest desire to rescue the others for the sake of nothing more than the sheer value of life; *that was something I'd thought impossible of a human.*

Had she never requested their rescue, I would have instructed my warriors to save them anyway. The decision of their fate did not lie on my shoulders alone; it was to be the responsibility of the entire Elder Council. Her genuine plea, however, ensured safety for her crewmates that they would otherwise not have had. My warriors would be commanded to spill no blood and cause no harm to any human alive from the destruction. *As for Tabitha Bartel, I would question her myself.*

I was taking her back to my parents' house. It was much closer than my own, and my house was also guarded and staffed. *I didn't want anyone knowing I'd brought back a human yet.*

When we arrived, I said, "Stop."

She froze immediately. I stepped in front of her and looked at her. I could tell she wanted to look around, but she kept her eyes firmly on mine. *It was a good choice on her part.*

"I will enter first. You will not run. If you do, you will die. There are creatures in the Plains that will kill you in an instant, and, if they don't get you, I will. Follow me closely," I instructed.

She nodded shakily, looking like her voice was stuck in her throat. I turned and opened the door, and I felt her presence within inches behind me.

The moment we stepped inside, my mother and father both looked up. They were near the cooking pot and appeared to be in a deep discussion. Upon seeing the human, however, they both responded at once. Mother sprung back and raced over to my siblings, placing her body firmly between them and Tabitha Bartel. My father had the opposite reaction; he jerked toward me in an attack stance. I coolly held up a hand to stop him.

"There was a crash. I assume it was the ship closest to Albaterra," I told them, looking at father as I spoke. "This human was the only one I found, but she thinks there are survivors inside the ruins."

"You didn't kill her?" My father hissed. He was staring aggressively at the girl, and I involuntarily stepped in front of her to shield her from him. *I didn't know why I did it, but it was my natural response to the expression on his face.*

"To kill her would undermine the authority of the Elder Council," I said. "That is a Forum decision."

"Why did you bring her here?" Mother whimpered. She was visibly trembling.

I glanced over my shoulder at Tabitha Bartel and saw she was looking between my parents and me with a mixture of fright and confusion on her face. I realized I had reverted back to A'li-uud dialect speaking to them, but I continued in the language, not feeling she should understand the conversation quite yet.

"I have staff and guards, mother. I don't want more people knowing I have her until necessary."

"Isn't *that* undermining the authority of the Elder Council?" Father asked pointedly.

I turned my gaze back to him, and I felt myself standing a little straighter with the power of my Elderhood. He seemed to shrink slightly beneath the weight of my expression.

"You may be my father," I said quietly, "but I am still your king."

He looked furious, but he kept silent.

"I need you to dispatch the warriors to the crash site. All survivors are to be extracted and brought to confinement. Any warrior who harms a human in the slightest will be executed; be sure they understand this. Tell nobody of this human."

Father looked as though he wanted to argue, but he turned to my mother with a small nod and exited the house, sidling past Tabitha Bartel cautiously. When the door closed behind him, I said to mother, "I will be taking her upstairs to my bedroom to interrogate her. Stay down here with Igno and Risa."

"Yes, son," she murmured, clutching my siblings to her.

I motioned for the human to follow me and led her up the staircase to what used to be my bedroom. Once inside, I closed the door behind us and pointed to the bed.

"Sit."

She obeyed. As she sat, she looked surprised by something, and I realized she was probably unfamiliar with virtually everything she saw, touched, and heard.

"Are you going to kill me?" She asked in a small voice.

For the first time since finding her, I was able to properly take in what I saw. Her hair was dark brown, much like the spots on hicorn, which fell past her shoulders in loose but bouncy curls. It looked as soft as the prairie grass, and I actually found myself wanting to touch it. Her eyes were fixated on me in wide, fearful rounds, but I noticed they were almost the same color blue of the mid-morning sky. She had a figure similar to Pugna'ta, but her human curves were slightly curvier. She didn't sport Pugna'ta's muscular ripples. *She was beautiful in a way I'd never considered before, beautiful in a way I had never been exposed to.*

"No," I said finally. "Not yet, at least."

I saw her eyes fill with liquid, and then a droplet leaked from the corner of one and spilled down her cheek. *It was an intoxicating sight to behold, almost majestic in a way.*

"What are you doing?" I asked.

She looked at me in confusion as a second droplet dribbled along her nose-line. "What do you mean?"

"Your eyes," I said, motioning toward them with one hand. "What is happening?"

"Oh," she said quickly, brushing her palm over both eyes and sniffling. "I'm crying. I'm sorry."

"Why are you doing that?"

She looked at me as if I was crazy. "Because I-I'm scared."

I leaned against the wall opposite her and watched as she wiped away more of the droplets. *I found her more fascinating by the second, but I didn't know why. Even stranger than that was my lack of fear. Nothing about her made me feel threatened. In fact, I felt an urge to reassure her, to let her know there was no reason to be scared, even though I couldn't be sure that that was true.*

"What is the name of your ship?" I asked, diving into questions to avoid any more of the strange emotions I was having.

"The *Paragon*," she said with a sniffle.

"What was the *Paragon* doing in Andromeda?"

"I don't know, exactly," she said, looking up at me. No more droplets were skimming her cheeks, but her eyes looked red-rimmed and a little swollen. "I was just the chef."

"Why were you onboard?"

At this question, her eyes dropped to her lap, and she looked torn between answers. When she responded, her voice was low and monotonous. "I didn't want to be on Earth anymore."

"Why?"

"Personal reasons," she said defensively, looking back up at me with a defiant glint in her gaze.

I took a step forward and grabbed her chin harshly in my hand, jerking it upward. "There is no room for personal reasons here."

She didn't reply. Instead, she stared at me with an expression of awe rather than fear or anger. I released her chin.

"Why do you look at me like that?" I asked, my tone slathered in suspicion.

"Your skin," she said in a voice of breathy amazement. "It's so...strange."

I furrowed my brow at her and crossed my arms. "What do you mean?"

She shook her head. "It's just so smooth and warm and hard." She flicked her gaze back up to mine. "What are you?"

"I told you. I am A'li-uud," I answered stiffly.

"Can—may I touch you?" She asked, extending her fingertips toward me.

I considered her request for a moment. To my knowledge, humans were innately unmagical, and there wasn't much she could do to me without weapons. Nevertheless, it seemed foolhardy to allow a prisoner, for all intents and purposes, to have direct contact with me. Despite my misgivings, though, I stepped even closer and held out an arm.

She pressed the pads of her fingers to my skin and slowly dragged them up and down the length of my forearm. She looked fascinated and almost excited. *Something about her touch made me want to close my eyes and just revel in the sensation*, but I kept my eyes fixed firmly on her as she explored. Her fingers drifted down to my hand, and she stroked down to the tips of my own fingers before caressing my palm with hers.

Everything she touched seemed to tingle. Her skin against mine felt cool and slick, and it relaxed me. I stared at her as she traveled up to the bend of my elbow and drank in the sight of her sun-white skin and sky-blue eyes.

"What's your name?" She whispered, still stroking my arm.

Something in her voice sent a jolt through my gut, and my response sounded huskier than I intended as I said, "Rex."

"It's nice to meet you, Rex," she said softly, looking up to me. She looked at my face more intently than she had thus far and asked, "May I see your eyes, please?"

I leaned down until we were level, and we stared at one another.

"Wow," she murmured, pressing her fingertips to my cheekbone just below my eye as she spoke.

"You have never seen A'li-uud?" I asked, equally as quiet. It was a question I had intended to ask in the interrogation, but it came out now as a personal inquiry.

"No. I didn't know you even existed."

Her hand moved up my cheekbone and came to rest at my temple. I raised my own hand slowly until I was close enough to touch her, and I stroked her jaw with just as much intrigue as she had for me. Our eyes locked again, and I leaned forward until I felt her breath on my lips. *She looked eager, intent, and slightly frightened, and I wanted to close the tiny gap between us.*

But I didn't.

I pulled back and straightened up, her hand falling limply from my face onto her thigh. She instantly seemed confused and hurt, and the slight fright on her features was now significant fear.

"I have to go," I said. "You will stay in this room."

"Where are you going?" She asked timidly.

I eyed her warily. "I am the Tribe Elder of this kingdom. I must confer with my warriors about what they have found at your ship's crash site. I must speak with the other Elders regarding what action we will take."

"Shouldn't—Shouldn't I go with you?"

In any other circumstance, I would have brought her. I couldn't understand why, but I couldn't reconcile bringing her with me for fear she would be harmed—or killed—on sight by one or several of the other Elders.

"You are still needed," I said in a clipped tone. "There are those who would kill you as soon as they saw you. I cannot take that chance."

Something in her face softened, and she nodded.

"You will stay in this room."

She looked rather disappointed as she asked, "Can't I just stay at the house? Do I have to stay in the room?"

I thought about the request. My mother was going to be terrified whether the girl remained in the room or not. My father would likely feel more comfortable with her *out* of the room so that he could keep an eye on her. She was no threat I could measure.

I nodded. "Fine. You may leave the room, but you *must* stay here."

"I will. I promise," she replied eagerly.

I moved for the door. Before I left, I looked over my shoulder at her and said, "I will be back soon, Tabitha Bartel."

The corners of her mouth turned up in a smile, and she replied, "Just call me Tabitha."

Chapter 6

Tabitha

I sat on the bed for a while after Rex left, reeling from everything that had happened. Fear still gripped my gut, fear of what was to happen to me as well as fear of what would happen to my surviving crewmates—*if they survived at all. Greater than the fear, though, was the powerful curiosity and awe I was feeling.* Rex, this strange alien creature, was fascinating and intoxicating to me in a way I'd never experienced before. *I wanted more of him. I wanted to be around him, to learn about this weird world from him. To learn about who he was.*

Finally, however, my curiosity got the better of me, and I stood. I crept slowly to the door, unsure if the other A'li-uud in the house were prepared to slaughter me the moment I stepped out. I heard sounds from the first floor which sounded like normal household activities, but I still didn't feel entirely safe to just wander. Nevertheless, I opened the door cautiously and peeked out.

Nobody was around. My gaze fell on the same strange staircase Rex had taken me up to get to this room. It seemed to be made of dirt, but it was solid and appeared to be crafted like any normal wooden or metal staircase. I tiptoed to the top step and began making my way down bit by bit.

When I made it to the bottom, I saw the two adult A'li-uud immediately. The female was hovering over a cooking pot, and the male was pacing around the space with his hands behind his back. Upon seeing me, both straightened up and seemed to freeze. I froze, too. I didn't know what Rex had told them before he'd left, and I didn't know if these aliens were trustworthy. Neither moved toward me, though. They both just remained rooted to their places with their eyes on me, though the female's eyes darted across the room intermittently at the two little children.

"Hello," I said uncertainly. My voice sounded loud and out of place in the room, and I almost wished I hadn't spoken.

I received no reply. I considered racing back upstairs and holing up in the bedroom until Rex returned, but I couldn't help myself.

"I'm Tabitha," I continued, my words trembling slightly with nerves. "Rex said I could stay here while he was gone."

"We know," the male said.

I was taken aback by his voice. It was deep and low, and, while he spoke in English with the same staccato mannerism Rex had, there was something almost foreign about the words. It was as if I could hear the clacking of his native tongue inside each syllable.

I understood him, though, and I nodded. "May I walk around?"

The female was looking at me with wide eyes now, clearly fearful, but the male seemed to be slightly more comfortable now that we were conversing.

"Rex says you are not a threat," he said. It wasn't exactly an answer to my question, so I responded to him.

"I'm not," I said. "I don't even know what you are or where I am."

"We are A'li-uud," the male replied, straightening up even further, puffing out his chest a bit.

It was a little difficult for me not to get snappish. Rex had just said he was A'li-uud, too, when I had asked about what he was. I wanted to say that knowing the name of something didn't explain what it was, but I was too far out of my element to do anything except nod again.

"Stay on the property," the male commanded. He sounded very similar to Rex in his dominant command. "You are not safe if you leave."

"I will," I promised. The two adults across the room remained frozen in their spots, just watching me, so I decided to move first.

Walking outside, I was able to breathe a little bit easier. It was unnerving to have two sets of eyes boring into me and assessing every little move I made. There was freedom in closing the door between them and myself, and the vast expanse of plains around me only helped to lift that feeling of freedom. I stood on the front path and just looked for a moment.

    The landscape was the same as it had been at the site of the crash, but, without the terror pulsating through me, it was even more breathtaking. The fluffy beige grass bent in synchronized dance with the whim of the breeze, making the ground seem to ripple like ocean waves, going on as far as the eye could see. A band of lilac-colored sky wrapped around the land where the horizon met the grasses, and, where there had been turquoise and lavender in the heavens, there was now a blanket of cobalt and swirls of varying eggplant hues. The stars were so bright in the fading light, I couldn't help but think of them as pieces of the weird white sun. The dusk brought with it blindness, but I could still make out the dark arms of the lifelike trees piercing the otherwise flawless skyline. It was beauty in its purest form.

  I turned to look at the house behind me. I'd seen it when Rex had first brought me to it, of course, but I'd been so frightened he was going to kill me, I hadn't been able to appreciate it. It was rounded in shape but with sharp angles and straight lines at unpredicted places. I extended a hand and pressed my palm to the wall. It felt like clay or mud, dried from the sun, but firmer and hardier. There was no flaking, chipping, or dust from the structure, as I would have expected. The house also had windows made of some kind of extraordinary, nearly invisible glass, and the door was of a wood I wouldn't have been able to name.

    Without really thinking, I walked a few steps down the path and propped myself onto the top rail of a fence which was made of similar wood to the door. The fence didn't seem to serve a purpose, as it had no gate to close and only stretched about ten yards, but it was a fitting place for me to have a seat and just relax for the first time since nearly plummeting to my death.

I was so lost in my thoughts about what would happen to me and what had or would happen to my crewmates that I didn't notice the sky continuing to darken until a noise made me jump. I swung my head in the direction of the source, but I could see nothing, and my heart leaped into my throat with fear. Before I could decide whether to run into the house or wait to see what the sound was, Rex suddenly appeared by my side.

"Oh my God," I said wheezily, putting a hand on my chest to steady my galloping heart. "Where did you come from?"

"We can move much faster than humans," Rex said calmly. "What are you doing out here?"

"Just thinking," I replied.

Through the darkness, I could make out his eyes staring at me intently. "Are you frightened?"

"Well, yeah," I said. "I didn't know it was you out there until you just popped up next to me."

"No. Are you frightened of your fate?"

The question caught me off-guard, and I had to think for a moment. I knew the answer. I was definitely afraid of my fate, but I wasn't sure I wanted him to know that.

"Yes," I finally answered honestly. "I don't know what you want with me. And I don't know what you'll do when you get whatever it is you want."

He continued to stare at me, and I desperately hoped he would reassure me somehow. I wanted him to tell me he wasn't going to kill me, that I would be okay, and he would help me get back to Earth.

He didn't, though. Silence spread between us for several long beats, and then he said, "Come inside. My mother has made dinner. That is what you call night-meal, yes?"

"Yes," I murmured. Then, tentatively, I asked, "Those people in there are your parents?"

"They are not people. They are A'li-uud," he said sternly. "And, yes, they are my parents."

He extended a hand to me, and I took it. He guided me gently off the fencepost to my feet and led me back inside the house. It was strange to me to enter this way since the first and only time I had walked into this house had been under the threat of death.

Both his mother and father looked up when we walked in, and their eyes landed on me immediately with the same kind of wariness they had had before. Rex clacked something to them before showing me to the table. It was made of wood, but a different kind of wood than the fence and the door. It seemed almost rubber-like in texture. I sat on the bench, which was also made of the rubber-wood, and waited in complete stillness for whatever was happening next.

Rex's mother was bustling around the cooking pot, and she handed him a misshapen bowl of something, which he then brought to me with a spoon. I looked at the dinnerware as he placed it in front of me.

"What is it?" I asked.

"Hicorn stew," he said.

I had been asking about the bowl and the spoon, as they were both cream-colored and had numerous imperfections, but this information distracted me from the original purpose of my inquiry. "What is hicorn?"

"A wild plains goat. They are a staple in our tribe's diet." He motioned to the bowl. "You eat from a hollowed hicorn horn, and you eat with a hicorn rib."

I swallowed hard. I didn't want to admit it, but I was horrified at the thought of eating off of bones. To refuse seemed like treason, however, so I carefully picked up the spoon, dipped it into the stew, and lifted it to my mouth.

It was odd but strikingly delicious. The meat was tender and gamey in flavor, and the broth had a hearty, earthen taste to it. There were bits of other things in the stew as well, what I presumed to be A'li-uud vegetables, and they added every kind of flavor imaginable: seductive sweetness, tangy tartness, pungent bitterness, savory saltiness. If I were to dream up the most perfect, satisfying dish in the universe, this would have been it.

I ladled another spoonful into my mouth, and Rex watched me eat it before he walked back to the cooking pot. He returned to the table with two more bowls, which he set down opposite me. He made another trip, and, when he placed a bowl beside me, he sat down before it. *I could feel his elbow brush against mine as he began to eat, and the touch made me shiver.* His parents sat down on the other side of the table, his father across from me, and they kept their eyes averted as they dined.

Rex exchanged brief conversation with them throughout the short meal in his clacking language, but his mother seemed unwilling to speak, and his father was looking at him with sternness on his face. I tried to eat as quickly as I could so that I could escape back to the bedroom and let them talk properly. *Of course, I was also extraordinarily hungry.* Just as I finished my food, however, Rex stood and extended a hand to me.

"Let us retire," he said. He clacked something to his parents, and they both nodded.

I took his hand, and he guided me back up the stairs to the same bedroom he had brought me before. Once inside, he closed the door and turned to me.

"You are to sleep here," he said. "Undress."

"W-What?" I stammered.

He stepped toward me, closing the gap between us, and moved a hand to my waist. I realized he was sliding my top up my torso, and I leaped back. He looked at me with surprise.

"What is wrong?" He asked. He sounded genuinely confused.

"You can't just undress me!" I cried, tugging my shirt back down.

His head tilted to the side, and he stepped up to me again. "You are to sleep now."

"Yes, but—" My voice died off as his hand skimmed the hem of my shirt again, his knuckles brushing along my waistline.

"You cannot sleep in these clothes. They are dirty and torn. We will get you new clothes tomorrow."

I nodded, and, this time, I didn't stop him as he slid the shirt up and over my head. His hands dropped back to my waist, and he eased my pants down the length of my legs. I stepped out of them gingerly, my heart beating faster than it had when he'd surprised me outside. My stomach was fluttering wildly, and my mouth was uncomfortably dry. Once I was reduced to my bra and panties, he looked me up and down. *His eyes were narrow and hooded, and I imagined I had the same expression on my face as I looked back at him.*

"Do you wish to remove those as well?" He asked, motioning to my undergarments.

For a moment, I imagined him unhooking my bra and sliding it from my breasts with the same gentleness he'd used to remove my other articles of clothing. I imagined the feeling of his strange skin against mine as he slipped my panties down my thighs, his mouth level with my most intimate place as he did. Then, I shook myself from the thoughts and responded.

"No. This is fine," I said softly.

He nodded once and motioned to the bed. I climbed onto it and lifted back the blankets. They weren't sheets and quilts as I was used to; they seemed to be made up of animal skins which had been beaten into buttery softness and furs exquisite to feel against my bare skin. I shimmied beneath them and pulled them up to my chin, rather self-conscious about being so naked in front of him.

"Where will you sleep?" I asked.

His eyes moved to the empty space in the bed beside me. Very seriously, he said, "There."

Again, my stomach fluttered, and I mummified myself even more with the blankets. It wasn't that I didn't want him to touch me. It was the exact opposite, and that made me nervous. I wasn't a promiscuous woman by any means, but something about this man—this alien—was making me quiver.

"Well, are you coming to bed, then?" I asked timidly.

He leaned against the wall across from the bed and crossed his arms over his unclothed chest.

I couldn't help but admire the way his muscles seemed to stand out, even through the darkness.

"When you sleep, I will sleep," he said.

I wanted to ask him more questions, to get some of the answers I so desperately needed to know, but I was more tired than I thought. Between the crash, the new planet, Rex, and my rollercoaster of emotions, the day was more than I could take. *I hadn't even opened my mouth to ask my first question before I fell into a deep sleep.*

Chapter 7

Rex

 A full moon cycle had passed since Tabitha had crashed into my kingdom and I'd brought her to my parents' house.

 My warriors had found thirty-three survivors inside the *Paragon* wreckage—which, counting Tabitha, made thirty-four captives. The humans had been brought to confinement within my village for holding until the Council decided what to do about them. Tabitha, however, had remained with my parents, to the knowledge of no one but them and myself.

The Forum on the captives had been, perhaps, the most turbulent yet in my Elderhood. The vote had been very divided on what to do with the humans, but it had been ruled they would be kept alive and tended to for questioning. In the meantime, it had been agreed we would halt our attacks on the ships inside Andromeda's borders. Vi'den had insisted that we learn what we could from the humans before continuing action, something I had agreed with wholeheartedly. It was unknown as of yet what would become of the humans after we had received all the information we could from them, but that was a subject for another Forum.

I had chosen to forego telling the Elders of Tabitha and her whereabouts. I wasn't sure why I kept her a secret; it went against everything I believed to be my duty as Tribe Elder. *For whatever reason, I couldn't bring myself to confess, and I wasn't entirely sure it was because I was concerned about the consequences the action would have to myself.*

She had become a strangely well-integrated part of the household. I hadn't been to my home since the crash, opting instead to stay at my parents' whenever I wasn't away on Elder work. For several days after bringing Tabitha there, my mother had been afraid of her and had stayed no greater than five strides away from my father. To my surprise, however, mother had been the first to warm to her—not counting my little siblings, of course, who knew nothing of threat and danger.

It had happened one day when I was out hunting. I returned with a hicorn ram and found mother and Tabitha around the cooking pot together. Tabitha was leaning over the pot, staring into it hard as though trying to memorize its contents, and mother was explaining the recipe to her in English as she dropped the ingredients in.

When I'd walked in, they'd both looked up at me and smiled brightly. *I had been so stunned to see them together that I'd just stared at them.*

"What is wrong, my son?" Mother asked, reverting to our native tongue. Tabitha glanced at her momentarily before swinging her gaze back to me.

"You are not afraid of her?" I asked surprised.

Mother flicked her eyes to Tabitha for a split second and then smiled warmly at me. "She has been no danger to us thus far. And I take great stock in your feelings for her, my boy."

"What feelings?" I said sharply.

She didn't answer. She just turned back to the cooking pot and resumed instructing Tabitha in English. I wanted to push the question, but I knew better. Despite being Tribe Elder, my mother was still an authority figure for me, and I wouldn't rudely demand anything of her, so I resumed bringing the hicorn to the back to be cleaned and harvested. *Her words remained in my mind, though.*

My father hadn't had an epiphany towards Tabitha, but he seemed to gradually take to her as he watched her play with my little brother and sister and help out my mother around the house. He no longer watched her with suspicion; on the contrary, he treated her as though she'd always been part of the family. He told her jokes and showed her various things about hunting tools. He also insisted that she come outside and learn about the animal anytime he brought home something she hadn't seen from a hunt. It reminded me greatly of how he'd taught me everything I knew about living off our land and respecting the gifts of the Grand Circle.

  At the end of the day, Tabitha and I continued to share the bed upstairs. Mother had lent her some new, undamaged clothes to wear for the first week of her stay, and father had gone on several extra hunts just to get new skins so that mother could show Tabitha how she could make them into clothing. When it was time to sleep, however, Tabitha still wore her own underthings to bed, rather than the traditional night-skins the A'li-uud of our tribe wore. I had awoken during several nights to find my arm or my leg pressed up against her, and it had stirred something inside of me which had made me salivate.

    She was so cool to the touch. I knew humans to be warm-blooded beings, but they weren't nearly as warm as A'li-uud, and it was almost refreshing to touch her. Sometimes, in the night, when I'd realize I was touching her, she would shift in her sleep and cuddle herself against me. *It was soothing and comforting, but it was also arousing, and I would spend the remainder of the night awake and alert.*

During one of those nights, I gave into my whims a bit. I looked over at her and admired the way she slept. Her back was to me, her dark, curly hair spilling out over the pillow, and she breathed slowly and deeply. I lifted my hand and gently brought my fingers to the blade of her shoulder. As I made contact, she mewed a bit in her sleep, and I gritted my teeth to keep down the desires roaring within me. Slowly, I trailed my fingers down her side, feeling each ridge of her ribs and each curve of her femininity. *It felt as though my skin buzzed against hers.*

That was when I realized my mother had been right. I had feelings for this human.

The next day, I studiously avoided both Tabitha and mother, occupying myself instead teaching Igno how to whittle vigibrach wood into pegs for building. I could tell, each time I passed on her, Tabitha was confused and a bit hurt by my behavior, but I didn't want to address the matter. *It frightened me that I cared for her. I didn't know what was to come of her or what the consequences would be for either of us if we were to pursue something deeper, and I wasn't prepared to be hurt.*

"Rex!"

I looked up at the call and saw my father knee-deep in the grasses a short distance away.

"You have to go! A Forum has been called!" He shouted at me.

I got to my feet, handing Igno the piece of vigibrach and the small knife, calling back to father, "Thanks!"

He nodded and turned around, presumably to resume doing whatever he had been doing when he'd received word of the Forum. I went into the house and found Tabitha sitting with mother at the table. Furs were scattered about between them, and both of them seemed deeply focused.

"I have to go," I announced, making them both look up. "There is a Forum."

Mother nodded, but Tabitha got to her feet. "Wait. I'll walk you out."

We exited the house together, and she smiled brightly at Igno as he showed her the peg he was working on. When we got to the edge of the front path, she put a hand on my arm to stop me.

"Is there something wrong?" She asked. Her eyes probed mine with obvious concern.

"No," I said. "Why do you ask?"

She shrugged. "It feels like you don't want to be around me."

I intended to reassure her while keeping as much distance—*emotionally and physically*—as possible, but I couldn't fight the feelings taking over. I reached forward and cupped her cheek in my hand. She looked back at me with a contradictory mixture of hope and fear in her expression.

"Tabitha," I said quietly, "I always want to be around you."

Her eyes seemed to melt, and she smiled. I could see in her eyes my own feelings mirrored back at me, and I realized *I probably wasn't the only one feeling things I would never have expected.*

"I need to go," I told her, just as quietly.

She nodded against my hand. I kept it there for another second, and then I jumped on the winds to P'otes-tat Ulti.

When I arrived, all of the other Elders were already present. I took my seat, and Vi'den took presence as usual. I tried to stay focused on where I was and why I was there, but I couldn't keep my mind from continuously reverting back to Tabitha and the look she had in her eyes. I was wrenched from the thoughts, however, when I heard Vi'den speak.

"It is time to revisit our action plan," he said grandly, arms extended to the side. "The humans have been our captives for a full moon cycle. We have received a substantial amount of information from those who have been interrogated, and there is likely to be much more to come, but we can no longer forego addressing the other ships in Andromeda that continue to travel nearer to Albaterra."

I sat frozen in my chair. The information we'd gathered from the humans, in my opinion, had been negligible; according to all of them, they had known nothing of us prior to their crash on our planet, and most didn't know the specific reason they'd been sent on their space mission in the first place. It occurred to me there may have been things learned I had not been told of, and, with a sickening swoop, I wondered if any of the other Elders had found out about Tabitha.

"We have enough humans to get what we need," the vicious cave Elder spat. "Blast the others."

"It is possible those on the other ships know things these humans do not," Ma'ris chimed in. "We would be unwise to destroy them without first questioning them."

"Enough questions!" The cave Elder barked back.

I could feel Duke's eyes on me from my right, and I knew he was waiting for me to say something. The humans had, after all, crashed in my kingdom, and it was expected from me to have particularly strong feelings one way or the other about our course of action. *I couldn't bring myself to say anything, though, for fear of blurting out something that would give Tabitha away.*

"We must come to a decision about the ships," Vi'den said sagely. "The humans here are confined and pose no immediate threat to us. It is to the Council to measure the risk the ships pose."

"Blast'em!" The cave Elder shouted.

"You are a foolish, narrow-sighted brute," Ma'ris hissed to him. "Your thinking is the kind that decimates races and worlds."

"And your thinking is what will have us all in shackles, doing the humans' bidding," the cave Elder roared back.

"Enough!"

I didn't mean to say it, and I certainly didn't mean to yell it at the volume I did, but silence fell in the chamber at once as my command echoed throughout. All eyes turned to me, and I sat up a little straighter in my chair.

"Bickering amongst ourselves solves nothing," I said. "And, if I recall, the *Paragon* landed in my kingdom. It was my warriors who found and brought back the surviving humans. It is my tribesmen keeping them confined and performing the interrogations. If anyone should have an opinion on the matter, it should be me, not either one of you in your ignorance."

Both Elders looked highly affronted, but Vi'den looked at me with an expression of obvious pride and approval.

"We would all greatly value your opinion on the matter, Rex," he said.

I didn't speak right away. I was going over my words in my mind, making sure I would say nothing relevant to Tabitha. When I finally did speak, it was slowly and calculatingly.

"The humans have, for the most part, shown no signs of aggression. Those we have seen have been symptoms of fear for their survival. I do not believe they were aware of Albaterra or the A'li-uud prior to their crash."

"That does not mean they weren't sent by those who *are* aware," Ma'ris cut in.

"Or that knowing about us now isn't dangerous," the cave Elder added.

Silence fell again as their assertions rang in my ears. I realized, with a dull pang, that they were both right. At the end of the day, I was a Tribe

Elder, and I had a duty to my tribesmen and my race. If I was unwilling to uphold my promise of safety and protection to the A'li-uud, I might as well have been executed for treason.

My chest suddenly felt hollow and achy as the truth sank into me. *My feelings for Tabitha were a distraction from the real problem, the real danger.* My feelings could be the catalyst for the decimation of the A'li-uud race and Albaterra altogether. At the very least, the safety of my family was in question the moment the Council found out about her.

"Let us vote," Vi'den said. I stared at the floor, feeling sick to my stomach, as he said,

"Those in favor of recommending our plans to destroy all human ships in Andromeda?"

Out of the corner of my eye, I saw hands lift into the air one by one. Duke, beside me, extended his upward as well. I swallowed hard. I had a choice to make, and, if I made the wrong one, it could literally mean life or death.

With trembling fingers, I raised my hand.

Chapter 8

Tabitha

I stood outside for several long minutes after Rex departed, just reveling in the way his palm had felt against my cheek and the husky way he'd said he always wanted to be around me. I'd been trying to ignore the tumultuous emotions I'd been feeling toward him which had been progressively growing stronger since he'd first brought me to his parents' house. However, the look in his eyes and the intimacy in his voice had finally made me come to terms with myself.

I was falling in love with him.

When we'd first met, he'd been very commanding and authoritative. That was natural, I suppose, given I was a strange being who had suddenly appeared in his world. I hadn't known it at the time, but he was also a Tribe Elder, and that meant he had a responsibility to his tribe to keep them safe. He hadn't known if I was a danger to them.

As time had gone on, though, he'd changed. I'd seen him loosen up and become more naturally casual in his interactions with me. He had seemed genuinely interested in learning about me as a person, not just as a human, and he'd appeared to take great pleasure in showing me his life—*or, at least, what I could learn about his life being confined to the house.* We still slept together every night, and there had been more than one time that I'd woken up out of a deep sleep to find some part of him pressing against me. Once, I'd thought I'd felt him stroke my back, but I hadn't been sure if it had just been a dream, and I'd never gathered up the courage to ask.

I wasn't just falling in love with Rex, though. I was falling in love with everything. His parents, once they got used to me and stopped thinking I was going to attack them at any moment, turned out to be utterly delightful. His mother reminded me very much of my grandmother in her ways of taking care of her home and family and her willingness to pass on the little gems of tradition. His father was disarmingly sweet behind his gruffness, and, though he attempted to be businesslike and emotionally distant from me, he had become very protective of me and my safety.

  Albaterra, or what I had seen of it, was a dream. I never tired of looking at the scenery around me. When Rex went for an afternoon hunt, I often sat in the tall, consuming grass and just stared at the sky around me. That was something I couldn't get used to but delighted in. The Albaterran sky wasn't *above* as it was on Earth; it was *around*, all-consuming. I felt as though I sat inside the sky like a little plastic snowman inside a snow globe. The turquoise and lavender heavens of the day, punctured by those incredible white stars, swallowed me whole and burrowed deep inside of me, while the cobalt sky of the eve pulled me into itself and wrapped around me like a blanket. The wheat-colored plains stretching for miles in every direction were inviting and threatening at the same time; *I found the contradiction invigorating.*

I finally moved from my spot at the end of the walk when Igno ran up to me and placed a finished peg into my hand. I studied it carefully, rolling it between my fingers, and I was surprised to find it was crafted as perfectly as if Rex had done it himself.

"This is wonderful, Igno!" I exclaimed, smiling at the little blue boy.

"Yours," he said with a nod.

"Thank you," I replied earnestly. I bent at the waist to plant a kiss of appreciation on his head, and he beamed.

I took him inside and showed the peg to Beni, who raved over it just as I had. Igno bounced away, thrilled with himself, to make more pegs, but I sat down at the table again with Beni and picked up the fur I'd been working on sewing.

"You seem to like it here," Beni said after a long quiet.

I looked up at her in surprise, accidentally pricking my finger with the bone needle. I stuck my finger in my mouth and lapped at the puncture with my tongue, but Beni shook her head and pulled my hand away from my lips by the wrist. She got to her feet and retrieved a little clay pot, which she brought back to the table and opened it. Inside there was a thick, grayish gunk. She took my finger and dabbed a very small amount of the gunk on the wound.

"What is it?" I asked.

"Boiled vigibrach bark and hicorn dung," she replied. I looked down at my finger with mild disgust, but she seemed unfazed as she returned the pot to its shelf by the rustic fireplace. "It will heal by tomorrow."

As she sat back down, she trained her eyes on me again. "Are you happy here?"

"Yes," I answered honestly.

"Do you wish to stay?" She probed.

I thought about the question. I wasn't sure if she was asking if I wanted to stay on Albaterra or if

I wanted to stay at her house, but the answer was the same either way. "Yes, I would like to, but I don't know what will happen."

"Rex will do what makes you happy," she said. She hadn't picked up her fur yet, and I could tell she wanted to have this conversation for a while.

Biting my lip, I averted my eyes from hers and stared fixedly at the table. "How do you know?"

"A mother knows." I looked back up at her again, expecting her to have a telling smile on her face, but she looked matter-of-fact.

"My staying may not be what's best, though," I said, finally voicing a fear which had been building inside of me all of this time. Hearing the words spoken aloud sent a shiver of worry through me.

"Best for whom?" She asked intently.

"For everyone," I answered. "Him, me, all A'li-uud."

She leaned forward over the furs and peered at me with unexpected intensity as she said, "It is not up to me what is best for the A'li-uud, and I cannot tell you what is best for you. But I don't think you need to fear that your staying is anything other than best for Rex."

I looked back at her, and something seemed to swell inside me so rapidly I thought I would burst. I felt both a strong desire to cry and a strong desire to laugh at the same time, but I settled to smile gratefully at her for her candor. She smiled in return and then sat back and picked up her fur.

We worked in silence for a long time until the door opened again and Rex entered. His eyes found me immediately, and I melted into a puddle beneath his gaze. He was shirtless, as usual, and the white sunlight spilling into the doorframe around him gave him an angelic appearance. His lips turned upward in a boyish grin that sent my stomach into the series of flutters I so often felt around him, and I actually giggled. In my peripheral vision, I could see a small smile of amusement spread across Beni's face.

"You are done with the Forum?" She asked.

"Yes," he answered, stepping all the way into the room and closing the door behind him. In the absence of the white sun, the room was noticeably dimmer, but it had an air of mystique which only served to heighten my arousal for him. An image of my body beneath his on top of the rubberwood table flashed through my mind, and I felt my cheeks warm with a sudden blush.

He crossed the room to where his mother and I sat, and, as he moved to join me on the bench, his hand casually brushed the nape of my neck. I quivered beneath his touch, noticing that my skin felt the warm imprint of his fingertips even after he had sat down and rested his arms on the table.

"Has something happened?" Beni asked him. She didn't sound overly concerned; rather, her tone was curious.

"The Council has decided to resume action on the ships in Andromeda," he said. I looked at him with questions in my eyes, but he only locked gazes with me for a second before looking away.

Beni, however, seemed intent on knowing more, and she didn't seem at all happy about what she'd just heard. "Why? There is no known threat."

I realized they were most likely referring to the other ships on the mission including the *Paragon*. I turned to him for his answer, as well as to ask more questions of my own. Before I could, though, he answered his mother in his clacking A'li-uud language. She spoke back to him with more clacks, and I looked rapidly between them in desperate hopes to understand what they said. I wasn't sure if they realized they had switched tongues or not, but it seemed unlikely to me they wouldn't notice they had. Rex was intentionally making sure I didn't know what he was saying.

It hurt me to realize that.

"Wait," I interrupted. Both of them looked at me. "Speak in English."

"It's nothing for you to worry about," Rex said dismissively, still keeping his eyes off of me.

I stared at him, trying to wrangle my mixed emotions. A part of me was hurt, but another part was furious he was keeping information about the fate of my human counterparts from me.

"I didn't say I was worried," I said in a clipped tone. "I just want to know. I think I have the right."

Without a word, Rex got to his feet and walked toward the door. I looked to Beni for advice, but the expression on her face told me she was torn between loyalty to her son and her feelings on my right to know. I looked back at Rex.

"What is going to happen to the ships?" I called to his back.

He whipped around suddenly, and I thought I'd crossed a line and had infuriated him. His eyes were dark and angry, and his posture was defensive, as though he was about to engage in a deadly battle. I flinched at the mere sight of the expression on his handsome visage and opened my mouth to apologize for butting into Council business, but he spoke before I could.

"Tabitha, go to the bedroom."

I blinked numbly; shocked he was actually sending me to my room as punishment for speaking out. When I didn't move right away, he yelled, "Now!"

"Go," Beni said in a hushed tone, pushing gently on my arm. "Go."

I got to my feet in a harried rush, stumbling over the bench in my hurry to stand. Beni stood as well and reached for me to steady me. Then, with one last look at Rex, I strode to the stairs and ran up them two at a time.

"Close the door," he ordered from the bottom of the staircase. I looked back at him, hoping to see some kind of explanation written on his face or any kind of telltale emotion in his eyes, but he was already walking outside.

I went into the bedroom and closed the door behind me as I'd been bid. Then, I made my way to the window to see where Rex was going. He was moving to the end of the walkway, and, in the distance, I saw the approaching figure of another A'li-uud. My stomach unknotted slightly as I realized his sharpness had been to get me up to the room to protect me, but it tangled up again as I wondered who it was and what they wanted.

As the figure drew nearer, I saw it was a female. She was beautiful, much like Rex but with more femininity, and there was a look of strong determination on her face. She wore skins tightly fitted to her muscular, curvy form, and it struck me just how pale she was compared to Rex and his family. Her skin was very light azure, and her hair was almost white, but she clearly wasn't an Elderly A'li-uud. In fact, she looked like she was around Rex's age, perhaps even younger. I watched as she walked up to Rex and stood close enough that there was nothing but a breath between them, and I saw her lift a hand and squeeze his arm affectionately.

My breath caught in my chest. This female wasn't a mere acquaintance, a simple tribeswoman. As I observed the way she stood with her chest extended out and her hip popped slightly, and as I watched her lean into him to whisper something in his ear, I realized she was something to him. *It hit me that this woman—this alien woman—might have been the reason for his sudden distance from me, and I felt like I'd had a sledgehammer thrown into my gut.*

When she tilted her face and pressed her lips to his, the first tear fell.

Chapter 9

Rex

I stood at the end of the walk and watched Pugna'ta come closer. When we were within earshot of one another, I opened my mouth to call to her it was a bad time, but I couldn't say the words. Knowing Pugna'ta, she would interpret that as a challenge rather than a simple dismissal.

When she came in front of me, she smiled suggestively.

"Well, well," she said, reaching forward and squeezing my forearm. "Awaited by the king himself. I'm a lucky girl."

"What do you want, Pugna'ta?" I asked. My tone was harsh and very unfriendly, perhaps too much so, but it did nothing to change her intentions. On the contrary, her eyes lit up, and I knew I had been right about her taking any rejection as a challenge.

She bent forward slightly until her lips brushed against my ear, and I heard her whisper coyly, "You, Wise One."

I didn't have time to respond. She pulled her head back, tilted it sideways to look at me with a flirtatious grin, and suddenly leaned in. Her mouth pressed against mine insistently as she began kissing me.

Furious, I yanked my head back and stepped away from her. I snapped, "What are you doing?"

"Getting what I want," she said, moving toward me again and trying to slip her arms around my waist.

"It's not going to happen, Pugna'ta. I've told you this a hundred times."

"Oh, you're just being stub—"

Her words didn't just die off into nothingness; they stopped short like they'd been chopped off by an axe. I looked at her, waiting for her to finish her sentence, but she was staring above my head with something like rage on her face.

"What?" I asked. I turned to see what she was looking at, and I realized, with the same sickening swoop in my stomach I'd felt in the Forum, that she was looking at the upstairs bedroom window. *I caught the flash of Tabitha ducking out of sight, but I knew it was too late.*

"You have a *human* in there?" Pugna'ta shouted. I swiveled my head back to look at her just before she shoved me. I stumbled back a bit but regained my footing. "You're keeping one in your *house*?"

"Shut up," I hissed, leaping forward again and taking her by the throat. "Do not question me."

"Our ever-faithful, ever-protecting Elder, hiding a *human* away for his own personal pleasure," she spat icily. Her voice sounded choked from the pressure I was putting on her throat, but I didn't release her.

"You know *nothing* of what I do," I growled.

"I know the Council will be very interested to hear about this," she retorted. Without warning, she swung her fist, and it connected with my temple. I let go of her at once, dazed, and she hopped back several feet.

"The human is not a threat," I said, holding my head as it throbbed in my hands.

"Oh, no? Is that why we have all the others locked up?" I could see her physically seething, her body trembling with her fury. "You are putting us all in danger! And for what? To bed that human parasite?"

I roared, irate at the accusation. "Do not tell me I am compromising my tribe!"

"You are selfish!" She screamed.

"And you are ignorant!" I shouted back.

"Well, we'll just see who the Council agrees with, then, won't we?" She snapped.

I struck out again, grabbing her by the neck and slamming her to the ground. I pinned her to the dirt by her throat as she scratched at my hand, desperately trying to get me to let her up and free her airway. My voice sounded hoarse and otherworldly as I spoke.

"I. Am. Your. King," I snarled.

She didn't answer because she was unable to do anything but gasp for breath and struggle against my grip. I pushed down even harder, and her eyes grew so wide they seemed to bug out of her head a bit.

"Don't you *ever* imply I care more for myself than my race," I continued.

Her body flopped wildly, her legs kicking at the air and her arms pushing against mine. Her nails dug into the back of my hand, but I didn't move even as blood rose to the surface of the wounds and started to spill in thin lines over my skin. She was making harsh gagging sounds that almost sounded like gurgles, and I could see her lips forming words she was unable to speak.

"Rex!"

My father's voice blossomed out of the still prairie air, and I heard his footsteps getting louder as he rushed up behind me. He grabbed me by my shoulders and pulled, trying to wrench me off of Pugna'ta, but he wasn't strong enough to succeed.

"Son! Stop!" He yelled, moving down to take my wrist in both his hands and tug.

With a growl, I released Pugna'ta's throat, and she scrambled away from me on all fours. Her breath was gritty and coarse, and she looked both terrified and irate. She reached up to her neck and massaged it roughly. I was still staring at her, and she stared back with equal hatred. My dad's hands had returned to my shoulders.

"You need to leave. Now," he said over my head, and I knew he was talking to Pugna'ta.

She didn't move her eyes from me, and, for a moment, I thought she hadn't even heard my father speak. Then, she slowly got to her feet, still massaging her neck. I, too, stood, and my father's hands dropped from my shoulders. Only the breeze could be heard in the stillness. There was thick tension filling the air, and I was sure Pugna'ta was going to attack me with vengeful rage. When she finally moved, though, it was to take off at a sprint away from the house and back toward the village. I didn't exhale until her back had become nothing more than a blurry haze.

"I'm sorry," my father said, breaking the silence. I turned around and looked at him. He looked back at me. "I'm sorry, son. You would have killed her."

"I know," I replied tonelessly.

He patted my shoulder and guided me inside. Mother was standing by the window, her eyes wide, and I knew she'd seen everything. The moment I entered, however, she hurried to get me something to drink, and father sat me down at the table.

"What happened?" He asked in a low voice.

I shook my head, angry at the fresh memory. Everything had happened so quickly and had been exactly what I'd been afraid of happening. It was hard for me to process the events. I could still see the image of Pugna'ta's face as she spotted Tabitha in my mind, the fury and the fear in her features. I knew that, had I not attacked her, she would have gone into the house and killed Tabitha herself, or at least taken her to the lock-up with the other humans.

"She came to persuade me into a relationship again, and she saw Tabitha in the window upstairs."

"What?" Mother whispered, horrified, as she brought me a mug of what I presumed was vigibrach root tea.

"She said I was putting everyone at risk, the tribe, and all the A'li-uud. She said she was going to tell the Council about Tabitha." I shook my head again and stared into the mug of tea. Steam rose up and clouded my vision, but I didn't care. "I lost control. I was angry, and I was scared."

"She wouldn't tell anyone," mother said. I looked up at her and saw the worry scrawled across her face. "Would she?"

I almost laughed at the notion that Pugna'ta wouldn't go running to the Council about this. "Of course she will. I'd bet my Elderhood she's on her way to P'otes-tat Ulti right now."

Mother just stared at me with wide eyes, but father asked, "How do the other Elders seem to feel about the humans?"

"They're divided," I said honestly. "Almost split down the middle. We all agree there is a potential risk to the A'li-uud if humans know about us, but there is contention about the level of risk—if any—if they don't."

"They're going to destroy the ships in the galaxy," mother told father. "Rex told me when he returned from the Forum today."

Father looked at me for confirmation, and I nodded. "There has been no vote on what to do with the captive humans once we have everything we can get from them, though."

"And the others do not know of Tabitha?" Father asked.

I breathed in a long, shaky breath, and then I shook my head with a hint of shame and an excess of defiance.

"Perhaps they wouldn't mind," mother said hopefully. "They made you an Elder for a reason. They trust your judgment. Maybe they will understand your decision."

"My decision, at first, is what I thought was best for the tribe," I said. I was starting to get angry again, but my anger was at myself for even getting into this situation in the first place. "But she has stayed here because I knew she would not be safe if I put her into confinement with the others. Too many A'li-uud would consider her a danger for her knowledge of us now."

"You haven't kept her here because you wanted her here?" Mother asked knowingly.

I looked away. I felt a strange heaviness in my heart, and my innards seemed to be twisted up in fear. "It's true. I wanted her here," I murmured. *It was the first time I had admitted my feelings out loud, and it both thrilled and scared me.*

My mother moved to the side to catch my gaze. "Then, don't you think the Elders would understand that?"

"It's not a risk we can take," Father answered brusquely. He seemed to have snapped into action.

His posture was very straight, and he looked deadly serious. "We have to protect Tabitha."

"Of course we do, but how do we—?"

"Take her to your house," Father said, cutting my mother off mid-sentence. His eyes bore into mine with more intensity than I had ever seen before, and I realized just how much he, too, cared for Tabitha.

I looked back at him, feeling helpless for the first time in my Elderhood. "I can't. I've kept her here this whole time because I can't take her there. The staff and the guards could tell someone, and it could be a disaster."

"The staff and the guards are the protection you need for her right now. They don't need to know they're protecting a human. They just need to protect." Father lifted his eyebrows at me with insistence. "Take her to your house, son."

"How am I supposed to get her into the house without anyone seeing?" I snapped. My fear was making me quick-tempered, and my heart was beating so hard I could hear it in my ears.

Mother reached forward and placed her hand lovingly over mine. When I looked at her, I saw a blend of worry and pride painted in her smoke-grey eyes.

"My boy," she whispered. "You're the king."

Chapter 10

Tabitha

When Rex came flying into the bedroom, I practically jumped out of my skin. He flew around in a frenzy, grabbing the pile of clothes Beni and I had made and even snatching up the burnt, ripped clothes I'd worn when the *Paragon* had crashed. I was so stunned I wasn't even able to move from where I sat on the bed. I just watched him race around, gathering all my things and not saying a word.

"Rex," I said tearfully after a minute of no conversation or acknowledgment. "What's going on?"

"We have to get you out of here immediately," he said. He didn't look at me as he spoke.

"Why?" I asked, sliding off the bed.

He didn't answer me, but the look on his face told me not to ask again. I just started grabbing the few things I'd accumulated since arriving that he'd missed. When we had everything, he jerked his head to motion for me to exit the room first. I did, hurrying down the stairs, where I found his mother and father in a tizzy as well. Beni was hovering over the two little ones and putting away the furs we had been working on while Rex's father trotted up to me with a huge bag made of sabrecat skin. He held it out, and I dumped the things in my arms into it. Rex came up behind me and dropped his gatherings into it as well. Then, he took the bag from his father and slung it over his shoulder.

"Be safe," his father whispered, giving him a quick, one-armed hug.

Beni bustled over to him as well and threw her arms around his neck, murmuring, "I love you, my son."

Rex opened the door, and I started to walk through it, but, before I could, Beni threw her arms around me as well. She pulled me to her warm body, and I could feel her trembling slightly.

"Take care of yourself," she whispered in my ear as she hugged me.

I felt tears prick in my eyes, and I felt a heavy weight of sorrow in my chest even though I didn't know what was happening. "I love you, Beni."

"I love you too, sweet girl," she said softly. She kissed me delicately on the cheek, and then she let me go. Rex's father stepped forward and hugged me briefly as well, but he didn't say a word. It looked like speaking would cause him pain. When he released me, Rex nudged my arm with his knuckles, and I walked out of the house into the sunset.

We hurried silently down the walk. When we reached the fencepost where I'd sat on my first day here, Rex stopped talking. He turned to me, and his face was grave.

"What I have to do is against A'li-uud law," he said without preface. "I don't know if it will even work, but we have to try."

"What are we doing?" I asked nervously.

He looked out over the landscape as though ensuring nobody was within earshot, despite there not being another tribal home for miles, and then turned back to me and said, "We are going to fly on the winds."

"That's not against the law. You do that to get to the Forum."

"It is against the law to take someone with me," he said. "And I assume the law is especially unkind to taking humans."

I swallowed hard. "Does it—will it hurt?"

"It doesn't hurt me, but I don't know what it will do to you," he replied. He was sincere, but the answer frightened me anyway.

I gritted my teeth and nodded. He held out his hand to me, and I took it. The feeling of his skin against mine was divine, even in the uncertain and terrifying circumstances, and I recalled the sensation of having his palm pressed against my cheek. I closed my eyes and took in a breath.

And then I was flying.

I heard everything and nothing at the same time. It was like having wind rushing in my ears and complete silence all at once. Bird chirps, rustling grass and prairie stallions galloping all seemed to sound repeatedly, but the sounds disappeared the moment I heard them and left me wondering if I even heard anything at all. I could still feel Rex's hand in mine, but it had no pressure or temperature. It just existed. I was too scared to open my eyes, and even when everything suddenly came to a halt, and I was jolted to a stop, I kept my eyes closed.

"Come," Rex murmured. I could feel his body up against mine now, pressed so closely that the heat of his front radiated up and down my back. Slowly, anxiously, I parted my eyelids.

We were in front of a house constructed of the same things like his parents', but it was much larger and grandiose in its size and architecture. My jaw actually fell open as I took in the burbling fountain before us, made of something like marble but much more exquisite and standing well over ten feet tall. The house itself was palatial, with massive, extravagant windows and beautiful balconies strung with strange, glittering lights.

I didn't have time to take in any more than that, though, before Rex ushered me forward. He was walking quickly but quietly, and I wondered if we were breaking into someone's home. He silently opened one of the double doors which served as an entrance. They were large enough to have been the doors of an old English abbey.

It was dark inside, but I was able to see there was a staircase before us so grand that I felt unworthy to step up on it. I didn't have a choice, though. He grabbed my hand and ran up the steps with me in tow. Once we reached the landing, he looked each and every way—*for what, or whom, I didn't know*—before tugging me to the right. We raced down a long, wide corridor with portraits of A'li-uud lining the walls before coming to another set of huge double doors. He opened them, practically shoved me through, and shut them behind us. I heard the click of a lock before he turned to face me.

"What's going on?" I asked him again for the first time since in the bedroom at his parents' home.

"I'm keeping you safe," he replied. He grabbed onto an armoire so big I could probably stand inside and twirl and started to pull. It moved an inch, and he yanked again. I hurried to the other side and pushed, and it began to give. I kept quiet until he straightened up again, and I realized we had moved the armoire in front of the doors.

He wasn't done, though. He went to a vanity of matching wood and pattern as the armoire and started to shove it toward the doors, too. I didn't help with this one. Instead, I pushed for answers.

"What do you mean, keeping me safe?" I asked. "From what?"

"Pugna'ta saw you," he grunted, shoving his shoulder up against the vanity as it eased its way across the floor.

"Who?"

He huffed as he got the piece of furniture in front of the doors as he wanted and turned to me. "Pugna'ta. She's one of my warriors, and she saw you today."

"Oh," I said slowly, realizing who he was talking about. "The woman that came to your parents' house."

"Yes," he said, walking across the room. I realized for the first time since entering that we were in a bedroom of such a size it would likely hold Beni's entire house and all of the things in it. He sat on the bed and looked at me, and he had such a defeated expression on his face that my heart actually ached. "She and I have a history she's always trying to rekindle. That's why she came by. She saw you in the window, and she's going to the Council to tell them about you."

My throat seemed to constrict at the news, but I tried to remain calm as I asked, "Why is that so bad?"

Rex's eyes narrowed at me through the darkness. "You don't understand. There are Elders who will have you killed, or will kill you themselves, the minute they hear about you."

"I thought you have to vote on things like that," I squeaked.

"There are those who would prefer to do first and pay later," he said. He got to his feet and walked to me until we were only inches apart. "I won't let that happen."

I looked up at him, shaking slightly with a new and powerful burst of adrenaline. "Where are we?"

"This is my house," he said, waving a hand around. "Well, it's the house of the kingdom's Tribe Elder. I don't own it."

I nodded in understanding as my mind raced with fears and questions. I could feel his eyes on my face, but I didn't look up at him until I found the voice to ask my next query. "Couldn't we just go to the Forum? Together, I mean. I could talk to the other Elders myself."

His face, somehow, grew even more serious than it had been since he'd burst into the bedroom at his parents' house. He said, "Tabitha, you would never get out of there alive. Like I said, there are Elders who would kill you the moment they saw you, and, even if they were able to restrain themselves long enough to hear anything you said, they would kill you after that just because you know so much about our kind and our world."

"So what?" I asked. My voice sounded about an octave higher than normal in my gradually rising panic. "Why does it matter if I know anything about A'li-uud or Albaterra or you or anything? What could I possibly do to hurt anyone?"

He shook his head, and I saw a mournful look take over his face. "It's not about what threat you pose individually, Tabitha. It's about what threat you pose as a species."

I felt as defeated as he had looked just moments before. He had an answer to every single one of my questions, and no answer was something we could work with. There was a dead end no matter which way I spun it. *I felt hopeless, helpless, and tired.*

"Wait," I said suddenly. "What does this mean for you?"

"What do you mean?" He asked.

"Won't you be in trouble for protecting me? I mean, especially if that girl tells the Council about me and they put a—a hit out on me or something. Wouldn't you be in trouble for, I don't know, obstructing justice or something like that?"

He looked back at me silently, and I felt my head start to swim. I was right. He was facing serious consequences for what he was doing for me.

"The ones who would kill me," I whispered, terrified to ask the question I was about to ask but even more terrified to hear the answer. "Would they kill you, too?"

Again, he just looked at me, and it was as if the walls around me were caving in. My heart stopped in my chest, and my breath caught in my throat. Black spots danced in my vision. *I couldn't hear anything except for his breathing.*

"No," I murmured. My voice started growing louder with each word I spoke. "No. You can't do this. They can't do this. I won't let them!"

With a cry of distress, I leaped forward. He caught me in the air, and I threw my arms around his neck. *Our lips crushed together in a kiss so deep and so passionate that I realized I had never truly been kissed before.* I tasted him, tasted the fruit of Albaterra on his lips, and relished the way his tongue intertwined with mine. My legs curled around his waist, and I felt his hands take hold of my rear end, keeping me held aloft. *Suddenly, we were moving, but I knew nothing except for him.* Our mouths were fused as one, and I felt his soul meeting mine.

    I loved him. I was no longer falling in love with Rex; I loved him, and the very thought of him meeting his end to protect me brought tears to my eyes. They spilled down my cheeks in torrents and made both of our faces slick as we kissed, falling deeper and deeper into one another. I wept against his lips and finally released the fear, the uncertainty, and—above all—the love I'd kept bottled up ever since I'd landed in a fiery heap on Albaterra.

"I can't let you do this," I sobbed, breaking the kiss in my failed efforts to restrain myself from saying the words. I became dimly aware he was carrying me across the room toward the bed. "I can't let you die for me."

"I have no choice," he said hoarsely. He wasn't watching where he was walking. He just kept his eyes pinned to me. "Without you, there's no life to live anyway."

I looked back at him, our eyes searching each other, and then I kissed him again with fervor. He kissed me back, his tongue gliding over my lower lip, skimming the path of my teeth, just as we tipped backward onto the bed.

Chapter 11

Rex

"The ones who would kill me," Tabitha whispered. "Would they kill you, too?"

I stared back at her, unable to form the words to answer her. My ears were pricked for any noise that would give warning of incoming danger. If she hadn't been looking at me with such desperation, I would have been pacing the room and looking out of each of the windows intermittently. When I didn't respond, her face crumpled.

"No. No. You can't do this. They can't do this. I won't let them!"

She cried out and sprang toward me, and I reached for her. She landed in my arms, and, the next thing I knew, we were kissing. I felt her legs wrap around my waist, but I couldn't process anything other than her. *She tasted exactly as I imagined the heavens would taste if I could pluck one of the lavender clouds from the sky. I was filled with that same sweet, delicate scent of hers I smelled every night as we slept beside each other.*

I carried her to the bed, and we fell onto the mattress clumsily. Her lips were against mine in furious passion and carnivorous lust. I blindly reached for her clothes and ripped them from her. *I was so hungry for her I was sure I wouldn't survive it if I didn't have her.* She reciprocated rolling my pants down my legs, whipping them off and throwing them to the side carelessly. Through the darkness, I could see her eyes widen as they focused on my nether region, and I looked down too. *I was erect and ready.*

"Is something wrong?" I whispered.

She shook her head. "I've just never seen— you're so *big*."

I looked down at myself again, still feeling the powerful urges of lust but now also feeling the impediment of nerves, and asked, "Are humans smaller?"

"Usually," she said. She crawled up my body, then, and pressed her lips delicately to mine in a kiss of sweetness rather than urgency. When she pulled back, she said, "I suppose you've never been with a human."

"No," I replied softly. "I don't want to hurt you."

She kissed me lightly again. "You won't. I'll show you."

My lust took over again, and I enveloped her lips with my own. She kissed me back with equal vehemence, and I felt her hand drop to my erection. Her fingers cool to the touch as her skin always was, wrapped around my girth and started to stroke so slowly it was almost torture. I groaned into her mouth, and I felt her smile.

"Patience," she whispered, lifting her face from mine, easing her way back down my body. When she was level with my groin, she exhaled softly, and I felt the breath caress me. *I shivered with desire.*

Her fingers continued to slide up and down my length, and I watched her. Despite the darkness, I had never seen her look so radiant. She was beautiful. Her dark curls hung down in imperfect perfection, framing her face in such a way I couldn't help but stare. I saw those eyes that had captivated me the moment I had seen her looking up at me at the crash site. *They had penetrated me to my very core.*

I was in love with this woman, this human, this Tabitha Bartel. That was the truth of the matter, and I was going to do everything in my power to protect her from the prejudices and fear-founded impulses of my peers.

She lowered her head down and took me between her lips, and I inhaled sharply. My hips lifted against my will, but she pressed down on my thighs lightly to keep me in place. *I had never felt anything quite like it, and I knew it was because it was she who did this to me. Tabitha was my beginning, and she would be my end.*

I felt her tongue caressing my hardness the way it had caressed my tongue when we'd kissed, and it sent me into such a frenzy of desire that I writhed beneath her. I wanted to take her, to be one with her not just emotionally and spiritually but physically as well. *However, I let her take control.* I wasn't sure how to be with a human; I didn't know if human intimacy was the same as with A'li-uud.

I reached down and stroked her curls. She moaned into me, so I tangled my fingers in her hair and felt the way she pleasured me through my palms. I watched my hands rise and fall repeatedly atop her head in tandem with the rise and fall of my chest as I breathed, and my head rolled back against the pillow. It was, perhaps, the most intense experience of my life, and any experience I had had prior to Tabitha didn't compare. With each burst of sensation that crashed through me came an even more powerful burst of emotion as the love I felt for her dominated my entire being.

When she lifted her mouth from me and looked up at me, I returned her gaze. I was breathless, wanting, but I didn't want to go alone. *I wanted her to join me; I needed her to join me.* I released her hair and held out my hand to her. She took it. Then, I pulled her back up until we were face-to-face again, and I claimed her mouth with my own.

    She rolled to the side without separating her lips from mine, and I followed until I was on top of her. Her hand dipped down again and sought my manhood. I growled, and she mewled in return. I felt her guiding me, and then I felt myself being pressed up against her most intimate of areas.

    "Go," she whispered against my mouth. "Slowly."

I did as she asked, easing forward so carefully that the movement was almost unnoticeable. Her hand remained in place at my base, and she pushed back against me after a second to indicate she wanted me to withdraw. I obeyed, and, when she gently guided me forward again, she moaned into me. It was the most intoxicating sound I had ever heard, and I engulfed her with a deep, soul-reaching kiss. This time, she didn't push me back, and I entered her fully.

Tabitha's back arched to the ceiling, pressing her breasts into my chest, breaking our kiss. I looked down at her, admiring the beauty of her face in ecstasy. Her mouth was parted very slightly to allow for the shallow breaths she panted to slip through her lips, and her eyes were closed, so her lashes kissed the shelves of her cheekbones. I grazed the tip of my tongue over her lower lip, and she opened her eyes again to meet my gaze.

"More," she murmured heavily.

Her voice alone was enough to spur me on, but the command was an order I was happy to obey. Our chest rose and fell together, our skin sliding back and forth over one another, and we kept our eyes locked. Her mouth opened a little wider as I took her and panting gave way to moaning. I couldn't keep myself from dropping my lips to hers, tasting the guttural moans on her tongue. She reached up and clawed at my back, her nails pressing unrelentingly into my skin, and I grunted with the onset of pain. *It hurt, but it was the most delicious kind of pain.* It was the pain of lust and love and promise and protection and trust and safety and fear and worry and all other things. It brought me to the edge, but I held back.

"Rex!" She cried, throwing her head back, scratching up to the nape of my neck.

My name on her lips was the most beautiful sound I had ever heard in my life, and I had to taste it. I lunged forward, plunging my tongue into her mouth, swallowing her passion into myself.

Making love to her was an experience I could have never understood before her, *something I could have never understood without her.* It was not just a meeting of bodies as times past had been; it was the meeting of souls. Her lips, her nails, her skin, her eyes, her entire being held me captive in a never-ending circle of enchanted love. *It was a circle that, in all its heresy, was the only thing greater in the universe than the Grand Circle.*

"I love you," I said. My voice was muffled against her, so I yelled it out. "I love you!"

"I love you too," she panted breathlessly.

The words sent me spiraling into the throes of euphoria, and I felt her join me. We rocketed together through time and space, leaving behind everything that was, greeting all that would be. *I knew of nothing but her.* As I groaned her name and stared into her angelic face, I knew nothing would ever matter to me again. She was beauty personified, and our love was as visceral as our love-making.

    I didn't stop moving until she told me to, and, when she did, it was with a voice thick with satiation. Her eyes were dark and hooded, and her skin felt warmer than it ever had. I looked down at her without withdrawing myself and brought my fingertips to her cheek, which was crimson and flushed.

"I promise," I whispered, "I will protect you. I will keep you safe."

She gazed back at me and murmured, "But what about you?"

"You're more important." I brushed my fingertips along her jawline as I spoke.

"No," she said, lifting her hand and pressing it against my own cheek. "It doesn't matter if I'm safe if you're not with me."

I stared at her, drinking in the vision of the human I'd fallen in love with, and then I nodded. "Then I will do what I have to do to protect us both."

She parted her lips and tilted her chin upward, and I leaned down to meet her mouth. I slid out of her as we kissed and eased myself down beside her, pulling her into my arms. When the kiss broke, I just continued to hold her, and she curled into my form in such a way it seemed my body had been meant for hers the whole time. We stayed like that in the darkness and silence and just listened to our breathing, letting our fears wash away in the undertow of our love.

I felt her chest slowing in its rise and falls, and I heard her breaths becoming deeper. I realized she was falling asleep, and I felt heaviness in my eyes myself. Just as she exhaled her last conscious sigh, I closed my eyes, buried my face in her hair, and allowed myself to drift.

Suddenly, I was wrenched awake by a sound. It wasn't particularly loud, but, in the stillness, it was very clear. I bolted upright and looked around the room in a panic. Tabitha didn't move right away, but she stirred when she realized I was no longer holding her and sat up sleepily.

"What's wrong?" She asked softly.

"I heard something," I whispered, putting a finger to my lips to indicate she needed to be quiet. Her eyes widened with obvious fright, but I climbed slowly off the bed and moved to one of the large windows, trying to remain in the shadows to prevent anyone outside from seeing me. There appeared to be nothing out of place or unusual at first glance, so I shuffled even nearer the window and looked out below.

I could hear Tabitha crawling out of bed behind me, and I extended a hand backward to silently tell her to stop moving. She obeyed, but I heard her voice waft almost imperceptible to my ears. "What is it?"

My eyes drifted down, and I saw a figure standing outside the front double doors.

Chapter 12

Tabitha

"There's someone here."

My heart was pounding so hard I was sure it was going to crack right through my chest and spill out onto the floor. I got out of the bed and scrambled for my clothes, which I threw on in a frenzy of disarray. Rex turned from the window and grabbed his pants. When he had them on, he looked at me, and he looked just as intensely serious as he had when we'd left his parents' house.

"You will stay here," he said. His tone left no room for argument, so I just nodded, frozen in place.

He left the room so quietly it was as if he was floating. I listened as carefully as I could for any sound of his movements, but I heard nothing. That was more terrifying than if I had heard a scuffle because I couldn't be sure what was happening. After a minute of panicked terror, I disregarded his command and fled from the room.

I raced down the corridor of A'li-uud portraits at lightning speed. I didn't even care if my footsteps made noise. By the time I reached the landing of the impressive staircase, I was gasping for breath and had actually broken a cold sweat. I could see Rex hovering by the door, carefully leaning to the side to try and make out the visitor through the window. He looked back as I started to descend the stairs.

"I told you to stay put," he whispered furiously.

His voice was low, but, in the absence of other sounds, I heard him as if he was standing right beside me. I didn't respond until I reached the foyer.

"I had to know what was happening," I said. My voice sounded shaky and weak, both from physical exertion and fright.

He shook his head angrily, but he didn't argue. *I was grateful for that.* He resumed peering through the window, and then I saw his form relax slightly. When he turned to look back at me again, there was an expression of relief on his handsome face.

"It's Vi'den," he said. Before I could ask anything, he opened the door.

Standing on the threshold, there was a very tall, very thin A'li-uud. He wore robes rather than skins, and they flowed from his shoulders to the ground in regal draping. The shimmer I had noticed in Rex's skin the day he'd found me was very noticeable on this alien; even in the darkness, he seemed to shine. I glanced at him, expecting to see a bright moon casting its glow upon him to bring forth the shimmer, but there was none. He simply gleamed.

Rex stepped backward, and the A'li-uud entered at once. There was no time wasted in Rex closing the door behind him. Even as he stepped into the shadows of the unlit house, the tall creature continued to glimmer slightly, and I could see his eyes were even whiter than Rex's. It was hard to make out his exact skin tone in the darkness, but it was evident he was paler than Rex, and I knew he was also older. I wasn't sure how I knew that, as his face showed no signs of wrinkled or weather-worn age, but it seemed inherently obvious he was ancient compared to my prairie king. Somehow, despite the grandiose house we were in, Vi'den seemed very out of place.

"Vi'den," Rex said. There was a level of respect in his voice I hadn't heard before. He almost seemed awed in the presence of the old A'li-uud.

"Good evening, Rex," Vi'den replied evenly. I was surprised to hear him speak English, but I was even more surprised by his pronunciation. He sounded like he'd spoken English his whole life, rather than learned it as a second language. "I dare say you know why I have come."

Rex's gaze turned to me, and Vi'den's followed. I suddenly felt as though I'd been placed under a spotlight, and I grew self-conscious about my messy clothes and tangled hair.

"Tabitha, this is Vi'den," Rex said to me. "He is also an Elder, and he is my mentor."

I expected to be afraid, but something about Vi'den calmed me. Without him saying it, I knew he had no intention of hurting me.

"It is an honor to meet you, Tabitha." Vi'den inclined his head as he spoke, a motion I mimicked involuntarily.

"Thank you," I said nervously. "It's good to meet you too."

He studied me for a moment in silence before saying, "There is no need to be frightened, Tabitha. I have not come to harm you."

I nodded, and Vi'den turned back to Rex.

"We must act urgently, however," he went on. "You are in grave danger, both of you."

"I know," Rex said quickly. "That's why we're here."

"This is not safe enough. Action must be taken." Vi'den started to walk, and Rex fell into step with him. They both took long strides that forced me to almost jog to keep up with them. We crossed into a room filled with luxurious cushions and a smattering of intricately-etched pottery. Vi'den sank onto one of the poufs. Rex followed suit. When I didn't sit, he shot me a look, and I dropped onto the nearest one.

"I happened across Pugna'ta. She told me you were keeping a human at the home of your mother and father." Vi'den's eyes swiveled back to me, and, again, I felt like the center of attention. "I was not inclined to believe her, but I see I was wrong."

"Pugna'ta came to my parents' house for personal reasons and saw Tabitha through the window," Rex explained. "She became angry and aggressive—"

"With good reason, Rex," Vi'den interrupted. I felt my stomach roll with anxiety at his words. "After everything that has been happening as of late, it would be unnatural for her to accept such a thing without question."

Rex bristled slightly, and, though he still spoke with respect, he sounded mad. "I am her king. She has no authority to question me."

"Every A'li-uud has the authority to protect our kind," Vi'den responded swiftly and sternly. Rex seemed to deflate slightly, but Vi'den continued. "I did not come to address your disagreement with Pugna'ta, Rex, nor did I come to question your decision to keep Tabitha."

"Why did you come, then?" I asked. Both of them turned to look at me, and I saw the surprise on Rex's face.

Vi'den answered in a slow, clear voice. "I came to try to save your life."

I just stared at him, waiting for him to go on, but he didn't. He stared back at me. It wasn't until Rex spoke that our eye contact broke.

"What do you mean?" He asked.

"Pugna'ta intends to go to the Council and reveal your secret. I would be surprised if she hasn't done so already, or at least hasn't made contact with several Elders." Vi'den leaned forward a little toward Rex and looked him squarely in the eye. "You must take Tabitha to the Forum at once."

In clear contrast to the way Vi'den leaned forward, Rex dropped back slightly. There was an expression of horror on his face as he said, "You don't really think that should be my course of action. Vi'den, that's a death sentence—for Tabitha *and* me."

"Going into hiding is your death sentence, Rex. Coming forward offers you a chance for redemption."

"Redemption from what?" Rex spat the words like a bitter tonic from his tongue. "I am a Tribe Elder. It was at my discretion to keep her with me. I thought it best."

"Your treason is not in your decision to isolate her and maintain close contact," Vi'den said quietly. "The betrayal is in hiding your decision from the Council. By doing so, you have effectively undermined the purpose of the Forum, of the Council, and of your Elderhood. We have not been aware of Tabitha's existence, let alone her casual captivity, and, throughout the time of our ignorance, she has been learning much of our planet and our race. Tabitha knows more about A'li-uud life than any human ever has. The Council views this as treason. Do you not see why?"

"I do," Rex said begrudgingly.

"Then you must take her to P'otes-tat Ulti immediately. If you go into hiding, an order will be placed on your heads."

Rex shook his head, and I could tell he was very conflicted. "I can't take her there, Vi'den. There are other Elders who would kill her as soon as looked at her because of their fear."

"I will make sure that Tabitha stays safe," Vi'den said. His voice was low, and he spoke in earnest. It was just words, but what he said was spoken with such calm confidence I found myself relaxing. *I believed him.*

"How?" I asked.

"I will enact the Law of Witness," he answered.

I saw understanding dawn on Rex's face, but I felt no understanding of my own. "What is that?"

"It ensures your safety," Vi'den explained. "The Law of Witness dictates that the guest in question cannot be harmed while at P'otes-tat Ulti. To do so would be punishable by death."

"It means I can take you to the Forum and the others have no choice but to listen to what we have to say," Rex said quietly. His eyes had a faraway look, and I knew he was deep in thought.

"Yes." Vi'den nodded, and he looked back to Rex. "But you must bring her immediately. You cannot afford for her to be found by anyone before she has a chance to speak."

"What am I supposed to say?" I asked, now feeling a slight rise of panic. "What am I supposed to tell them?"

Rex lifted his gaze to me, then got to his feet and offered a hand to help me to mine. I took it as he said, "We tell them the truth. We tell them you pose no threat to the A'li-uud, that I brought you back to ascertain what you knew and, over time, we fell in love. We tell them you're innocent."

"What could I possibly be guilty of?" I murmured.

"Exactly," he said, cupping my face in his hands, kissing me gently.

Vi'den rose from the pouf on which he sat and approached us. "We must go now. Take her by the winds; we don't have time for you to make the journey. Bring her straight to the antechamber before she can be seen. You will wait there with her until you are called."

Rex and I both nodded our understanding, and Vi'den walked back to the double doors. The moment he opened them and stepped outside, he was gone. Rex took my hand, and we also walked outside, but we didn't disappear right away. He led me to the fountain before turning to me.

"This is still very dangerous," he said. "I wouldn't do it if we didn't have another choice. I want you to know that."

"I do know that," I reassured him.

He bent forward and kissed me again, and, before our lips parted, we were flying. When my feet hit the ground again, I gasped. Before me, there was a massive castle-like structure, complete with ornate doors as tall as a house. It was breathtaking in its beauty, but it was also dark and foreboding like the descriptions of castles in gothic romance novels. I shivered involuntarily as my nerves set in.

"This way," Rex said, grabbing me by the wrist, pulling me away from the doors.

We rounded part of the castle until we came to a much smaller, single door of ordinary construction. He opened it for me, and I entered first. The room was a big one, but it felt cramped somehow. Statues and shelves lined with tomes and wall-hanging tapestries seemed to fill every single inch, and the gray stone walls felt like they were sinking in on me. There was just one other door in the room, and I was certain it was the door that would bring me before the Elders. *I eyed it with trepidation.*

Rex came up behind me and wrapped his arms around my waist, saying nothing. We stood there together without saying anything. Very faintly, I could hear the low rumble of multiple voices speaking at once on the other side of the door, but I couldn't make out anything being said. It wasn't until the door swung open—*so unexpectedly that I jumped back against Rex—* that I could properly hear everything.

"You're choosing a human's safety over the safety of our race, Vi'den," a male was saying furiously. "The Law of Witness was not written to protect terrorists!"

"We won't know if she's a terrorist until we speak to her," another voice chimed in. This one was strange, almost gurgling in its syllable.

"Please bring forth Elder Rexstrenu'us Et'Herba Cam-pes'tribus and the human."

I recognized the third voice as Vi'den's. I looked over my shoulder at Rex, and he nodded at me. I turned back toward the door, and the small, young A'li-uud who had opened it brandished a hand, motioning me to walk into the chamber.

"I love you," Rex whispered in my ear.

I swallowed hard, choked back my fear, and said, "I love you too."

The Unfolding

Chapter 1

Rex

The Forum was always a solemn, somber affair. It was not a place for light-hearted quips and exchanges, and most of the Elders saw it as the ideal opportunity to air their grievances, no matter how large or small. But I had never felt such thick tension and animosity in the air as I did when I walked into the circle with Tabitha.

It was strange to stand in the center of the stone room, surrounded by Elders with faces as hard as the walls around them, and to see my seat beside Duke empty. Never in my short time as an Elder had anyone been called into the Forum as a witness, and it was surreal to be my own first. In truth, Tabitha was the one being called, but I was an accessory to her and was required to be at her side. We stood upon a heavy, round, stone slab which had been placed over the fire pit in the very heart of the room, and I was surprised to see how dark the space was in the absence of flames. To rectify the problem, the small hall boy brought forth six torches mounted on thin, stiff poles and thrust them into the dirt floor in equal increments around us. Then, he went from one torch to another and lit each until the glow was so bright I could see only silhouettes of the A'li-uud sitting around us.

    Beside me, Tabitha was trembling. Her hand brushed against mine, and I could feel its quaking tremors against my skin. She felt warmer to the touch than usual; I knew it was because her adrenaline was rocketing through her like a bolt of lightning. *I wanted to comfort her somehow, but I remained still and straight-backed as I awaited the interrogation.*

I didn't have to wait long. Once the hall boy scuttled away and the sound of the door closing behind him echoed all the way up to the twenty-foot ceiling, there was a very light shuffling sound, and then I heard Vi'den speak.

"The Forum has called forth a witness of the human species, accompanied by Elder Rexstrenu'us Et'Herba Cam-pes'tribus." His calm, deep voice filled the chamber like gas, swirling around me, coming to rest on my ears. Even through the torches' glow and smoke, I could see his tall, thin form standing regally before his chair. "Human, what is your name?"

There was silence; it was so loud as the other Elders waited that it practically made me deaf. Then, I heard the sweet, girlish voice I loved ring out.

"Tabitha Bartel," she said with a tremor.

I didn't look at her, but, out of the corner of my eye, I could see her chin was lifted even as her limbs shook. I felt a swelling of pride in my chest for the woman's bravery, and the pride was joined by searing adoration when she curled her pinky finger around mine discreetly.

"Tabitha Bartel," Vi'den continued. "You have been brought before this Council to explain your purpose for infiltrating the boundaries of the galaxy Andromeda and entering the atmosphere of our planet, Albaterra."

"I didn't infiltrate anything," Tabitha said at once, her voice steadying in her sudden defensive anger. "My ship crashed, and I ended up here. That's all."

I squeezed my pinky around hers as a warning. I knew there were Elders in the chamber who would relish a reason to condemn her and the other humans for the smallest of reasons. Her aggression and lack of cooperation would only serve to enforce their bloodthirsty cause.

"You were aboard the ship *Paragon*, which crashed in the Kingdom Campestria of Albaterra nearly two moon cycles ago. Is that correct?"

"Yes," Tabitha replied huffily.

I tried to see Vi'den's face through the smoky haze, but I couldn't make out any of his features. He stood as elegantly still as usual. Ma'ris, however, who sat to Vi'den's left, was distinguishable. His round face was puffed up in suspicious indignance, and he was staring at Tabitha as though she were a puzzle to be solved. I didn't try to look around at the other Elders, but I could hear mutterings beside and behind me, and they didn't sound promising.

"Where have you been kept since you were recovered from the crash site?" Vi'den questioned.

Tabitha turned to look at me, but I kept my eyes trained firmly forward. I could feel her uncertainty wavering from her body, and I was sure she was hoping I would answer for fear she would say something that would cause me trouble. When I kept my mouth closed and refused to look back at her, though, she responded.

"With Rex."

"At his home?"

She made a noise that was a cross between a whine and a sniff of frustration. She knew that Vi'den was aware of where she had been, but she didn't seem to understand it needed to be stated for the Council.

"No," she said finally with reluctance. "At his parents' house."

The mutterings grew noticeably louder, and Vi'den stayed quiet until they subsided. I could feel angry gazes and glares being tossed at me from some of the Elders.

"Were you imprisoned?" Vi'den continued.

Tabitha shifted her weight from one foot to the other, but her pinky remained firmly entwined around mine. "No."

"You had freedom to go where you pleased?"

"No," she said again. "Not exactly. I wasn't allowed to leave the property."

"But you were free to go and do as you pleased within the property lines?"

"Yes." She nodded once.

From behind me, I heard a bark. "Blasphemy!" There was immediately an outpouring of agreeable chatter, and I saw the dark silhouette of Vi'den's arm rising into the air to silence the speakers.

"What did you do during your stay?" Vi'den asked calmly.

Tabitha's voice had started to tremble again, and I could feel her fear from the enraged Elders around us. "I don't know. I learned how to cook some things, helped Beni make clothes and took care of the little ones."

"Traitor!" The roar came from my right, and I knew the voice to be that of the war-happy cave Elder. He was a squat A'li-uud who appeared to be nothing but a ball of muscles. He had a rough, gritty voice that could be identified by the blindest of beings. I turned to look at him, but I couldn't see him through the smoke. He rectified the problem, though, leaping off his chair and seizing the two torches nearest him before yanking them from the ground and whipping them furiously against the wall. They were extinguished immediately, and I could make out his face clearly. It was mangled into an ugly sneer, and his small, beady eyes flashed with rage.

Several other Elders leaped to their feet as well to stop him, but he was close enough to me to lunge and close his fingers around my wrist. Duke wrenched at the Elder's forearm, but it didn't give, and I was pulled forward from the stone slab onto the dirt floor of the chamber.

"You've shown a human our ways! You let'em get close!" The cave Elder bellowed, knocking Duke back with a swing of his free arm. "You'll die for your treason! I'll kill you myself!"

"Enough!" Vi'den boomed.

Usually, it would have been enough to bring peace back to the room, but the Elder was beside himself. He looked at Vi'den for the briefest of moments before letting out a snarl like a sabrecat and charging at Tabitha.

"No!" I shouted, flinging myself back onto the slab and throwing myself in front of her. His fist landed squarely on my temple. I grappled with him in a daze as Tabitha hunched down behind me, sobbing in terror.

Duke had wrapped his arm around the Elder's neck and was yanking him back while two others pulled insistently on the Elder's thick arms, but it didn't hinder him from yelling. "You'd save a human instead of your own! Traitor! Traitor!"

"Torik!" Vi'den's voice was no longer a boom; it was an explosion. It shattered the confrontation like glass and left everyone still and panting. The cave Elder, Torik, stared daggers at me, but he finally didn't say anything else, and Duke loosened his hold.

"This is a disgrace," Ma'ris warbled, shaking his head solemnly. I wasn't sure if he meant Torik's behavior or my choices regarding Tabitha, but I didn't care.

"Everyone will sit," Vi'den said slowly and firmly. "Now."

Torik shook off Duke of him and dropped back onto his chair, his chest heaving in great bursts. The other Elders found their seats again as well, and I returned to my place beside Tabitha on the slab in the room's center. She was shaking violently, and her sobs were so deep they were nothing more than desperate gasps for breath. I knew I was to stand stoically beside her and wait for the interrogation to continue, but I couldn't leave her in such a frightened despair. I wrapped my arms around her and pulled her to me, as she wept heartily against my chest.

"Disgusting," Torik spat. "He cares about it."

"That will do, Torik," Vi'den said harshly.

Silence filled the chamber once more, broken only by Tabitha's wracking sobs.

I pressed my lips to her ear and whispered, "I'm so sorry."

Her cries became even stormier, and she practically vibrated in my arms with the intensity of her tears. I held her tightly, but I was rapidly becoming more worried.

"Tabitha," I murmured. "We're not done yet. You have to collect yourself."

Another few minutes passed in which her weeping lessened until it was just a series of sniffles, and then she straightened up. She wiped her eyes, glanced at me fearfully, and then faced Vi'den again. In the absence of the two torches Torik had thrown, the glare from the flames was no longer too great, and I could see Vi'den's face. He looked very, very serious and rather intimidating. When he made eye contact with Tabitha, however, there was a shadow of kindness beneath his aged features.

"I apologize for the interruption," he said, inclining his head as a show of regret. "You have my word it will not happen again. You are safe here."

Torik grunted, but Vi'den ignored him, as did everyone else. Tabitha sniffled, nodded, and said softly, "Thank you."

"Are you prepared to continue?"

"Yes," she agreed.

Vi'den sent a look around the room that clearly indicated he would not tolerate another outburst from anyone, and then he asked, "You are from Earth, correct?"

"Yes," she repeated dully.

"Why were you aboard the human ship *Paragon*?"

Tabitha hesitated. The chamber was so quiet now that I could hear the slow, bated breaths of the Elders surrounding me as they waited for her reply.

"I wanted to get away from Earth," she admitted eventually. Her tone was carefully measured and well-controlled as though she didn't want to give anything more away than necessary.

"Why?" Vi'den pressed.

I could feel her unwillingness to answer him, and I wanted to tell her she had no choice. To refuse would be death, both hers and mine, once we got on the other side of the gates separating the protected Elder city of P'otes-tat Ulti and the rest of Albaterra. Thankfully, she chose to speak.

"My life had become very bad," she said simply. "I didn't know how to fix it, so I just wanted to start over."

"Were you a space explorer before this mission?"

"No," she said with a shake of her head. "I was a chef. A NASA recruiter asked me to join the *Paragon's* crew."

There was a very brief pause, and then Vi'den asked, "What is NASA?"

"The National Aeronautics…and…Space…Administration?" What had initially started off as a confidently-spoken answer quickly turned into Tabitha looking around uncertainly and finishing her answer with a question mark. No one, including myself, knew what she was talking about, and it must have been evident on each of our faces because she explained, "It's the part of my country's government responsible for space travel and such."

All of the Elders exchanged looks, and I was sure they were thinking the very same thing that had popped into my head. NASA was our target, whether for elimination or for interrogation. The piece of information was an invaluable step in the right direction for securing our galaxy and the safety of the A'li-uud from human colonization—*or worse.*

Vi'den's voice seemed to bring everyone back to the questioning at hand. "What was the mission of the *Paragon*?"

Tabitha looked at me again, but, this time, it was with uncertainty as to why she would even be asked such a question. "I don't know," she said honestly.

I expected to hear scoffs of disbelief around the circle, but there were none.

"Your government did not disclose the purpose of sending you and your crew into space?" Vi'den asked. Even he didn't sound entirely convinced.

"Not to me," Tabitha said. "I'm sure the captain and some others knew more. I only knew that NASA had been looking for new resources in space for some time."

"What kind of resources?"

"You know," she said, waving her hands about a little. "Fuel and things like that."

Again, the A'li-uud in the room exchanged looks. Tabitha shuffled her feet nervously and waited for her next question, but it didn't come. After a sufficient silence, Vi'den looked at me.

"Do you trust your warriors to keep her confined?"

"I do," I said confidently.

"Then the Council will release Tabitha Bartel into your care."

"Thank you," Tabitha burst out in a grateful breath. Vi'den inclined his head to her as acknowledgment before continuing to address me.

"Was the captain of the *Paragon* recovered from the crash?" He asked.

"I do not know," I told him. "Most of the survivors were severely injured and in need of intense treatment to recover. Some are still struggling to recover. Only in the last few days have any remaining crewmembers been able to speak with my warriors, and I did not want to exacerbate their condition with an intense interrogation for fear they would not survive."

There were murmurings again, but, this time, they were more thoughtful. Vi'den considered my words carefully before speaking.

"You will take Tabitha Bartel to your home. She is not to leave, and you will have a guard on her at all times," he said. There was a look in his eyes that told me he intended the guard to protect her as much as anyone else, and I was thankful for that. "You must find out if the captain was amongst the survivors. If so, you are to do the interrogation yourself."

"I understand."

"Tabitha Bartel, thank you for your cooperation," Vi'den said, turning to her.

"Of course," she murmured. There was a look of unhappy curiosity on her face which surprised me.

Extending his arms outward to signal his address to the entire Council, Vi'den said boomingly, "We will continue as agreed to eliminate the threat of remaining ships in the Andromeda galaxy. Our plans beyond that would be dependent on the *Paragon's* captain if he survived."

Then, swiveling his eyes onto me, he added, "You may take her back to your home, but you are to return to P'otes-tat Ulti immediately to answer charges against you for treason."

Tabitha's mouth opened in horror, but I grabbed her hand. "Thank you, Vi'den." Then, before she could ask any questions, I pulled her out of the room.

Chapter 2

Tabitha

When we left the building and stepped outside, it was very dark and rather cold. I was still shaking from everything that had happened. The interrogation, the fight, and most certainly what I had heard at the end about the rest of the *Paragon* crew. Further, I had a hard lump in my stomach of fear about what it meant for Rex to return to the

Elders and be tried for treason. I spun on my heel and faced him.

"What just happened?" I demanded, not able to put my questions into more specific terms.

He looked at me for just a moment before tilting his face to the sky and closing his eyes. I knew what he was doing; he was preparing to take me and fly on the winds back to his home, rather than traveling by foot. I stomped my foot like a childish little girl and grabbed his wrist.

"Rex, I mean it. What just happened?"

"I have to take you back," he said. Then, closing his free hand around the hand I'd secured over his wrist, he jumped upward, and we were flying.

I had traveled with him this way twice before, but it was still just as jarring as the first time. It was like being catapulted into the space between everything and nothing. I was unable to see or hear, and the only thing I could feel was his hand on mine. It terrified me to think what would happen if either of us let go of the other, but I had a pretty good feeling he would just keep flying while I plummeted to my death.

When we landed, I was even more scared and furious than I had been at P'otes-tat Ulti. I tried to pull myself free of him and step back, but I stumbled because I hadn't gained my footing again. He reached forward to help me, but I shook him free with a glare.

"You need to tell me what's happening right now," I said firmly.

"Not here. I need to get you inside," he replied in a low voice.

I hadn't realized he'd taken me back to his house. It was strange to think that, only a couple of hours before, we'd been inside that house making love and preparing to run for our lives. I saw the outline of his massive, palatial home through the thick, navy blue darkness and flicked my gaze to the double doors marking the entrance. I wanted to resist, to demand that he tell me, but I knew he was right and I didn't want to put him in any more trouble than he already was, so I let him lead me inside and take me up to his room.

It was just as we'd left it. The blankets of the bed were wrinkled and mussed, and I sniffed and could have sworn I smelled our passion in the air. I actually felt sad realizing that everything seemed to have changed in just a few short hours.

Instead of asking him again to tell me, I just sat on the end of the bed and crossed my arms, staring at him and waiting. He stood by the door, and, when he reached for the knob, I stiffened.

"Where are you going?" I asked through gritted teeth.

"I was ordered to return," he said. He sounded rather dull and exhausted, and I wanted to feel pity for him—*or to at least feel sympathy*—but all I could feel was frustration and fear. "I have to go."

"You will not go!" I cried, springing to my feet again, crossing the room to block the door. "You can't leave me here with all of these questions while I'm waiting to find out what's going to happen to you! That's not fair!"

I felt my eyes start to burn with tears I didn't want to shed, but I didn't look away from him as I normally would have because I wanted him to see how serious I was. He looked back at me, and he lifted his thumb to the corner of my eye where a small droplet was forming. *His touch was very warm, as it always was, and I was struck by how beautiful his azure skin was even in the darkness of night.*

"You are crying," he stated simply.

A'li-uud didn't cry, and if they did, it wasn't in the same way as humans. The first time I had wept in front of him, it had been because I was afraid he was going to kill me after he'd found me at the *Paragon's* crash site. He'd been befuddled by the liquid coming from my eyes and had asked me what I was doing. It was just one of several glaring differences between humans and A'li-uud.

"Of course I'm crying," I snapped, irritable I wasn't stronger. "I'm confused and scared, and you won't give me an answer to anything I ask you."

He sighed and looked at the large floor-to-ceiling window that lined the wall opposite the bedroom door. "I need to fetch a guard. When I get back, I'll explain as much as I can, but I won't have a lot of time."

"Fine," I agreed.

I was left alone in the room with my thoughts, and I walked to the window. Looking down, I saw Rex disappearing out of the courtyard and out of sight completely. Fear was swirling in my heart, but greater than the fear of what was to happen to him was the fear of what had happened to my comrades from the *Paragon*. From the small bit that I'd heard Vi'den say, the ones who had survived the crash were being kept somewhere, and they were to be interrogated. I didn't know if it was the same as what had happened to me—standing amidst a group of A'li-uud with questions flying at me left and right—or if it was something more sinister, *but I knew I needed to find out.*

    When Rex returned, I was pacing the room. He swung the door open, and with him, there was a very tall, nearly naked alien. Compared to the other A'li-uud I had seen, he had strikingly dark skin, almost as dark as the nighttime sky of Albaterra, and his abdomen was somehow even more chiseled than Rex's. While both men were bare-chested, this new A'li-uud was wearing only a pair of bottoms which looked like a Speedo or like the minimalistic trunks professional wrestlers wore. I immediately averted my eyes.

"Tabitha, this is Ca-es'a. He is my most faithful warrior. You can trust him," Rex said, motioning to the dark-skinned warrior beside him, who bowed his head to me by way of greeting.

"Nice to meet you," I murmured.

He didn't speak, but he inclined his head again. I wondered if he could understand English before remembering that A'li-uud had the ability to speak whatever language was spoken to them. Rex looked at him and said something in his native language of clicks and clacks. Ca-es'a said something back and left the room, closing the door behind him as he went. Rex turned to me.

"What did you tell him?" I asked.

"I told him I needed a moment alone with you," Rex said. "And it truly is a moment, Tabitha. I have to get back."

"I need to know where the other crewmembers are and what you're doing to them,"

I said at once. I wanted to make the most of whatever limited time I had with him.

Rex studied me carefully. Even though there were no lights or flames in the room, I could see his white eyes probing me, considering me. Finally, he said, "The survivors are receiving medical treatment for their injuries. Many were near death. Several have died despite our best efforts."

"Where are they?" I asked.

"They are in the holding cells underground." His voice was soft and quiet. "There are guards on constant watch."

"For whose protection?" I snapped, crossing my arms.

"Tabitha, you cannot be so stubborn as to believe I would naively allow strange beings to walk freely amongst my people," he cut in a little angrily. "I am entrusted to protect my village and those who call it home."

I glared at him. "You think we're here to kill you all or something?"

"You could be," he shot back. "You said yourself you didn't know why you had been sent on your mission in the first place."

I stared at him silently, biting the inside of my cheek. I was furious, but he had a point, and that only made me madder than I already was. "What are you going to do when you interrogate them?"

"I'm going to ask them the questions I need to be answered," he said. He stated it like it was the most obvious thing in the universe as if he couldn't understand why I would ask such a question.

"You're not going to…" I gestured randomly with my hands. "…stick hot pokers on them or anything?"

He blinked. I could tell I'd stunned him with the very notion. "No."

"Okay." I kept my arms crossed, but I softened my tone a little. "Can I see them?"

"No," he said again. He didn't offer any further explanation, and I felt my temper flare once more.

"Why not?"

"You heard Vi'den. You are to stay here."

"I don't care," I said heatedly. "I need to tell them they'll be okay."

"You need to stay here!" He roared. I actually stepped back in surprise. He had never raised his voice to me, and it was just as frightening a sound as the way Torik had screamed at him. Rex's eyes were narrow slits of rage, and I could see his fists clenching and unclenching. "Don't you understand that, if you disobey, you will be killed, and I will be next? I'm trying to protect you!"

"From what? Vi'den said I was safe!" I yelled back, spurred by his outburst.

"At P'otes-tat Ulti, you were safe," he hissed. "Here, you're nothing but a target and a threat."

We stared at each other for a moment, our chests rising and falling with the intensity of our argument. Neither of us broke eye contact, and I was thankful I wasn't crying now. Eventually, Rex turned toward the door.

"I have to go," he said emotionlessly. "Caes'a will be outside the room if you need anything."

"What are you going to do to the other ships?" I asked suddenly.

I hadn't intended to blurt it out so bluntly, but I'd panicked when I'd realized he was leaving. His hand froze halfway to the doorknob, and he turned back to me so slowly that it was almost painstaking. He looked me directly in the eye again, but, this time there was something in his gaze that seemed restrained.

"There was a vote," he explained softly, "before your ship crashed. We had learned that humans were in our galaxy, and it was our duty as Elders to decide what action we should take. It was agreed that we would destroy all human ships in

Andromeda to protect our race from any immediate threat. What you heard tonight was Vi'den acknowledging that the vote still stands."

Even though I couldn't see myself, I knew my face had gone pale. I felt my hands become cold and clammy, and there was a moment when I was certain whether I was going to pass out or not.

"You—you're going to destroy them?" I whispered, utterly horrified.

"Yes."

I shook my head, trying to wrap my mind around the words but I was completely unable to get a grasp on what I was hearing. *It was barbaric, nothing like what I had come to know of the peaceful A'li-uud.*

"But...*why?*"

"They pose an immediate threat," he said again with a small shrug of his shoulders.

A thought hit me, then, that almost knocked me entirely off my feet and stole my breath right out of my chest. "Oh my God," I said in a shocked, strained voice. "That's why the *Paragon* crashed, isn't it? You shot the ship."

Rex didn't respond. He didn't look away from me, but he also didn't say anything, and it was enough of a confirmation for me to sink to my knees from the sheer weight of the news.

"Oh my God," I said again.

There was a moment of silence that was so mournful in its existence I actually ached. Then, Rex murmured, "I must go, Tabitha."

"You killed them!" I cried, looking up at him through thick, pearly tears. "Everyone who died, all those people who were blown up or burned or severed, you did that, and for no reason! And you're keeping anyone who survived as *prisoners*!"

Again, he didn't say anything, and I burst into a tidal wave of sobs. My heart seared with horrible, gut-wrenching pain for all the crewmembers who had lost their lives simply because they were in the wrong place at the wrong time. Just because they were considered dangerous without any proof of such. I wept as I thought of my sous chef, the captain, Leanne, even Trey, and I cried even harder because I didn't know if they had suffered or made it at all.

When I looked up again through misty eyes, Rex was gone.

Chapter 3

Rex

The look on Tabitha's face when she found out the truth had cut me to the quick. I had never seen so much pain in someone, not even when I'd watched the late chief of Campestria take his last breath. *It hurt me all the more to see the pain ripping through the lovely, delicate features of the woman I loved.*

But I had to go. It would have been worse for both of us if I didn't.

I'd left her wailing on the bedroom floor, which made me feel even worse than I already did. When I silently closed the door behind me, Ca-es'a laid his hand on my shoulder and gave me a look of stoic sympathy. Without speaking, he told me he would watch over her, and I pressed my hand over his as thanks. Then, I swept out of the house into the courtyard and leaped into the wind to travel back to P'otes-tat Ulti.

Upon my arrival, the hall boy immediately ushered me back into the room Tabitha, and I had been bidden to wait in until called earlier. It had been strange then not to be in the chamber during the Forum, but it was stranger yet to be in the cold, unforgiving room alone. I stood in one place rather than paced as I was inclined to, primarily because my nerves wouldn't allow me to move but also because I didn't want my footsteps to overwhelm the little bits of conversation I was able to pick out through the door to the chamber.

"...protected her..."

"It's treason!"

"I'm sure we can come to..."

Frustrated, I closed my eyes. I understood why the Council wanted to try me for treason, and I knew it wasn't a formal trial or I would be brought into the chamber by several guards and restrained. Nevertheless, it frustrated me that some of the Elders allowed their fear to overcome their compassion and understanding for other living beings, no matter how different from us.

Of course, I had been one of those Elders. I had raised my hand in the vote to destroy the human ships.

The hall boy opened the door, and then stood back. I could see that the stone slab Tabitha and I had stood upon before was still present, but the torches had been removed, and the chamber was disarmingly dark. I realized they had only added the torches for Tabitha's sake. A'li-uud had much sharper eyesight than humans, and I could see sufficiently in the absence of the flames.

"Please bring forth Elder Rexstrenu'us Et'Herba Cam-pes'tribus," Vi'den said solemnly from his place around the circle.

I was gestured forward by the small A'li-uud, and I swept past him with my chin tilted rather higher than normal. In my indignance over the matter, I felt a strong surge of prideful arrogance, and I knew it showed with the swagger of my steps and the disdainful expression on my face. When I took my place in the center of the stone slab, Vi'den got to his feet.

"Elder Rexstrenu'us Et'Herba Campes'tribus, do you understand that you have been called before the Council to answer accusations of treason against you?"

I looked at him with a face as stony as the slab upon which I stood. "I do."

"May the Council note that this is not an official trial and will not be treated as such," Vi'den said, looking around at his counterparts.

There was a disorganized synchronization of nods.

"Then, let us begin." Vi'den looked back to me. "Rex, you took actions regarding the keeping of an individual human captive, namely Tabitha

Bartel, without the consult and consent of your Elder brotherhood. What do you have to say for yourself?"

I frowned. I respected Vi'den with every fiber of myself; he had been my mentor upon my being made an Elder, and he was well-known to be extraordinarily fair. Despite this, I couldn't keep the haughty lilt out of my voice as I answered him.

"I found Tabitha at the crash site immediately upon my arrival. She was the only human who had made it out of the wreckage alive, and she was practically uninjured. I took her to my parents' home at once, because it was nearer than my own to the ruins, to find out what she knew. I knew I could trust my parents to keep her confined as I saw fit when I departed to inform the Council of the crash."

"But why did you fail to inform us you had a human?" Ma'ris gurgled. It took me a moment to understand what he'd asked. As the leader of Albaterra's underwater Kingdom, Ma'ris sounded like he had bubbles in his mouth, and I stared closely at him while he spoke to try to read his lips and understand better what he had said.

Reluctantly, I replied, "I did not want the Council to make a hasty decision."

"You wanted to protect her," Torik said snidely from my right. "Just like you did tonight."

I turned slowly to look at him. If my eyes could have shot fire, they would have. "Yes," I hissed. "I wanted to protect her."

"Why?" This question came from Duke, who was behind me. He sat in the chair beside my empty one, and, when I looked at him, I couldn't read the expression on his face. Duke was, for all intents and purposes, my friend, but he was hard-headed and quick to battle, and I wasn't sure he would find the truth a suitable answer for himself. Nevertheless, I was before the Council, and I couldn't lie.

"I love her," I said softly.

The sudden hum of sounds the Elders made was like screams compared to how quietly I'd spoken. Torik made coarse, crude comments of disgust while Ma'ris burbled something unintelligible. Even Vi'den murmured something I couldn't hear clearly. As for Duke, his features went through a series of changes, starting with horror, transitioning to anger, and settling finally on deep contemplation.

"You love a human?" He asked. His voice was low, almost as though he intended for the question to be a conversation between him and me alone.

"Yes," I affirmed truthfully.

"Traitor," Torik spat in revulsion.

"If I may," Vi'den interjected. I spun to face him once more, and he met my gaze with a thoughtful, calculating look. "It is not at the Council's discretion who you love, and you are entitled to love whomever you like." He looked around at the others with stern eyes, almost as though he were telling them off before continuing to speak. "The issue at hand is your acting independently regarding a matter of A'li-uud safety."

"How are you so calm about this?" Torik snapped, rounding on Vi'den. "We're lucky she didn't decimate the entire planet!"

"You're pathetic," I snapped. I couldn't help myself; it flew out of my mouth before I could reign in my irritation. I had completely forgotten I was on trial with the Council and needed to comport myself appropriately. All I cared about at that moment was Torik's seemingly endless assault on Tabitha and her character. "You know as well as I do that she couldn't hurt me, much less the entire planet. You just have a prejudice against anyone that isn't like us, and you like to see people die."

Torik opened his mouth in a wide, toothy grin of maliciousness, but Vi'den silenced both of us with a loud clearing of his throat.

"While I may not agree with the extreme claims Torik makes," Vi'den said slowly, "he has a point which cannot be ignored. By acting independently, you chose to dismiss the authority of the Council, and your decision could have had unnecessary and unpleasant consequences. At the very least, it is important to us that the humans don't know more about us than we know of them, and Tabitha Bartel has gained very intimate knowledge of A'li-uud daily life since being in your care without the approval of the Elderhood."

"I understand," I said, lowering my head slightly. I didn't say it to pacify him or the others; I truly understood the weight of my actions and knew they had every right to question my loyalty and dedication to my position of leadership.

"However," Vi'den continued, holding up a solitary finger. I looked back up, surprised. "As Tabitha Bartel has stood before us and we have released her back into your care, it seems we can all agree that no damage was done."

"That we know of," Torik said grudgingly.

"Quiet," Duke hissed at him. I felt a surge of gratitude toward my friend, even if we often didn't see eye-to-eye.

"It is my personal opinion that we need not mete out punishment for what could have been," Vi'den said stoutly. "I do not believe Tabitha Bartel to be a threat to our kind. Moreover, I believe you acted as you saw best when you brought her to your parents' home in Campestria rather than bringing her to us."

"You're an old fool," Torik hissed at Vi'den.

Unexpectedly, Ma'ris swelled in his chair and turned toward Torik with narrowed eyes. In a voice clearer than I'd ever heard from him, he thundered, "You. Will. Show. Respect."

Ma'ris was the oldest of all the Elders of the currently sitting Council. So old, in fact, that he'd been made an Elder two entire Councils ago. I had never realized he was sensitive about his age, or perhaps he simply demanded respect from those of us who would be considered youth, despite our being of equal authoritative status as him.

"Those in favor," Vi'den continued as though nothing had occurred, "of absolving Rex of all treason accusations?"

His hand rose first, followed by Ma'ris and several others. I wanted to appear unconcerned about the outcome, but I couldn't resist turning around to see if the Elders behind me had opinions in my favor. I saw Duke's hand amongst them, and I breathed an internal sigh of relief when I saw that the hands raised were of the majority.

"So be it. Absolved of all accusations," Vi'den said. He nodded at me. "Please take your seat, Elder Rexstrenu'us."

With a nod back at him, I wound my way off the slab and around the circle to my empty seat. As I lowered myself into it, Duke nudged my arm with his, though he didn't look at me. *I understood it as his way to show his support.*

"Now, to another important matter." Vi'den's eyes were still on me. "The prisoners are in your kingdom, Rex, and the Council is entrusting their interrogations to you and your warriors. As discussed earlier, you are to perform the interrogation on the captain of the *Paragon*, assuming he survived the crash."

"Yes," I agreed.

"I ask the Council to come to a consensus as to what to do with the captives after all information, valuable and invaluable, has been extracted."

The musing of the other Elders was nothing but noise to me as I realized there was a chance it would be deemed that the surviving humans should be killed, and it would likely be my warriors, on my word, to carry out the deed. Tabitha's face flashed through my mind, the face I had seen when she'd found out about everything—

the ships, the survivors, and the Council's plans. For the first time since initially learning humans were in Andromeda before the *Paragon* even crashed, and before I had even known Tabitha, I felt doubt.

    Had I never met Tabitha, my decision would have been clear-cut and unwavering. *The safety of the A'li-uud came first.* Now, however, while I still valued the safety and preserved existence of my race, I couldn't dismiss the consequences to my relationship with Tabitha of eliminating her people. Worse, I knew I wouldn't be able to obey the Council if it were ruled that she was to be eliminated as well.

Her words sprang fresh in my mind. "You killed them! Everyone who died, all those people who were blown up or burned or severed, you did that, and for no reason!"

"Rex?" Vi'den's voice brought me back to the present. "The prisoners are under your supervision. What say you?"

I took in a deep breath, and then I said, "I think we need to find out what they know first."

Chapter 4

Tabitha

I stayed on the floor with silent tears streaming down my face for what felt like hours. I knew I had lost all track of time because, when I finally clambered to my feet and wiped my cheeks clean of moisture, it was still dark outside, which meant that too much time couldn't have passed. Nevertheless, I felt as though I'd just returned from battle; my muscles were weak, and my emotions were utterly spent.

    My inclination was to crawl into the bed where Rex and I had made love not so long ago and sleep until I couldn't sleep anymore, but I didn't. I couldn't make myself relax as long as I knew my fellow *Paragon* crewmembers were being held prisoner somewhere in the very village where I was staying. While I understood why Rex hadn't allowed all of the humans to roam freely after they were nursed back to health, I was filled with pain and fear over the conditions of their captivity. I needed to know they were okay, that they weren't spending their days or nights being tortured or neglected. At the very least, I needed to make sure they knew I was going to do everything I could to get them released.

Rex's words about staying put in the room flashed through my mind, but I dismissed them at once. I didn't want to put myself in danger, and I certainly didn't want him to be in danger because of my actions, but I felt as if I had no other choice. So, with trembling knees, I opened the door.

Standing just outside the bedroom there was the warrior Rex had brought to me, Ca-es'a. He turned to me in surprise when I appeared, and we stared at each other almost awkwardly.

Then, straightening myself up boldly, I said, "I need to see the human captives."

"You are to stay here," he answered. He spoke with a strange accent, unlike Rex who sounded just like me except being a little bit more staccato in his syllables. I wondered why there was a difference if they were from the same village, but I didn't have time to ask.

"No, I need to go now," I said firmly. "I need to see them."

"I cannot let you leave," he replied. His response was just as firm as mine had been, and there was a rather dangerous flash in his eyes which told me he would make me stay if I didn't do it on my own.

I was slightly intimidated, but I was not deterred. Trying to seem friendly, I asked, "Can you come with me? That way, you'll know where I am."

Ca-es'a looked uncomfortable with the suggestion. "I was instructed to keep you here."

"Please," I implored, starting to feel desperate. My only other option was to try to escape Rex's guard which would mean either running past him and hoping he couldn't outrun me—*which I was sure he could.* Or breaking the window in the bedroom and jumping, which likely meant I'd be hurt or paralyzed anyway because the second floor was so high from the ground. *I needed to convince him.* "I don't want to free them or anything. I just need to see they're okay."

"I have seen them," he said. "They are safe."

"I need to see them," I said again, looking at him with wide, pleading eyes. "Please, let me just see them."

He shuffled uncomfortably, and then he gave me one short nod. "You stay by me."

"Okay. Yes," I agreed eagerly, flooded with gratitude for his cooperation.

We left the house and stepped out into the night air together. Even though the breeze was gentle and uplifting, I felt smothered by the broad, dark sky, and I had to count my breaths as I inhaled and exhaled to make sure I was still able to breathe properly. Ca-es'a guided me out of the courtyard through the gate which allowed entrance to Rex's palace and into the main part of the village.

I had never seen it for myself. When Rex had found me after the crash, he had brought me straight to his parents' house, and I had been bidden to remain there. I'd learned they were on the outskirts of the village anyway, so I hadn't been able to even see the village from their property. Then, when Rex had brought me to his house, he'd taken me by the wind, and I couldn't see anything when we traveled that way. We'd landed directly into the courtyard, and we'd gone up to his room to make love. I realized as I took in the view of the village for the first time I really hadn't seen anything of Albaterra yet, and I'd been here for over two months.

    The houses were scattered rather haphazardly in a messy kind of circle. They looked nearly identical to Rex's parents' house as they were made of the same foreign mud-clay substance, though some were single-story and others climbed two or three stories high. Most had rickety fences made of unfamiliar wood around their yards, and all had various elements for skinning animals and cooking outdoors placed around the homes. A thick dirt road ran from one end of the prairie as far as the eye could see into town, where it curved into a circle like a cul-de-sac and continued on the other side to disappear into the opposite horizon.

In addition to the houses, there were what appeared to be shops. They had no doors, just wide, undressed openings through which I could see the wares. Inside one, I could see the hanging carcasses of the odd plains goats that wandered the area surrounding the village, as well as shelves upon shelves of raw meat. In another, there were skulls and bone creations like dishware on display. A third was full from wall-to-wall with weapons of varying sorts, including scimitars which looked like the one Rex carried—except Rex's had a fuchsia glow, and these were ordinary. I was teeming with curiosity and wanted to go into each shop and examine all of the goods, but I was on a mission.

Ca-es'a pointed to the center of the dirt road circle, where a solitary tree with exceptionally long limbs and odd, twitchy, brownish-green leaves grew rather regally. "They are there."

"In the tree?" I asked, taken aback. My eyes lifted to the branches, but they were long and lean, and I would have easily been able to see if my crewmembers were hanging like cocoons or sitting on the boughs like playful children. *I saw nothing but what was I supposed to see? A tree?*

"The vigibrach tree marks the entrance," Ca-es'a explained. He grabbed my upper arm and pulled me along gently as he started to walk toward it. "It grows over the dungeon."

"You're keeping them in a *dungeon*?" The very word made me sick to my stomach, and I turned to look at him with disgust on my face.

He didn't look at me, though. He kept his gaze forward and continued holding onto my arm as we drew nearer to the tree. "It is the safest place. It protects our villagers, and it also protects the prisoners from any vigilantes."

I hated to admit it, but that made sense. Falling into a grumpy silence, I let him lead me all the way up to the tree. Then, he stopped, standing only a few feet from the trunk, and said sternly, "Stay here."

Before I could ask any questions, he rounded the tree to its other side. The trunk was so thick I couldn't see him, even when I leaned in either direction to watch what he was doing. When he reappeared, he took my arm again and showed me what he had done. There was a staircase descending into the ground, much like a normal cellar, at the base of the tree. I didn't see a door or a lid flipped off to the side, so I scanned the ground to see if I could find one lying nearby, but there was nothing other than the fluffy beige grass.

"How did you do that?" I asked suspiciously.

"You do not need to know," he responded, looking at me with a rather scolding expression. "Go."

Feeling a little nervous, I started going down the stairs. *I had an unexpected sense of foreboding, and I was rather anxious as to what I was about to find.* Ca-es'a stepped down as well, remaining one stair behind me as I walked.

It seemed to go on forever. As we drew further and further underground, the moonlight started to disappear. In its place, there was a flickering blue glow from torches mounted on a wall, lit with cerulean flames that popped and wiggled like normal flames but seemed almost transparent. It actually gave the dungeon the illusion of being underwater, which I found absolutely disconcerting. Finally, however, I stepped onto solid, firm, flat ground, and before me, there was a long corridor.

"Straight ahead," Ca-es'a instructed with a single nod of his head.

"Maybe you should go first," I murmured nervously.

He looked down at me like a parent disciplining a child. "You asked to come here. Now, find what you seek."

Letting out a big breath in a whoosh, I started walking again. The corridor was plain with nothing on either side but dirt walls and the mounted torches with blue flames. It seemed to stretch on just as long as the staircase had until a massive wooden door came into sight at the end. When we drew close enough, Ca-es'a held out a hand to stop me.

"You cannot open it," he said.

Moving the hand he'd thrown in front of me to the door, his pressed his fingertips to a broad, sweeping curve in the tribal design of the wood. Then, with his other hand, he reached for a knob in the very center of the door. I wouldn't have noticed it had he not wrapped his hand around it. It was made of the very same wood as the door and appeared to be nothing more than part of the pattern. He turned his hand, and the door swung open much more smoothly than I would have expected.

The same blue glow I'd been washed in since entering the dungeon filled this area, too, but there were thick bars of an odd, corroded metal on both sides of me. I realized that the light was coming from large bowls of fire dangling from the ceiling like medieval chandeliers, but that held my attention for a mere second before my eyes drifted from side to side to see inside the cages to my left and right.

They were there.

Sleeping on thin cots pacing back and forth along the length of the cells, and pressing their faces up to the bars were my crewmembers—*the ones who had survived, anyway.* I immediately recognized each and every one. Having been the chef, I'd served every person aboard the *Paragon* several times a day and, while I hadn't learned all their names, I had certainly become acquainted with their faces. I spotted the captain first, who was one of the few pacing relentlessly with his hands locked behind his back and his eyes lowered to the ground. My sous chef was several cells down with his nose poking through the bars and his eyes wide and frightened. I even saw Trey, the ship mechanic who had persistently tried to hook up with me, curled up on a cot asleep.

Then, I saw Leanne.

Seeing my best friend for the first time in over two months sent a bolt of lightning through me I never would have anticipated. *I'd spent so long wondering if she'd even survived the crash, and to see her face looking back at me from an underground alien prison cell was perhaps the most intense, surreal thing I had ever experienced.*

I raced down the corridor to her, disregarding Ca-es'a's command to stop. When I reached her, I threw my arms through the bars in a strange, awkward hug, and she returned the hug with vehemence. Tears welled up in my eyes from the sheer gratitude I felt for her survival.

"Oh my God," I whispered hoarsely. "I thought you were dead."

"I thought the same for you, too," she murmured back. We both let go of one another, but I didn't step backward. Just inches apart, our eyes slid almost hungrily over each other's faces.

"I'm so glad to see you," I said tearfully.

She smiled. It was a genuine smile, but it severely lacked in its normal, Leanne-like brightness, and it hurt me to see the unhappiness lurking beneath her features.

"How did you get out?" She whispered, her eyes darting over my shoulder.

I looked back, and I saw that Ca-es'a was behind me. He looked very uncertain and incredibly irritated, but I ignored him and turned back to Leanne. "One of the Elders found me right after the crash. He had me staying with his family."

"What?" Her eyes widened in shock, and I was certain I could see desperation and jealousy in her gaze as well. "You just *lived* with them?"

"Well, kind of. I had to stay in certain boundaries and—you know what, it's not important," I said hastily, waving a hand. "I had to come here, to make sure all of the survivors were okay."

Her expression hardened slightly. "It depends on your definition of 'okay.' They're feeding us and keeping us warm if that's what you mean, and they're treating us for our injuries from the crash. But we're not allowed to talk to each other very much, and we don't get out of our cells at all."

"Well, I'm going to get you out of here. All of you," I said, my tone insistent and determined. "I'm going to have Rex—"

"Rex?"

"The Elder who found me," I explained hurriedly.

"He's an alien named Rex?" Leanne asked incredulously.

I shook my head. "No, he has a really long, complicated name. He just goes by Rex."

"And you're on a first-name basis with him?" She had a very dubious, rather suspicious expression on her face which made me draw back a little bit in surprise. "I mean, Tabitha, it sounds like you're friends."

If we'd been sitting inside of Rex's house eating and drinking and chatting, I would have told her every last detail of my strange and unexpected relationship with him. As we were in a dungeon and she was behind bars and Ca-es'a was nudging me repeatedly in the back, however, I didn't have the time.

"Leanne, I'm going to make sure I get you all out of here," I whispered. "I promise."

"We must go," Ca-es'a said loudly in my ear. I felt his fingers close around my upper arm again, and he started to pull me back toward the door.

"I promise," I said to her again. She didn't say anything in return. She just watched me being dragged from the room with a blank, emotionless look on her face.

Chapter 5

Rex

When I returned to my home after the Forum, I was surprised to see Ca-es'a standing outside the front double doors. I was struck with sudden fear, and I raced up to him in just two or three strides.

"Is Tabitha safe?" I demanded at once.

"She is safe," he answered solemnly. "I must tell you something."

I looked at him with narrowing eyes. He didn't seem panicked or intense as he would if something terrible had happened, but I could definitely see nervousness in the way he stood. He avoided my gaze and seemed rather sheepish.

"What happened?" I asked, suspicion coating my voice.

He shifted from foot to foot uncomfortably as he said, "Tabitha wanted to see the prisoners." I immediately felt a surge of anger, but he continued to speak. "She asked me to take her to the dungeon. I did so, as I thought it better to escort her safely rather than denying her. She was very determined. I was sure, if I hadn't taken her, she would have found a way to get there herself."

"I told you to keep her here," I hissed furiously, stepping toward him. He held his ground, but he appeared to shrink slightly beneath my glare. "It was not just my order; the Council wishes her to be contained as well."

"I thought it best," he replied with an abashed lowering of his head.

"It was not up to you." I stalked past him and into the house. The truth was that I knew Ca-es'a had made the right decision as Tabitha was stubborn and determined. She would have likely gotten past him any way she could to get to the dungeon. I still had the utmost respect for him as my warrior, but I was furious with the risk of what could have happened to her regardless.

Ca-es'a followed me inside and up to the bedroom. When I opened the door, however, he stood stiffly outside the room. I closed the door behind me and left him to stand guard in the hall. I turned around and saw Tabitha sitting on the bed.

Her back was very straight, and her eyes were pressing into me like irons. She almost seemed like a statue. Her expression was painfully serious, and I could barely see her chest moving with her breaths. I walked a few steps forward toward her before going still and waiting for her to speak. I was still angry, furious even, and didn't want to open my mouth for fear of saying something I would regret.

She stared at me in silence for several long moments. Then, she said, "I see Ca-es'a told you."

"He's a good and faithful warrior," I replied tightly. "He would never have kept it from me."

Tabitha didn't say anything, and I suddenly let everything pour from my mouth.

"I told you to stay here!" I burst out. "I told you, and Vi'den told you! How *dare* you go against my orders?"

"I'm not one of your warriors!" She shot back. Her tone was just as angry as mine, and her face suddenly creased with rage. "I don't answer to you or your Elder Council!"

I stepped forward again, this time involuntarily. "You don't have a choice. You landed on my planet—"

"I didn't *land* here; you bombed us! All I did was survive a crash which should have killed us all like you wanted!" She shouted.

"It doesn't matter!" I was bellowing now, completely out of control and utterly seething from the adrenaline racing through me. "You're here! This is my planet, my people, and my kingdom! You will do as you're told!"

Tabitha looked as though she'd been slapped. She pulled back slightly, still sitting, and gazed at me with wide, flashing eyes. "I will do as I please," she responded coldly.

"Then you will die," I snapped. "And you'll kill me in the process."

She tossed her head. I realized my hands were shaking and I clenched them into fists as I took deep, shaky breaths to calm myself.

"Don't you understand I can no longer picture a life without you?" I asked quietly.

"I thought I did," she murmured, her voice just as soft as mine. "I thought I knew you, but the

Rex I know wouldn't be keeping innocent people as prisoners."

"They are well cared for. You saw that."

Tabitha's eyes flashed again, and, with anger in her voice once more, she said, "They're in *cages*, Rex. Like animals or criminals."

"What do you propose I do?" I demanded. "Send them back to Earth with knowledge of us so that your government can swoop in on our planet and take over? That's condemning my race to death. The entire history of humans is bloodied by genocide and hostility amongst its own kind. There would be no mercy for us."

"You could wipe out the human race in about a week, and you know it," she said dismissively. "We're not a threat to you. That was your whole argument to the Council, wasn't it?"

"As individuals, you are no threat to us," I clarified. "However, the population of your species outnumbers that of the A'li-uud exponentially. There is strength in numbers, Tabitha."

"Fine. Then don't send them back. Let them live here."

I crooked a sardonic brow. "Oh? Let's overlook that humans are beings of destruction to their environment for a moment. Let's overlook that, while the number may be small now, the human population on Albaterra will multiply when they start to breed—"

"*Breed?*" She spat in disgust. She was looking at me as though she had never seen anything or anyone so repulsive before. "So you *do* think we're animals, then!"

"Enough with the dramatics," I growled. "What you're suggesting is inevitable murder for your people. Even if they were to stay here and lived peacefully beside us and amongst us, there would be those who wouldn't stand for it. There would be mutiny until every last human was slain. Think of Torik, how he tried to attack you. Think of how he tried to attack me for protecting you.

He's not alone, Tabitha. There are many, many others who would not tolerate coexistence with humans, and they would take action independent of the Council's orders."

"So what are you going to do to them, then?" She asked heatedly. "After you've questioned them and drained them of all pertinent information, what will happen to them? You won't send them back to Earth, and you won't let them live here. What does that mean? Death?"

I looked at her and answered evenly, "That is yet to be determined."

"I don't believe this," she said, shaking her head, looking confounded. "I can't believe you would do something like this."

"I haven't done anything yet." I moved toward the door, and she watched me with confusion in her eyes and anger scrawled on her face.

"Where are you going?" She demanded.

I wrapped my fingers around the doorknob. "I'm going to sleep in another bedroom. I need to visit the dungeon in the morning."

She turned around without a word, pulled back the covers on the bed, and crawled beneath them. Then, she threw them over her head, and I saw just a lump beneath the blankets. I left the room without saying goodnight.

***

The next morning, I dismissed Ca-es'a to get some sleep and left his replacement outside Tabitha's door with strict instructions to keep her in the room. Then, I went straight to the dungeon.

The torches along the underground corridor danced despite the stillness of the air and emitted a flickering, white-gold glow. During the night, the torches were dimmed and blue to simulate the natural light of late hours and encourage sleep amongst the captives, but they shimmered with pleasant, pearly flames during the waking hours to brighten the space and offer the illusion of daylight. I wondered if Tabitha had been so angry about the dungeon because she'd seen it in the heart of the night.

When I walked through the door to the cells, I saw a dozen human faces looking back at me. No one said anything, but I could sense their fear and frustration as though they were screaming it out. The A'li-uud guard stood at the opposite end of the aisle, one on either side and both standing erect with alertness. I moved past the humans to the guard.

"Is the captain here?" I asked.

One of them lifted his hand to gesture back toward the door again. "He is in the first cell, Wise One."

I looked back to the first face peering out at me and then turned to the guard again. "How bad were his injuries?"

"He is still receiving treatment. He was nearly dead when we found him."

"Thank you," I said, feeling slightly disheartened. I still intended to interrogate him, but it was possible I'd have to stop the questioning earlier than I would have liked if his condition was uncertain.

"Are you Rex?"

The voice came from a cell about halfway up the aisle. A pretty human was looking intently at me through the bars, and, when our gazes met, she repeated the question. I glanced at the guard, who seemed completely bemused and walked back slowly to the girl's cell.

"How do you know me?" I asked her suspiciously.

"Tabitha is my friend," she replied, sounding eager and nervous at the same time. "She told me you took her into your home."

I studied her warily, and then said, "Tabitha should not have come here."

"Why not?"

I didn't answer. Instead, I stepped closer to the bars and lowered my voice so that the conversation was more private. "What is your name?"

"Leanne," she answered at once. "I was the seamstress on the *Paragon*."

"What do you want, Leanne?"

Her eyebrows knitted together, and she looked at me like I'd asked the most obvious question in the world. "I want to get out of this jail."

"I'm afraid I cannot do that," I said emotionlessly. I started to turn away, but her hand shot out from between the bars and grabbed my wrist. I was surprised to find she felt much colder than Tabitha ever had.

"Please, you can't leave us down here," she whispered. Her voice sounded choked and strained the way Tabitha's did when she cried, but there were no tears in her eyes. "Tabitha said she would talk to you about getting us out of here."

"Tabitha does not get to make that call."

"Who does?"

"I do," I said, straightening my shoulders and lifting my chin slightly.

To my surprise, Leanne yanked on my wrist to pull me closer to her. She wasn't nearly strong enough to do much more than wavering my balance, but I stepped so close to her cell that the bars pressed against my face anyway.

"Are you hurting her?" She hissed, her eyes narrowing into almost imperceptible slits.

For some reason, I was offended by the question. It shouldn't have mattered to me what the human thought, but the suggestion I would ever hurt Tabitha was beyond my comprehension, and it angered me.

"No," I said icily. "I would never."

She continued to look at me dubiously, and then she asked, "Do you care for her?"

My inclination was to ignore her. *I had no reason to tell her the truth.* On the other hand, my feelings for Tabitha were no longer a secret to the highest authority of my race, and I could see no harm in being honest to Leanne either.

"Yes. I love her," I replied, still speaking coolly.

Her eyebrows lifted so high they practically kissed her hairline, and she released my wrist out of sheer surprise. "Oh."

"If you'll excuse me," I said, starting to move away again toward the captain.

"Wait!" She cried out. I stopped and looked back at her. Her expression had become imploring, pleading. "Please, be good to her. She's been through enough."

"What do you mean?" I asked. I approached the cell again until Leanne and I were separated only by several inches of air and the metal bars.

She frowned. "She never told you?"

"Told me what?"

"Why she joined the *Paragon* crew." She looked regretful now, as though she wished she hadn't spoken at all.

"She said it was for personal reasons," I responded. Against my wishes, my curiosity was manifesting, and I found myself no longer interested in the captain for the time being. *I wanted to know what Leanne knew.*

Leanne dropped her voice to a near whisper to prevent the other humans from hearing her as she spoke. "She murdered someone. Her boyfriend."

I blinked. I had never expected to hear the word "murder" in relation to Tabitha, especially after her reaction to learning what the Elders had planned for the humans.

"You must be mistaken," I said dismissively.

"I'm not mistaken," Leanne growled. I could tell she was rather affronted by the comment. "Ask her yourself."

I didn't know how to respond, so I remained quiet as the news tried to reconcile itself in my mind.

"She had a good reason," Leanne went on. "Believe me, it wasn't a cold-blooded kill or anything. Like I said, she's been through enough."

My insides felt dry and hollow, like a dead vigibrach branch, and I wasn't able to form coherent thoughts. All plans to interrogate the captain had dissipated in light of this information. All I could focus on was Tabitha rather than my duties as an Elder.

Finally, I looked back to Leanne and inclined my head respectfully.

"Thank you, Leanne. You've been most useful."

Chapter 6

Tabitha

When I woke up the next morning, I was sprawled across the bed horizontally and felt horribly alone. It was the first night I had spent in Rex's house, which discombobulated me enough, but it was also the first night of the crash I'd slept without Rex beside me. At his parents' house, we slept in the same bed each and every night. I'd grown accustomed to feeling his warm, tall form curled up behind me like a comforting cocoon.

The odd white sunlight of Albaterra was spilling through the massive window, bathing me in a heavenly glow, but I found it intrusive and unnerving. All of the other mornings, I had been fascinated by the sunshine and the way it made the technicolor turquoise Albaterran sky seem to glow, and I had always felt refreshed and invigorated by its pleasantness. *This particular morning, however, I just felt exhausted and drained and, more than anything, miserable.*

I didn't know if Rex had left for the dungeon yet. I'd expected him to wake me up before going, but the sun was so high in the sky I was certain he'd departed hours ago. That realization brought with it a loneliness that, in conjunction with the other awful feelings, brought a lump to my throat.

Clambering off the bed, I straightened my clothes and made sure I was semi-presentable. Then, I padded to the bedroom door and swung it open without preface. Standing outside, there was a warrior I didn't recognize. His head whipped in my direction so quickly it was a blur, and we just looked at each other for a moment without saying anything.

Finally, I greeted him. "Good morning."

He didn't speak. His expression made it clear he wasn't interested in conversation. In fact, I felt rather certain he wasn't interested in me at all. There was a shadow of hostility in his gaze, hidden behind a curtain of suspiciousness which he made no effort to hide. I cleared my throat uncomfortably.

"Is Rex here?" I asked, attempting to sound friendly.

Again, he didn't speak, and I felt frustration flare up inside of me. He just continued to stare at me with the same expression on his face; he didn't even twitch or fidget. To a third party, he would have looked like a statue.

"Look," I said irritably, dropping all pretense of charisma, jamming a hand on my hip. "I don't know if Rex told you not to talk to me or something, but, if I were you, I would answer my question. Otherwise, I'm just going to find out for myself. Ask Ca-es'a. He'll tell you I get what I want."

The warrior's eyes finally moved, flicking away from me for the briefest of moments. Then, in a gravelly, reluctant voice, he said, "No."

"No?"

"Rex is not here," he said firmly. He seemed angry, either with me for insisting he speak or with himself for speaking, but I didn't care.

"Well, did he say when he'd be back?"

His mouth tightened into a thin line, and he replied stonily, "No."

"Fine," I said. I stepped back through the doorway to the bedroom. Before I closed it, I said a little kindlier, "Thank you."

He dropped his head slightly in acknowledgment of my gratitude, and I shut the door. I went to the window and peered out at the grounds below, hoping I'd see Rex lingering outside or walking toward the front doors. All I saw, however, was the lush grass swaying in a gentle breeze and the fountain burbling cheerfully in the very center of the courtyard. I sighed heavily and went back to the bed, falling onto it face-down.

The first thoughts that drifted into my mind were the vivid memories of last night. So much had happened it was more like recalling the events of a month's time rather than a night's. It had all started by a female A'li-uud seeing me in the window of Rex's parents' house. The next thing I'd known, Rex was whisking me off to his house to keep me safe from those the woman told about me, and, in our terror for our lives, we'd ended up making love on the very bed I was laying on now. Then, we'd been visited by the very tall, very thin, very old Vi'den, who, in all of his wisdom and understanding, urged us to go before the Elder Council immediately before any decisions about our fate could be made. Rex had taken me to P'otes-tat Ulti, the walled city where Elders held the Forum, and I'd been questioned and nearly attacked. Finally, when he'd brought me back to his house before he went on trial for treason, we'd gotten into a huge fight, and I'd snuck into the dungeon to see my fellow crewmembers from the *Paragon. All that had resulted in my waking up alone this morning.*

It was almost too much to stomach, but I *had no choice.* I had to be able to think rationally if I were to have any hope of convincing Rex to stop the Elders from killing the *Paragon* survivors and decimating the other spaceships in the galaxy.

I still loved Rex. In fact, I loved him so deeply I realized I never knew what love was until Rex. No matter how I tried to spin it or justify it in my mind, though, I simply couldn't justify allowing my captive crew members and the others on the mission still aboard their ships to die for the sake of preserving my relationship. They were innocent people, and if I had knowledge of their destruction and did nothing to stop it, I may as well be wielding the weapons myself upon their demise.

Pain rocketed through me as I realized that my only option was to save the other humans, and I would have to do it with or without Rex by my side. I recognized the pain as heartbreak, but it still seared my chest like a knife plunging through my sternum, and I was rendered breathless for a moment.

	As if he sensed my anguish and was coming to my rescue, Rex suddenly stepped into the room. I looked up, startled. His face wore a strange expression, one I couldn't quite identify. He certainly seemed upset and bothered, which was to be expected after the previous night's events, but there was something else mixed in as well.

Something I had never seen in him before.

Despite the look on his face, his voice was calm, low, and steady when he spoke. "Did I wake you?"

"No," I said, shaking my head and sitting up. "I've been awake for a little bit."

"Good," he replied. He crossed the room and joined me on the bed, taking a seat at the very foot, so we were still out of arm's reach of one another.

"Were you at the dungeon?" I asked as I eyed him quizzically.

He nodded, glanced at the door, and then turned his eyes to me. "I would like to discuss some things."

"Me too." My heart started to pump madly in my chest as I climbed up onto my knees and leaned toward him earnestly. I felt horribly certain this would be my only chance to sway him to my side, to get him to help me rescue my people from the uncertain fears of the Elders, and the heaviness of the moment weighed on me like bricks. "You know you have to do something, Rex. You know you can't let the Council go through with their plans."

"I am only one member of the Council. I don't get to make the decisions myself," he said. He sounded distant like his mind was far away, so I reached forward and took his face between my hands to look him right in the eyes. I wanted to avoid another fight like last night's, but I needed him to know how serious this was.

"You may not get to make the decisions, but you get to influence them," I said firmly. "We both know Vi'den will at least hear you out, and I'm sure there are others—"

"You know nothing of us," Rex interrupted harshly.

I stared at him, struck in the heart by his words. He was not speaking words of anger or confrontation; he was stating what he believed to be the bald truth. It hurt me so savagely he would feel I was so ignorant to his plight that my lips turned down in an injured frown and my throat seemed to close up in response. He just looked back at me, his expression blank and his eyes hard. *This was not the Rex I loved.*

Finally, I mustered the strength to murmur, "I know you, Rex, and I know you can't in good conscience let the Elders kill hundreds of innocent people."

"You don't know me," he responded bitterly.

Again, I just stared at him, struck dumb by the slash of his words and honest tone. Frustration and despair started to bubble up in my gut, and it poured forth as anger.

"How could you say that?" I demanded, my voice growing louder. "After everything we've already been through after you made love to me, how could you say that?"

"Because it's true," he said, getting to his feet. He was louder, too, and I could definitely hear anger in his tone that matched mine. "You don't know me, and I know I don't know you."

"Of course you do," I whispered, stung.

He quirked a brow. "Do I? I think your friend Leanne knows you much better than I know you."

I gaped at him and asked softly, "You met Leanne?" Where the frustration had been bubbling now flourished hope that perhaps by meeting someone I held so dear, he would be more apt to change his mind about helping me rescue everyone.

"She told me about what you did."

Immediately, it felt like I had swooped from miles high in the sky toward the earth at speeds faster than sound. My stomach lifted and plummeted in a matter of a millisecond, stealing my breath and making my head so light that the edges of my vision became white and furry. I blinked rapidly to try and regain my composure, and then I asked hoarsely, "What are you talking about?"

"I'm talking about the fact that you murdered your boyfriend and joined the *Paragon* crew to get away from what you did," he growled. Then, spinning on his heel until he was facing away from me, he clapped his hands to the back of his head and roared with such fury he sounded like a lion calling to its pride. When he turned around to face me again, his face was contorted with rage, and his ghostly white eyes seemed to flame. "How dare you name me a murderer? Who are you to accuse me of murder when my only aim is to protect my race? Meanwhile, there you sit, pointing fingers and making me a villain when you willingly took the life of your own kind?"

"You don't know what happened!" I shouted. I could hear blood pumping in my ears, and my hands had started to tremble. I felt a strong desire to cry, but I felt an even stronger desire to defend myself, and I couldn't stop my chest from heaving.

He made a sardonic noise in his throat and said, "I don't think it matters what happened, Tabitha. I have a duty to the A'li-uud above all else, and I'm certainly not going to be persuaded otherwise by someone who doesn't even value a life of her own species, much less the lives of mine."

"You're just trying to justify your genocide," I hissed venomously. "You're not even interested in knowing the truth about what I did. You just want a reason to validate doing it yourself."

"I don't intend to do what you did. A'li-uud life is precious to me." His words were challenging and judgmental, but, rather than angering me further, they deflated me.

I looked at him through eyes which had started to swim with tears and whispered, "My life was precious to me."

His face changed, then. It softened slightly, and his mouth hinted at sympathy. Nevertheless, he remained stiffly upright and commanding in tone as he replied, "I will do what is best for my race, Tabitha."

Again, I felt the sting of heartbreak shoot through my chest, and my tongue burned as I said the words I had never wanted to say.

"Then, you need to kill me too, because I can't love someone who would kill innocent people, and there is no life for me without you."

Chapter 7

Rex

I wanted to cry out, to run to her and clasp her to my chest and never let go. I wanted to tell her it would be all right and I would stop the Elders from decimating all humans in Andromeda or die trying. I wanted to soothe her tears or comfort her until she could cry no more.

But I couldn't.

I was filled with so many conflicting emotions I was simply rooted to the spot. I could do nothing but watch her weep her pain into her hands, and I realized she was essentially letting me go. *My entire body seemed to still, first with shock and then with the most excruciating ache, I had ever felt.* The very idea of losing Tabitha was debilitating, but it was almost bearable beside the complete and utter implosion of my soul at the notion of killing her. Worse still, the sincerity in her words had been undeniable, and I knew she intended to die with her comrades if that was to be their fate.

Unbidden and unexpected anger manifested in my core and billowed out to every inch of me until I was fairly shaking with its power. *I was angry with her for insisting I choose between her and my Elder brothers. I was angry at myself for feeling anything at all and getting myself into such a situation. I was angry with the Council for being so frightened by the humans and the unconfirmed threat they pose. I was angry at the universe for the course of events which had led me to this point. My rage was so great in fact, I had to force my lips and tongue to form the words I needed to say.*

"You will stay in the house. I will have food prepared for you. You are welcome to entertain yourself as you desire, as long as it is within the confines of these walls. The guards will be alerted to my orders, and under no circumstances are you to try to sneak by them or convince them to let you leave. Am I understood?"

"I'm not your prisoner," she said defiantly.

"You are for now," I replied, rigid ice in my voice. I was in such emotional pain I couldn't afford to be softer with her. "I will return by nightfall."

She glared at me so fiercely that, if it were possible, she would have shot me dead on the spot with just her eyes. I looked back at her, drinking in the vision like it would be the last time I'd ever see her. My gaze caressed her long, dark brown curls and creamy skin, skimming down to relish the feminine curves of her figure. *Even in the midst of our dark hour, she was still the most beautiful creature I had ever seen.* Then, before I could give in to my desires and lunge forward to take her in my arms, I left the room.

After giving my orders to the guards around my palace, I stepped out into the sunlight and tilted my face up to the sky. The wind kissed my cheeks like a loving mother, and I knew where I needed to go. Bending at the knees, I jumped, and

I took flight on the winds to my parents' home on the outskirts of the village.

It was strange to arrive and find everything as it had always been. Because everything had seemed to suddenly turn on its head, I had expected disorder and chaos, perhaps broken windows and the door hanging off its hinges. There was no disorder, and there was no chaos, though. The same two-story home I had grown up in looked back at me with unnatural serenity, almost smiling and welcoming me back. The air in my lungs flowed out from between my lips in a great sigh of relief, and I strode up the entrance path.

Mother opened the door before I could even lift my fist and rap my knuckles on it, and, the moment she saw me, she threw her arms around me and crushed my face into her shoulder.

"I was so worried!" She exclaimed. Her voice was choked, cracking with emotion. She clung to me so tightly I had trouble breathing properly. When she finally released me and stepped back, she said, "Are you safe? How is Tabitha?"

"We are both fine," I reassured her, stepping into the house, allowing her to close the door behind me. "It's only been one day, mother. How much could change in a day?"

The irony of my words wasn't lost on me.

"Everything was just a mess, Rex. Your father hasn't stopped pacing around the house, and I couldn't get a thing done because I've been so scared that…"

Her voice died off, and I realized she was still frightened for me, despite my being right in front of her alive and well. My heart went out to her, and I pulled her into a hug again, which she returned with vigor. I imagined her crying the way Tabitha did when she was emotional.

"I never did like that Pugna'ta," she finally muttered, and I couldn't help but laugh. It felt rather unfamiliar to laugh, as though I hadn't done it in years, but the heavy weight in my chest seemed to suddenly lift as the chuckles rolled from my mouth.

There was a thump, and I looked over her shoulder to see my father entering the house from the back door. He looked like he'd aged a century. When his eyes met mine, however, I watched as relief flooded his face. He instantly seemed revitalized. He crossed the room in two long strides, and I let go of my mother to hug him too.

"It's good to see you, son," he said gruffly, banging his hand on my back as we embraced.

"Good to see you too, father," I replied.

It amazed me my parents had been so concerned about my welfare, particularly because I was an Elder. I'd been so preoccupied with ensuring Tabitha's safety it hadn't occurred to me how my mother and father would be wishing they could do the same for me. When we broke apart, he pounded my back once more and looked me up and down.

"Well, you're in one piece," he said. He, too, sounded rather choked, just like mother had. "That's something to be celebrated."

I decided not to tell them about nearly coming to blows with Torik at the Forum. They were worried enough as it was.

"I was hoping you'd have some time to talk," I said to my father. Then, rather reluctantly, I admitted, "I need advice."

"Of course, son." His answer was immediate and without hesitance. He motioned to the back door. "I'm just cleaning a hicorn for tonight, can we talk outside?"

"That's fine," I agreed. I squeezed my mother's hand reassuringly as I walked past her to the door, and then went back outside with my father on my heels. There was a large, muscular hicorn dangling from a gambrel with its skin already removed, leaving its thick pink muscles exposed. Father went to the hicorn and picked up his harvesting tools, made from the bone of the very species he was dissecting. He then looked at me through the glinting sunlight and waited for me to speak.

"I was tried for treason," I said bluntly.

His hand froze in midair on its way to the wild goat, and his eyes widened until he appeared to have two white holes in his face. His mouth, too, opened wide, but no sounds came out.

"I was cleared," I continued. "Vi'den saw to that."

"Praise the Grand Circle," father groaned gratefully, dropping his tool-holding hand down to his side and looking up at the sky. I looked up as well, admiring a particularly lovely lavender swirl amidst the blanket of turquoise. When I looked back down, Father was pressing his fingers to his forehead, looking at me warily. "Is that what you wanted to discuss?"

"No." I stepped nearer to him and dropped to the ground, ignoring the dust that clouded up around me as I did. "A lot happened last night, father, and I'm not sure what to do about any of it."

"Go on," he said as he resumed cleaning the hicorn.

I sighed heavily, trying to decide where to start. I opted to just launch into my woes. "I brought Tabitha to the Forum to speak to the Elders herself before Pugna'ta could spread the word, under Vi'den's advice. We didn't want them to decide our fates before we had a chance to talk to them directly."

"Of course," father said, nodding.

"Tabitha was brought before the council and questioned. They seemed to feel she was no threat and released her to my care, under the chaperone of myself and my warriors. Then, they talked about the other survivors of the crash, as well as the other ships in Andromeda, and, when I brought Tabitha back to my home, she confronted me about both."

Father pursed his lips slightly. "Had she been unaware of the Elders' plans prior?"

"Yes," I admitted. "I didn't feel it was wise to tell her."

"Hmmm." I could see he disapproved, but he didn't comment.

I filtered through the events of last night, trying to pick out the relevant bits to tell him. "After I was tried and cleared, I returned home and learned that Tabitha had convinced Ca-es'a to take her to the dungeon to see the humans."

"Oh, no," father said, straightening up and looking at me with concern. "I can't imagine Ca-es'a wavering from your orders."

"I couldn't either until it happened." *I was still rather bitter about it, regardless of my love for Ca-es'a.* "It upset her greatly to see them. She insisted I let them go, but I told her that was impossible because we couldn't send them back to Earth with knowledge of us, and allowing them to set up residence here was simply out of the question."

"Why?" My father tilted his head, and I could see he was interested to hear my response.

I blinked, surprised to hear him question something that seemed so obvious to me. "Well, because we can't be sure that the A'li-uud would be safe, and I'm certain the humans wouldn't be safe from vigilante A'li-uud who want to eliminate them."

Father frowned, leaving large creases in the corners of his mouth, and he looked at me dolefully. "It saddens me, son," he said, "that even you are tainted by the prejudices and fears of our history. Have we not taught you to love and accept all as the children of the Grand Circle?"

"Humans do not believe in the Grand Circle," I replied. "They believe in deities and science."

"Many believe in fate," father corrected me. "And what is fate but the Earthling's Grand Circle?"

I frowned then too, thinking deeply on his words. What he said made sense, but I couldn't shake the feeling that allowing the humans to live out their lives, procreating and developing and growing, on Albaterra was too great a risk to our own race.

"A conversation for another time, perhaps," father said. There was a small smile on his face, one I recognized as smug pleasure for having made me think. "You were saying Tabitha wanted you to free the survivors."

"Yes," I said, returning to my previous thoughts. "I went to the dungeon today to find out about the captain's condition and to question him, as directed by the Council, but I was intercepted by a human woman named Leanne. She told me she was Tabitha's friend and asked me to release her and her crewmates. I declined, of course, and, in the course of our conversation, she revealed to me that Tabitha had joined the *Paragon* crew after killing her boyfriend."

Again, father's hand froze on its way to the hicorn, and he looked at me with a furrowed brow. I could see him trying to process the information, and I was certain my face looked almost identical when I had heard the news myself.

"I can't imagine Tabitha doing something so terrible," he said finally. There was reluctance in his voice I felt within myself.

"She did," I said. My throat felt swollen again, and I lowered my eyes to the ground. "I confronted her about it."

"To take the life of another is a grave transgression against the Grand Circle," father murmured.

"I know."

"Perhaps there was a reason. A'li-uud have killed their own. It has been a rare occurrence in our history, but it has happened, and there was always a reason," he mused.

I lifted my gaze to him again. "She said I needed to change the Elders' mind about destroying the ships and that I needed to ensure the safety of the survivors even after the interrogations were finished. She said that if I didn't, I would be murdering innocent people and I should kill her too because she couldn't love someone who killed innocent people."

Father looked back at me, and he didn't speak. He was visibly pained by what I told him, and I knew he hurt for me, but I didn't want his sympathy. I needed to know something.

"If you had to choose between the Council and mother, what would you choose?" I asked softly.

His face crumpled slightly with thought. I watched his eyes lift to the sky again, and I sat in silence to allow him time to contemplate the question. As I waited, my mind slid back and forth between the options, the Elders or Tabitha. I was grateful when he looked back down at me again.

"I would choose Beni," he admitted, his voice as soft as mine had been when I'd posed the question to him. "I would always choose Beni."

I opened my mouth to say something, but he cut me off.

"Something you need to remember, though, son, is that you are in a position of authority. You swore to protect your kingdom, your planet, and your people. It is your duty to make decisions for those whose well-being is entrusted to you," he said sternly.

"Yes, but you'd choose mother," I murmured. "And I want to choose Tabitha."

"If you have to choose, there is only one right decision to be made," he told me. Then, leaning forward to look me clearly in the face, he added, "Before you make a hasty decision, however, perhaps you ought to consider that a decision may not have to be made after all."

Chapter 8

Tabitha

For at least an hour after Rex left, I had no desire to leave the bedroom. I just sat on the bed and stared out the window overlooking the courtyard walls, staring into the abundant sunlight without a care for the health of my eyesight. When my stomach finally emitted a loud, unpleasant groan of hunger, however, I knew I needed to get something to eat and pull myself out of my despair. I would be of no help to anyone, Rex or my crewmates, as a starving waif.

I left the bedroom and walked past the guard, feeling rather unnerved he didn't try to stop me. I'd already become accustomed to being a prisoner of sorts. I descended the massive, exquisite staircase of alien wood and intricate carvings, stepped into the foyer, and realized I had absolutely no idea where I could find the kitchen.

A guard appeared in the arch on my right leading into a room that appeared to be just as grandiose as the staircase behind me. His eyes were pinned to me, and I knew Rex had made sure every member of his staff had been made aware of my presence and his orders for me to remain on the property. I didn't like the feeling of being watched, so I turned to the tall, well-sculpted A'li-uud and asked, "Where do I find the kitchen?"

"I do not understand," he answered in cropped, choppy words. His hands were empty, but they were flexed by his sides, and I realized he had a bow strapped to his back. I wondered if he intended to shoot me if I were to make any sudden movements.

"The kitchen?" I said again, waving my hands around haphazardly as though to indicate stirring and eating. I tried to remember if Beni,

Rex's mother, had called her kitchen area anything in particular. "The—the cooking pot?"

"You are hungry?" He asked. He no longer seemed defensive as his hands became limp and his head tilted curiously to the side. Rather than appearing intimidating now, he actually looked fairly innocent and childlike. It was almost endearing. I nodded in response to his question, and he motioned back through the arch he'd entered from. "This way."

I followed his gesture through the arch into what looked like an enormous and well-furnished sitting room. The warrior remained close behind, though I didn't know if it was to watch over me or to continue guiding me. I wanted to stop and examine the things I saw, including a carved bone sculpture. It hung above a gray stone fireplace so deep and wide I could have sat comfortably inside it, but I figured I ought to keep walking since the warrior was sticking so hot on my tail.

  The next room I entered was through an arch that was similar in shape but smaller than the one leading into the foyer. In the center of the space, there was a table which looked like the rustic, hewn table in Rex's parents' house, but it was about three times as big, stretching from nearly one end of the room to the other. On either side of the table, there was a bench of the same wood and the same carpentry technique. With the nude-toned mud walls and medieval-style metal lanterns dangling symmetrically from the ceiling over the expanse of the table, I was easily able to picture feasts and parties of respectable size and decadence being held in the room.

When I turned left through a third arch, I knew I had reached the kitchen. It looked very much like Beni's had, but, just like the table; it was significantly larger and much more awe-inspiring. There were not cabinets and countertops as human kitchens had; rather, long, planked tables lined the walls from end to end with free-form shelves mounted on the walls above them that held numerous vials, lidded pots, and skin pouches, all of which were certain to contain herbs and other basic ingredients. There was a basin made of marbled, silvery metal atop one of the tables. Upon closer inspection, I could see it was much deeper than it looked at first glance. A human toddler could have comfortably sat in it like a tub for a bath. There was not one, but two cooking pots in the center of the kitchen, both with their own fire pits beneath, and cooking utensils made of what I presumed to be hicorn bone hanging from the ceiling above them.

    I could smell a robust and meaty aroma in the air. Embers beneath the cooking pot nearest me were still glowing, though there was not an actively burning fire. I turned to the warrior, who was watching me look around the kitchen with an expression of amusement on his rugged face. "Has someone made food?"

"Yes," he said plainly. "Rex instructed Gorlah to make you a meal. She is the cook for the Elder palace."

"The Elder palace?" I asked, intrigued by the term. "Is that where I am?"

"Yes," he said again. He walked to the nearest corner where two of the plank tables met, and I saw a dish covered with an odd, off-white cloth resting there. Plucking the cloth from the top, he scooped up the dish and brought it to me.

"Thank you," I murmured, taking it gingerly and looking in to see the contents. I was expecting stew or something similar, as that had been the entrée of choice at Rex's parents' house, but what I saw was actually something which looked like it could have come from any Michelin-star restaurant on Earth. A beautifully cooked slab of meat sat in the center of the plate with dark char marks on its surface and a thick, smooth bone jutting out of one side, much like a lamb chop. Surrounding the meat, there was a cream-colored something that reminded me of whipped potatoes, and an emerald-green sauce with flecks of herbs in it drizzled over the top of the entire plate. *It smelled heavenly.*

The warrior held several utensils out to me, and I took them as well. He motioned to the dining room we had just walked through, and I went back into it, sliding onto a bench, placing the plate before me. I expected him to sit as well, but he just stood beside the arch and watched me closely.

It was uncomfortable to sit at the giant table by myself and eat alone while an A'li-uud stared at the back of my head, but I was too hungry to put too much thought into it. I began to eat, and, once the first bite hit my tongue and flavor burst in my mouth, I started shoveling the food in unceremoniously. My stomach gurgled first with confusion upon receiving sustenance, then with appreciation as, bite by bite, the plate emptied, and my appetite was satisfied. When I was finished, I placed the utensils down beside the dish and exhaled heavily, completely sated.

Before I could get up, however, there was a loud shriek from outside. It sounded like a panther about to strike, high-pitched and wailing. The warrior behind me leaped to my side and ripped his bow from his back, holding it aloft with an arrow poised and ready. I was so unnerved by the odd shriek I didn't even study the odd, wavy-shaped, purple arrow as I ordinarily would have. I just sat on the bench and stared into the fancy sitting room, waiting for someone to come bursting in. Only seconds later, an A'li-uud raced into the room, and I was struck motionless with shock as I recognized the face.

It was the woman who had seen me at Rex's parents' house.

"Pugna'ta!" The warrior bellowed. He sounded surprised and commanding at the same time, and he didn't lower his bow. "You must leave!"

She clacked at him in her native tongue, and he responded back in the same language. I looked between them with no inkling as to what was happening, but then the white eyes of the female—Pugna'ta—turned to me. *They were more evil and aggressive than any eyes I had ever seen on an A'li-uud before, even Torik.*

"What are you?" She spoke to me in English, and she said the words as though they were both bitter and sour on her tongue.

"I'm—I'm human," I stammered, completely nonplussed by her combative attitude.

She made an odd snarling sound reminiscent of a scoff and tossed her head. "I know you are human, stupid girl," she spat. "Why is Rex protecting you? What is so important about you?"

I shook my head and held my hands up a little as though surrendering. "I don't know. I never asked him to protect me. He just found me at the crash site and kept me with him, and—"

"Stop talking," the warrior interjected suddenly. His voice was sharp, and I fell silent at once. His eyes remained on Pugna'ta, even as he spoke to me, but then he addressed her. "It does not concern you what our Elder intends to do with the human. You will leave now."

Pugna'ta cackled, and it was the cruelest sound I had ever heard in my life. Her gaze slid to the warrior, and she looked at him with such disdain which was almost embarrassing. "Do not threaten me, Surlif. You are but a child. I could remove your head and feed it to your corpse before you could shoot that arrow."

He didn't lower the bow, but he seemed to slacken a little. "What do you want, Pugna'ta?" He asked carefully.

"I want to stop this betrayal before we all feel the consequences," she answered, her voice a growl and her eyes swinging back to me. "Rex has fallen under the enchantments of this inferior creature, and I will not have it."

Suddenly, it dawned on me what Pugna'ta was angry about. I stood slowly from the bench and faced her, understanding coursing through me.

"You want him," I said, sounding rather awed. "You want him, and you're angry I have him."

"You have *nothing*," she hissed. She punched the last word with such force I was sure she was trying to convince herself of it as much as me.

"I have Rex," I told her, tilting my chin up in a show of defiant confidence. "He loves me, and I love him."

"Stupid human." She was hunched slightly now, poised in an offensive stance and I realized this A'li-uud would not hesitate to try and hurt me if provoked further. "You are naïve and foolish, and I will not stand by while our Elder condemns us to certain death for a romance with a germ of a creature."

"I'm not out to hurt you," I said insistently. "None of us are. We didn't even know about you until our ship crashed here!"

"Lies!" She screamed.

Then, in a movement so fast and so unexpected I didn't see it coming, she launched herself from her place in the sitting room all the way to me. I was so stunned by the sheer strength and distance of her jump I didn't even react. She sent me flying against the wall with a powerful strike to the chest. My body landed flush against the wall with a sickening crack before I fell in a crumpled heap to the floor. The warrior, Surlif, lunged forward to seize Pugna'ta around the middle, but she threw her arm back and met his temple with her elbow. He stumbled sideways, clutching his head. She turned her wicked gaze back to me and leaped again, landing atop me.

  Her legs gripped my sides in a vice-like hold. I shot my hands up in the air above me, plunging my fingers into her eyes, and she roared like a wounded tiger. Her own hands came down in claws, dug into my cheeks, and ripped, tearing strips of flesh clear off my face on both sides. I moaned with pain and immediately pressed my palms to the wounds. Blood soaked my skin at once, running in beaded rivulets down to the back of my skull.

    Pugna'ta was not satisfied. She took my face in both of her hands and pulled upward, then slammed my head down onto the floor with such force that I saw stars. She pulled me up again to deliver another blow, but Surlif leaped onto her back and curled his arm around her throat. Pugna'ta released me, croaking strangely, and clawed at his arm desperately, but he held tight. I wanted to swing at her, but I was too afraid of hitting Surlif in the process, and my cheeks were in so much pain I was nearly paralyzed.

With a swift, graceful swoop, Pugna'ta rolled backward and off of me, effectively surprising Surlif into loosening his clutch on her throat. She pummeled her fist into the side of his temple, which sent his head flying into the leg of the bench beside them, and I watched in horror as he went limp. Realizing I was on my own to fight her off, I scrambled to get to my feet, but Pugna'ta whipped around and pounced on me again. She straddled me with as much force as she had before, and then her fingers curled around my skull once more. I knew she was going to smash my head into the ground again, but I didn't know if I would survive it.

And then, in the blink of an eye, she was off of me. My body was alone on the floor, aching horribly, and the sounds of a scuffle took over my senses. Groaning in pain, I turned my head and saw Rex. His hand was around Pugna'ta's throat, and she was dangling several feet off the ground. Her fingers tried to pry at his, but he was relentless. On his face, there was an expression of such fury that it made Pugna'ta look like a timid little kitten, and even she seemed frightened of him.

"If you ever touch her again," he whispered, "I will kill you with my bare hands."

Chapter 9

Rex

Seeing Pugna'ta assaulting Tabitha was like seeing my worst nightmare brought to life. Tabitha's face was bleeding profusely, and her body lay beneath Pugna'ta's in a misshapen form. Surlif was lying by Pugna'ta's feet, unconscious, but I could tell he had tried to defend Tabitha. I had no time to feel grateful, however, as Pugna'ta had lifted Tabitha's head off the ground to deliver what would likely be the final blow.

I had never moved faster in my life. My hand was around Pugna'ta's throat before I realized I had even reached her. She choked for breath and tried to free herself from my grasp as I held her above my head. *It was the first time I wanted to kill another A'li-uud, and, were I not an Elder, I probably would have.*

I released her by simply letting go, and she dropped to the ground with flailing limbs. There was a crunch when she hit the floor; I didn't know if she'd broken any bones, and I didn't care. I moved swiftly to Tabitha's side; she clawed desperately at my chest with pain. When I looked around again, Pugna'ta was clutching her neck and gasping for breath while staring at me with hatred on her sharp, well-defined features.

"You will leave here, and you will not come back," I said in a low, dangerous voice. "Get out. Now."

"You're going to kill us all," she panted. She didn't make any moves to get to her feet. "Your *love* for that simpleton human is going to be the end of our race."

My reaction was instinctual, not purposeful. I stood in one smooth movement, stalked over to her, wrapped my hand in her pale, wispy hair, and dragged her across the floor through the social room to the foyer. At that moment, several warriors burst through the front doors with weapons raised and alert expressions on their faces. I sneered at them in disgust. "There will be consequences for this."

"She got past us, Your Highness—"

"Pugna'ta is a skilled warrior—"

I held up a hand and closed my eyes briefly. My other hand, still wrapped in Pugna'ta's hair, shot forward as an indication for one of the guards to take her from me. As I reopened my eyes, the nearest stepped forward and took a fistful of her hair, and I let her go. "I want this abomination out of my house. If she ever comes within these walls again, you will kill her on sight."

Pugna'ta snickered, and I knelt down in front of her. Taking her chin in my fingers, I tilted her face up to mine and murmured, "You don't have to worry about my love for Tabitha ending our race. Your arrogance will kill you long before that ever happens." Then, with a sweeping motion of my hand, I dismissed them all from my presence. They turned back through the double doors with Pugna'ta dragged behind them, and I returned at a sprint to the dining room, where Tabitha remained on the floor.

"Is it just your face? What else hurts?" I demanded, feeling her all over for tenderness or broken bones.

She winced repeatedly and said hoarsely, "She threw me into the wall. Everything hurts."

I watched as her eyelids drooped, and I immediately grabbed her face in my hands. She screamed out in agony as my skin settled over her open, bleeding wounds, but I didn't let go. "Tabitha, I need you to stay awake. You cannot go to sleep, do you hear me?"

"Yes," she whispered miserably.

I eased my arms beneath her; with one supporting her back and the hooked under her knees, I lifted her from the floor. With slow, even steps, I carried her through the social room into the foyer, up the stairs, and down the corridor until we reached the bedroom. The warrior I had placed outside the room earlier was still there, though his eyes were wide and he looked alarmed. I knew he had heard the sounds of the fight but had been reluctant to leave his post, and I wasn't angry at him for that.

He opened the door for me, and I carried Tabitha to the bed, where I laid her down gently. "Bring me two poultices and some damp rags," I told the meek A'li-uud. He nodded and rushed away. *I would have gotten them myself, but I was too afraid of Tabitha falling asleep in my absence.*

When he returned with the items, I dismissed him from the room and began to carefully mop the blood from her face with the rags. She moaned each time I brushed the fabric over her cheeks, but I had to see the severity of the lacerations. As the blood was wiped away, I was relieved to see they were mainly surface wounds which would likely heal without leaving scars behind. Then, I placed the poultices on either side of her face and ran my hands lovingly through her hair.

"I'm sorry," I said softly. "I'm sorry I let this happen to you."

"You're all paranoid," she groaned. She didn't meet my eyes, and I realized she was still angry with me.

"Why do you say that?" I asked, my hand pausing on her hair.

She shifted with obvious discomfort and another groan, and then croaked, "You all think I'm going to destroy you. Humans don't deserve that much credit."

My mouth tightened, and I exhaled slowly. "You don't realize how easily you could destroy me, Tabitha."

"For a race that claims to be so close to nature," she said, looking up at me through squinted, pained eyes, "there's a lot of prejudice against anything or anyone that isn't like you."

I was instantly reminded of my father's words to me, how he'd expressed his sadness that I'd been influenced by the prejudices of others, and I felt a sudden stirring of guilt. Shaking my head sadly, I murmured, "You just don't understand."

"What don't I understand?" She asked as she lifted a hand slowly to move one of the poultices over the apple of her cheek.

For a moment, I considered not answering the question. I wondered if I should let her rest and discuss this further when she'd recovered. Tabitha, though, was not someone to let things wait, and I knew she'd only do more damage to herself and slow her recovery by following me around until I did answer, so I spoke.

"You're asking me to choose between you and my people," I told her quietly. "You're asking me to choose between my love and my race."

Her eyes drifted up to mine so slowly that it seemed to take several full minutes. Despite the scratches marring her perfect face, I could see she wore a thoughtful, almost cynical expression. Her lips parted, and she said simply, "So are you."

I stared at her for a moment, trying to process what she'd said, and then I asked, "What do you mean?"

"You're asking me to choose between you and *my* people," she replied.

There was a moment when I considered she might have lost a little comprehension from the intensity of the fight, but then I was smacked with the reality of what she meant. *It was true; I was asking the exact same thing from her she was asking of me. I wanted her to sit back and stay out of things when she knew exactly what would happen to the other humans if she did, effectively putting her in a position to either choose to do as I wished and be with me or go against my orders and be with her crewmembers. It was identical to how I felt, and I was at once comforted by the realization we were both experiencing the same thing for the same reason.*

I couldn't help it. I laughed. My head tilted back, my mouth opened wide, and I guffawed to the ceiling so loudly that my warrior opened the door to make sure everything was okay. The corners of Tabitha's lips turned up in a smile, and she grimaced, but I could tell she wanted to laugh along with me. *There was so much relief flooding through me I found it hilarious. I imagined she felt the same way.*

When I gathered myself, I looked back down at her with a broad smile on my lips. "So we're both facing the same decision, just on opposite sides."

"Yes," she agreed softly. "We are."

"Then, the question is, how do we eliminate the need for a decision and join sides," I said confidently. My father's words were ringing so loudly in my mind I could almost viscerally hear his voice, and I finally grasped exactly what he'd meant by them.

She breathed in, and I could hear the scratchiness of the air hitting her throat. "I think we need to start by being completely honest with each other. Full disclosure."

I looked at her pensively and said, "Okay. What do you want to know?"

"I want to tell you about what happened first," she rasped. "What I did on Earth."

"Oh." My eyes popped open wide in surprise, but I quickly collected myself and nodded. "Okay."

She moved her arms to her sides and pressed, trying to sit herself up. I hurriedly pushed her back down again with as much gentleness as I could, but she waved me off.

"You shouldn't sit yet," I chided.

"I don't care. I want to sit for this," she said, that familiar defiant twinkle in her eye. I yielded to her wish and helped her settle into a comfortable upright position. When she was ready, I pulled both of my legs up onto the bed and crossed them beneath me, prepared to hear whatever it was she was going to tell me.

Her lips parted again, but, this time, it seemed to hurt her. I almost told her we didn't need to have the conversation now, but I realized it wasn't the movement that hurt her; it was the words she was about to say. So, I kept my mouth closed and waited.

"I am a murderer," she began. She spoke slowly and purposefully. "I killed my boyfriend almost a year ago, and I got away with it."

She went quiet, and I thought perhaps that was all she had to say. Then, however, she closed her eyes, and I could see her falling into the memory of her story. I reached forward and took her hand in mine as comfort while she talked.

"Before I tell you everything, I need you to know I didn't plan to do it," she whispered. A sparkling, crystal tear bloomed on the inner corner of her eye, trembled at the end of her lashes, and fell gracefully into her lap. "It just happened in the heat of the moment. But I'm glad I did it. The bastard deserved to die."

"I believe you," I whispered back. I squeezed my fingers around her hand reassuringly, and she gave me a weak squeeze of her own in return.

With a shuddery breath, she dove into her tale.

"It started about two years ago. I was in college—"

"I'm sorry," I interjected. She opened her eyes and looked at me. "What's college?"

The corners of her mouth turned up again, very slightly this time. "School." I stared at her, still confused, and she added, "It's a place where teachers educate students who are new adults."

"Oh," I said with a nod of understanding. "Thank you. Continue, please."

She closed her eyes again. "I was in my final year of college, and I was only about three weeks into classes when I met this guy. His name was Patrick. He was the kind of guy every girl—well, an Earth girl, anyway—wants. Tall, muscular, athletic, handsome, charismatic. He was really wealthy, too, though I didn't care about that. Basically, I was really attracted to him, and he was interested in me, too."

"We started dating, and everything was great, the way all relationships are at first. We went out to amazing dinners and took walks around campus and stayed up all night talking. It was the way things were supposed to be. I actually started to believe he could be *the one*, the guy I was supposed to marry."

"Then, he hit me."

Chapter 10

Tabitha

"What the hell is this?"

I shrank the moment I heard his voice in the room. It was a habit for me to shrink when I heard him now; I'd learned from past experience I needed to put as much distance between myself and his hands as possible without being obvious. I hadn't realized he'd come home because he'd gotten a ride to work that day, so I hadn't heard the garage open, and his car pull in like I normally would have. It was an unwelcome surprise.

He brandished a stack of mail at me. The top envelope had my name and address stamped across the center. In the upper left corner, the return address indicated it was a letter from Sterling Creek Apartments. Patrick didn't know I'd gone there before work a week ago and filled out an application for an apartment. I'd been hoping he wouldn't find out.

"I don't know," I lied, tripping over my own tongue. "Probably junk mail. Just throw it away."

He threw the rest of the mail onto the floor, giving the carpet a skewed rug of envelopes, flyers, and postcard advertisements. With his teeth, he ripped the top of the Sterling Creek envelope open and spit the paper from his mouth before freeing the letter inside. He unfolded it and began to read aloud.

"'Dear Ms. Bartel, we are pleased to inform you that your application for Apartment 3 at Sterling Creek Apartment Complex, Building 1, has been processed and approved. Enclosed, you will find a copy of this year's event calendar for residents, the latest newsletter, popular FAQs, rules, and regulations for common areas, and an automatic withdrawal slip for you to fill out should you wish to sign up for monthly autopay. Welcome to Sterling Creek Apartments!"

As he read, his face gradually contorted from anger to rage. I didn't realize I'd already started trembling until he held the paper out to me and I reached forward to take it. Before I could grab it properly and tug it away from him, however, his other hand shot forward and circled around my arm. He yanked me forward with such force I stumbled over my own feet and fell against his chest. The impact left me slightly stunned, but more than stunned I was terrified.

"You lying bitch!" He shouted, grabbing both of my shoulders and shoving me back. I lost my balance and collapsed on the floor, looking up at him with wide, frightened eyes. He lifted the paper again and waved it in my face, leaning over me. "You were going to leave me? You were going to just get up and go without a word?"

"No!" I cried as I shook my head wildly. "No, I just—"

"Don't lie to me!" He bellowed. His free hand swung down and connected with my nose, blinding me with white-hot pain, setting forth a gush of blood from both nostrils. I yelped involuntarily, and blood streamed from my nose into my mouth. I tried to spit, but he slapped my cheek with a flat palm to stop me.

"Patrick!" I whimpered plaintively. "Please stop!"

Again, his knuckles descended upon me, this time crashing into my jaw. I heard a sickening crunch and felt an even more sickening shift of my teeth. The sound that came from me was so inhuman, so unearthly I didn't even realize I was the one making it. My mind had gone blank as it tried to cope with the level of pain I was feeling. The contents of my stomach were rolling around, threatening to spew out of me the same way the blood did from my nose.

When his fist collided with me for the third time, I realized he might actually kill me. Every time he'd hurt me before, it had been an outburst of one strike—two if he was drinking. Never had he hit me three times in a row, and I could see through swollen eyes he was winding up for a fourth. Perhaps, in the face of losing me, he was ready to end it all. At that moment, I hoped he would.

    The fourth punch had barely landed when he roared, "Two years! We've been together two years, and this is how you want it to be? You're too much of a coward to tell me you don't want to be with me anymore?"

    I couldn't tell if it was tears or blood soaking my face anymore, but I didn't bother to respond. I had told him several times I wanted to part ways, and every time had ended up with me sporting bruises for the next few weeks. Going to Sterling Creek had been a last resort, an escape from him I had desperately hoped it would work. He wouldn't know where I lived, and there were people at work who would call the police if he showed up there. I would've been safe, if only he hadn't found that letter...

"You're a conniving, selfish bitch!" He continued. He tangled his fingers into my hair and got to his feet, pulling me upright with him. "You're not leaving! You made me like this! It's your fault I ever ended up this way! You don't get to leave!"

My scalp felt like it was on fire where he was holding as the hairs were ripped out by the roots, but it was the only part of me that hurt anymore. The rest of my body had gone numb in some kind of self-preservation. I tried to lessen the pain by standing on my tiptoes to allow for some slack in my hair, but he wrenched me this way and that like a ragdoll being whipped around, and all I could do was hope to God he didn't pull my head right off.

Suddenly, he struck me with his knee directly in the small of my back and let go of my hair at the same time. I was sent careening forward until I fell flat on my face just inches from where the living room carpet ended, and the kitchen linoleum began. My nose, which I was certain was already broken, smashed against my face, and I screamed out in a fresh wave of pain. He delivered a kick to my ribs, rolling me onto my back, and grabbed the front of my shirt by the collar. Slowly, almost ritualistically, he lifted me to my feet again. I could see my blood coating his hand like a glove, and there was even some blood smeared across his forehead flecking his cheeks.

"Clean yourself up," he snarled, shoving me into the small, meticulously clean kitchen. Droplets of blood fell from me to the white floor, leaving a trail even Hansel and Gretel couldn't miss. Shaking so violently that I could barely stand, I limped to the sink and leaned over it like a drunk in a toilet. I turned the tap on and just shoved my face under the stream of icy water, not even noticing how much it stung.

    Without warning, I felt his hand clutch the back of my head and thrust downward until my forehead cracked into the bottom of the sink with a metallic smack. Water filled my nose and mouth, gagging me as it went down into my lungs instead of my stomach. I knew, at that moment, he wasn't going to stop until I was dead, and something inside of me clicked.

My hands flew out on either side of me, slapping against the countertops for anything I could grab. The tips of my right-hand fingers grazed something smooth, and I realized it was the knife block. Choking and desperately trying to get air, I swiped a knife from the block. Then, in one swift, clean movement, I swung the knife back and heard a chilling crackle.

Patrick's hands lifted from my head, and I wheezed as I drew in as much oxygen as I could. Whirling around, I saw him hunched over with both hands pressed to his side. Blood was seeping through his shirt, and he was looking down at the injury in horror. Before he could look up and lunge at me, I raised the knife and plunged again. One of his hands shot out and reached for my wrist, but the blade sank deep into the side of his neck just as his fingers closed around me. A second later, he fell, gurgling as blood bubbled out of his mouth. His grip on my wrist loosened slightly, but, even as his face went blank and lifeless, he didn't let go. I stood over him, panting and bleeding and barely able to stand, the knife still in my hand.

***

When I finished speaking, I opened my eyes again and looked at Rex. He was watching me with something like awe on his face, though it was hard to tell because my eyes were rather swollen from the fight with Pugna'ta. His hand was still holding mine, but it had tightened considerably since the start of the story, and he looked like he was having trouble swallowing.

"Do you think I'm a cold-blooded killer?" I asked tentatively.

Rex shook his head and replied gravely, "I think it was your life or his. You made the right choice."

"I'm glad you think so," I said, speaking softly now. The reminiscence was not a pleasant one, and I felt emotionally drained. I slid back down on the bed from my sitting position to lie once more, placing the poultices back on my wounds from Pugna'ta.

Rex looked contemplative about something, but I didn't ask. The pain was beginning to subside in my limbs and muscles, though my cheeks still stung, and all I wanted to do was sleep. I remembered, however, that Pugna'ta had slammed my head against the floor, and Rex had banned me from falling asleep just yet.

"I went to see my father," he said without preface. He was looking at me, but his eyes still appeared to be lost in a faraway thought. "I told him about everything that happened last night."

"He must have been worried," I murmured. "Beni, too."

"I needed advice," he continued as though I hadn't spoken. "I wanted to know if he would have chosen my mother over the Elders."

I lifted my gaze to him. "And?"

"He said he would choose my mother." Even though they were the words I was hoping to hear, the solemn way Rex said them didn't reassure me.

"Why does it sound like you're not going to choose me over them?" I asked in a meek voice.

He turned his head toward the window, looking out over the courtyard. The sun was still shining, but it had gone down a little from the last time I'd left the room. I found myself wondering what time it was.

"Father said there may not need to be a decision at all," Rex said. "I'm hoping he's right, that I'll be able to choose both."

"How?" I was desperate to know the answer, both because I wanted Rex to choose me without defying his Elder brothers and because I wanted to be able to choose Rex without forsaking my people.

He turned back to me again, and I saw a flicker of hope in his face. "I think you are right that destroying the ships would be killing innocent people, Tabitha. I didn't want to hear it because I didn't want to be the reason to show mercy and turn out to be very, very wrong to the detriment of the A'li-uud. But I can't embrace the fear anymore."

"You're going to try to change their minds?" I asked, the hope in his eyes now devouring me as well.

"Yes," he replied. He looked serious and intense, but I was so overjoyed I felt a smile stretch across my lips from ear to ear. He narrowed his eyes at me. "It won't be easy, though. You were there at the Forum. You saw how many of them perceive humans."

"I know," I said earnestly. "But we have to try."

Chapter 11

Rex

Despite Tabitha's pleas, I insisted that we spend the night at my house. She was wildly eager to get started on talking with the other Elders and trying to persuade them to leave the humans alone, but I was too concerned about her injuries to permit it. I stayed in the bedroom with her as the sun went down to make sure she didn't fall asleep before nightfall to ensure she had no lasting head injury. Then, when we were bathed in darkness, I curled up beside her under the blankets and held her as she drifted off to sleep. Unfortunately, I couldn't stop thoughts from parading through my head about how we were going to go about convincing the Elders to look past their—*using Father's word*—prejudices and what our odds of success were, so I lay awake for hours after Tabitha's breathing had become deep and slowed in sleep.

It felt like I had just dozed off when I was roused by the brilliant white light of the morning bathing my face. Blinking rapidly and trying to clear my head of grogginess, I looked over at

Tabitha. Her cheeks had stopped bleeding, though the scratches were still bright red and angry, and several bruises had begun to bloom on her smooth, creamy skin. I frowned and hoped she wouldn't wake with much pain.

"Tabitha," I whispered in her ear. She groaned a little but didn't speak, so I kissed her shoulder and tried again. "Tabitha."

"What?" She grumbled.

"It's morning. We need to go see Vi'den."

As though an explosive had been placed under her rear, she shot out of bed horizontally and landed unsteadily on her feet. It would have been comical to see had she not wailed in pain. I immediately bolted upright and scrambled across the mattress reaching for her.

"I'm okay," she said hurriedly. "I'm okay, I'm okay."

"You're not okay," I replied, giving her a stern look, running my hands over her legs as I had done the day before to check for broken bones.

"No, really, I'm fine. I'm just stiff, that's all. I just need to walk around, stretch a little."

"Tabitha, you're injured," I said. I finished pressing and prodding her legs and moved on to her hips. "Maybe we should wait for a few days."

She glared at me, jamming her hands on her hips and wincing. "We are *not* waiting a few days.

In a few days, all of the ships could be destroyed, and the *Paragon* survivors could be beheaded."

"This isn't the French Revolution," I said pointedly. She tilted her head, surprised, and I couldn't help but flash her a grin. "I know a lot more about humans than you'd think. We've been studying your kind for a millennium, which is the basis for everything we are about to go up against."

"God," she said, pressing a palm to her forehead. "No wonder the A'li-uud are so paranoid about humans. If you've been studying us for that long, you've seen the most terrible things humans have ever done."

"Yes, we have. So, if we're going to try to combat one thousand years of knowledge and observances, you need to be healthy."

Tabitha shook her head. "I understand what you're saying, Rex, but we just don't have the time. How long after you initially decided to destroy the ships in your galaxy did the *Paragon* crash?"

I sighed heavily. It hadn't been long at all, a matter of hours. "You're right. But maybe I should go alone," I said insistently.

"No." She had dug her heels in and was growing impatient, crossing her arms over her chest, swaying from side to side with repeated grimaces. I sighed again, climbed out of bed, and pressed my lips delicately to hers.

"Fine, you stubborn human," I said. She smiled smugly.

We cleaned ourselves up, and I informed the guards we would be leaving the palace for a while. I reiterated to them that they were to kill Pugna'ta if they saw her on the grounds again, and then I took Tabitha's hand and led her into the courtyard.

"Are we going to P'otes-tat Ulti?" She asked as the beams from the sun cast down upon us.

"That's only where the Forum is held," I answered, lifting my face to the sky to feel the breeze. "Vi'den is the Elder of Finiba."

She suddenly looked dubious. "That's not in a volcano or something, is it?"

I chuckled and glanced down at her. "No," I said reassuringly. "It's actually my favorite of the kingdoms, aside from Campestria. It's as green as your Earth emeralds, and it has hills as far as the eye can see. The horizon with the green of the hills and the turquoise of the sky is just lovely."

"Like Scotland," she commented thoughtfully. I gave her an inquisitive look, but she waved a dismissive, impatient hand. "Let's go."

I stood behind her and wrapped my arms around her torso. Normally, I would have only taken hold of her hand, but, in her weakened state,

I wasn't certain she could hold on. Then, I bent my knees, gripped the wind, and flew into the air.

When we landed, Tabitha looked woozier than usual after traveling by the winds, and I didn't let go of her right away for fear her knees would give out. We had arrived in the middle of a clearing in a valley surrounded by five hills with softly rounded peaks. In front of us, there was a door built into the base of one of the hills. Cheerful red and yellow flowers with hundreds of petals apiece lined either side of the door and seemed to wave at us in greeting, and a thin chimney poked out from the hillside, emitting a strand of silvery smoke. *It was the kind of place that immediately filled one with optimism.*

"Is this where Vi'den lives?" Tabitha asked timidly. Her eyes were wide, and she was looking around in whimsical wonder.

"Yes."

"Wow," she said. "I pictured something much more—I don't know—castle-like."

"You mean, like P'otes-tat Ulti?"

"No, that's too dank and depressing. Something like Cinderella's castle." I crinkled my brow at her, and she added, "It's a fairy tale."

"Are you well enough to walk?" I asked, still holding her tightly.

She nodded, and I slowly let go to make sure she wasn't mistaken. Her stance was a little wobbly, but she took several steps forward successfully, so I walked alongside her without holding her. When we reached the door, I knocked and waited. Tabitha looked at me nervously.

The door creaked open after a brief moment, and Vi'den stood on the threshold looking very surprised. When he saw Tabitha, however, his face creased with concern, and he held out his hands to take hers.

"My dear girl," he said rather breathlessly. "What happened to you?"

"Pugna'ta attacked her," I answered in Tabitha's place. Vi'den looked over to me, and I could see anger flash behind his peaceful face.

"Come in, come in," he said, ushering us forward into the Hill-house. "I have something to fix that up for you."

"Actually, that's not why we've come," I told him. He gave me a curious look, but helped Tabitha onto a chair and bustled over to a tall, wide cabinet.

As he pulled out herbs and potions and powders, Tabitha turned to me with pleading eyes. I knew her primary concern was discussing our plan, but she didn't want to be the one to start the conversation, so I obliged her.

"Vi'den, we need to talk to you about the human space crafts in Andromeda," I said, moving behind Tabitha and resting my hands delicately on her shoulders. "We need to stop the Elders from having them destroyed."

Vi'den returned before Tabitha with several pots and a vial in his hands. He lifted his brows at me as he began to apply remedy after remedy to the long scratches on either side of her face.

"I'm afraid a Forum vote cannot be overturned without another one, Rex," he said, dabbing a strong-smelling yellowish ooze to Tabitha's right cheek.

"Yes, I understand," I said, "but we need to get that vote. We cannot kill innocent people."

Vi'den paused. His eyes darted between Tabitha's and my own, and his mouth turned down in a slight frown. "If I recall, you were one to vote for the ships' destruction."

Tabitha turned to look up at me, but I didn't return the gaze. *I didn't want to see the disappointment scrawled across her lovely, marred features.* "I know," I said with a nod. "I was wrong. We cannot murder those people without first having proof they intend to harm us."

"I agree," Vi'den replied sagely. "That is why you were instructed to interrogate the *Paragon's* captain. Did you do so?"

I dropped my eyes, feeling slightly ashamed. I had intended to, but my conversation with Leanne had distracted me so much it had slipped my mind. "No," I admitted. "I...was waylaid." Vi'den narrowed his eyes slightly, but I hurriedly asked, "But shouldn't we wait to put offensive plans in place until we have a reason to, rather than seeking a reason to call them off?"

Tabitha piped up. "There is no threat to your people or your planet, Vi'den. We didn't even know you existed until we crashed here."

"Unfortunately, dear girl," Vi'den said, turning his gaze to her rather sorrowfully, "while *you* may not have known of our existence, that does not mean those above you were unaware as well."

"But they were. I promise you, they were," Tabitha went on. She was speaking so quickly that her words seemed almost conjoined. "We didn't even have any weapons onboard, except for a couple of pistols and knives."

Vi'den's head whipped up to me so quickly I thought he'd snapped his neck. This was clearly very valuable news to him, and I was intrigued to learn that as well.

"Did you know of this, Rex?" He asked.

"No," I answered truthfully. "I would have informed the Council if I had."

Tabitha was looking at me over her shoulder, and I could see eagerness written on her lips. Already, the scratches that had been so brazenly red when we'd awoken that morning had faded into a soft pink hue, and the bruises on her face were merely pale lilac shadows now. I tried to tell her to calm down with my expression.

"Did your warriors recover any weapons from the wreckage?" Vi'den asked me.

I shook my head. "All that was found intact were the survivors and some pieces of furniture.

Everything else had been destroyed or lost in the atmosphere when the ship descended."

"Tabitha Bartel, how can you be certain there were no weapons aboard?" He pressed, now looking at Tabitha.

"We all took tours of the ship before launch and during our first week in space," she explained. "Also, being the chef, it wasn't unusual for me to deliver meals to various people while they worked. I would have noticed if there was an arsenal of cannons or missiles or something."

Vi'den nodded slowly. "I wish you would have told us this when you were brought before the Council, but, alas, what's done is done." Then, he flicked his ivory eyes to mine. "I believe you are right to reconsider the vote, Rex, but I fear it may be too late. You'll have to work quickly, and you'll have to start at once if you hope for any chance to appeal the vote."

"Well, let's go," Tabitha said, getting to her feet at once. It was the swiftest and easiest movement I'd seen her make since Pugna'ta attacked her, and I was relieved to see she was feeling better. "Who do we start with?"

"I think it's best that you do not assist Rex in this," Vi'den told her gently.

"I'm not letting him do this alone," Tabitha replied, rather heatedly. "That fat little alien will attack him again!"

I had to force myself not to laugh, but I was certain I had seen the corners of Vi'den's lips twitch upwards for the briefest of seconds.

"It would be useless to try to persuade Torik down any path than the one he is on," Vi'den said. "Thankfully, it is only necessary to sway a majority of the Elders to overturn the vote, not all of them. There are others who will prove more worthy a trip."

"Then, I want to go to them," Tabitha insisted stubbornly. "This isn't just Rex's battle."

"Indeed," Vi'den agreed. "But it will be most efficient and with greater impact, if you fight the battle separately."

Tabitha and I exchanged confused glances, and then she asked, "You mean, you want me to go talk to some of the Elders by myself?"

"Oh, no." Vi'den shook his head, and, again, I saw the corners of his mouth turn up momentarily. "No, your fight, Tabitha Bartel, is not on Albaterra. It is back to space with you."

Chapter 12

Tabitha

Vi'den's plan was for Rex to go to each of the kingdoms in Albaterra with Elders who had potential to be sympathetic to our cause. In the meantime, I was to be sent back into space to meet up with the other human ships in the galaxy and warn them about the potential destruction in the event that the vote did not get overturned or that another missile was released before a new vote could be taken.

    Truth be told, I was very frightened about the idea of going back into space. *The first and most important reason was because I didn't want to separate from Rex.* I was concerned that his plea to the other Elders would be met with aggression and that one of them would take matters into their own hands. I had also learned to rely on him in the last few months, and being without his leadership—*or any leadership, for that matter*—wasn't something I was used to anymore. *The second reason was because, the last time I had been in space, I'd nearly crashed to my death. Obviously, the cause of the crash had been identified, but I was scared nonetheless.* It was not unlike those people who got into a car accident and were afraid to drive for some time afterward.

I knew, however, that Vi'den was right in his thinking. Rex was better suited to approach his kind with the proposal, and it was necessary for me to give warning to the other humans in Andromeda. That way, if the vote were not appealed, the ships would hopefully have enough notice to turn around and escape safely before harm came their way.

We left Vi'den's kingdom shortly after coming to an agreement. He offered for us to stay the night, as it was almost dark, but Rex insisted that we return to Campestria to organize his warriors and collect a crew for me. It seemed I had impressed upon him just how delicate our time was, so we departed from Vi'den's little hill house, with plenty of thanks for his medicinal treatments, and hopped on the winds back to the plains.

    When we arrived in Rex's courtyard, he told me to go to the bedroom while he informed his guards of his return and assigned them with the task to get a ship ready for my journey. I obeyed, but I desperately wanted to stay with him. In the face of our impending separation, I was experiencing a powerful bout of clinginess.

Rex joined me in the bedroom just after the sun had completely disappeared beneath the horizon. "I have good news," he said. He tried to sound cheerful, but his tone was strained and falsified. *It was evident he was as worried about what was to come as I was.* "Ca-es'a has agreed to captain your crew. I know you bonded with him a bit."

His attempt at humor was lost on me as I looked at him with concern. "I thought Ca-es'a is your most loyal warrior."

"He is," Rex confirmed. "That's why I trust him to go with you and ensure your safety."

"But I'm going to be in space. What can Ca-es'a do to keep me safe there?" I asked, wringing my hands with worry. "I think he should go with you. You're much more likely to encounter a confrontation than I am, and Ca-es'a would be able to defend you."

"I have other warriors as capable in battle as Ca-es'a," he told me. "I do not, however, have other warriors as willing to lay down their lives for a human simply because I asked them to."

"But—"

"Tabitha, if what I was looking for was a deadly assassin to send with you, I would have chosen Pugna'ta. She is a living weapon in battle.

Besides, Ca-es'a is an extremely accomplished pilot and is very familiar with the ship you'll be taking. Please, trust me in this."

"Okay," I yielded, nodding. "I trust you."

"Thank you." He stepped up to me and pulled me into his arms. I breathed in his strange, alien scent, an aroma like warm honey, and pressed my cheek against his bare chest. My face no longer burned from the scratches; in fact, I felt nothing more than slight tenderness. The rest of my body, however, still felt like I'd been run over by a truck, though it was significantly more tolerable than it had been when I'd woken.

"So, what do we do now?" I asked.

"Now you go to sleep," he said firmly, looking down at me, pressing his lips to my forehead. "You're still injured, whether you like to admit it or not."

I frowned. "What are you going to do?"

"I need to assemble your crew."

The clinginess in me cried out in protest, but I maintained my composure and asked, "How are you going to pick a crew?"

"There are A'li-uud in my army with skills relevant to your journey, and I was thinking of releasing some of the *Paragon* survivors to join the ranks as well. How do you feel about that?"

I was certain my face was glowing because I felt a pleasant heat radiating from me and a smile took over my lips. "Will you let Leanne come?"

"Does she have any piloting, navigational, or other necessary skills to help you?"

"She supports me," I said resolutely. "That's as necessary as anything else."

I saw his mouth tighten slightly with disapproval, but he nodded. "If having Leanne will bring you comfort when I cannot, then she shall join you."

Standing on tiptoe, I kissed him. I intended it to be a gentle peck of thanks, but he deepened the kiss by probing my lips open with his tongue, burrowing into my mouth passionately. It was a surprise, but I was more than delighted, and I reciprocated with fervor. His hands encircled my waist and crushed my front to his. I secured my fingers at the nape of his neck, bringing his head down closer to mine to kiss him with lustful intensity.

I was reluctant to break apart, but he gently untwined my fingers from his neck and guided me toward the bed. "You must rest," he said. "You have a much greater task before you than I have."

"I'm not so sure about that," I murmured, brushing his bluish cheek with my fingertips. I wanted to look at him forever, to simply drink in his vision and plaster it before my eyes for eternity.

He kissed me again, lightly this time, and pulled the blankets over me. "Sleep, my love."

***

"I have to tell you," Leanne murmured in my ear. "I never thought this would be my life."

"That makes two of us," I whispered back.

We were standing near the entrance ramp to a small but impressive alien ship. It was nothing like the UFOs in drawings or doctored pictures. Actually, it wasn't a far cry from a human rocket. Rather than being circular or oblong, it was bullet-shaped, though much squatter than a typical rocket. Its top was as rounded as the hills in Finiba, and blindingly bright cyan lights glared all the way around the craft. It was constructed from a metal completely foreign to me, though it seemed to be much sturdier and more uniform than any metal I was familiar with.

    Rex was speaking with Ca-es'a and seven other A'li-uud, all of whom were gathered in a small group a short distance away. Leanne and I were with two other humans, both of whom I recognized, but whose names I had never learned. *I was surprised not to see the captain among us, but, then again, I supposed there was no need for him since Ca-es'a would be captaining this mission.*

"Their language is so weird," Leanne said softly, her eyes on the group of aliens nearby. They were within earshot, and the varied clacking sounds they were making sounded almost like tap dancing.

Finally, Rex split apart from the others and strode over to me. His expression had been tight and stressed all day, and I knew it was from his worry for me, but I wished at that moment he would smile. The other A'li-uud scattered in several directions and gathered bags and crates of items which they carried up onto the ship one after the other.

"You can trust this crew," Rex said, speaking English again. "They do their jobs well, and they don't fear humans the way many of our race do."

"Well, I should hope not," Leanne interjected. I shot her a look, and she silenced.

"I don't want to leave you," I told him in a murmur. Out of courtesy, Leanne walked a few feet away to give us a moment of privacy.

Rex pulled me up against him gently. "I don't want to leave you, either, but we have to do this. You're the one who made me see that, remember?"

"Yes," I said, burrowing my face in his shoulder miserably. Then, voicing what I'd been feeling inside, I added, "Rex, I'm scared."

"I know. I'm scared too," he admitted, kissing the top of my head.

I tilted my face up to him, and he pressed his lips to mine. I threw myself into the kiss, giving him all of myself, tasting him so thoroughly I would never forget the taste again. As his tongue swirled around mine, I felt my eyes begin to burn, and tears started to roll freely down my face.

When we broke apart, he took my cheeks in his hands and said firmly, "I *will* see you again soon. We will do what we need to do, and then we will be together."

I nodded, kissed him one last time, and stepped back. Ca-es'a walked up to us tentatively, not wanting to interrupt, and he stared at me as I wept silently. I knew he had never seen tears before, but now was not the time to educate him about human sorrow. "Are you ready?" He asked me quietly.

"Yes," I whispered. I didn't believe it as I said it, but I needed to go before I changed my mind and flew back into Rex's arms.

Rex brought my hand to his mouth and pressed his lips against the back, looking at me through eyes I was certain would be crying if they could. Then, he let go, and I walked to the gangplank. As I reached the door of the ship, I looked back at Rex one last time.

We were going to save both of our worlds. Together.

The Releasing

Chapter 1

Rex

The Montemban Mountains stretched before me like snow-tipped claws intent on plucking the lavender flourishes from the turquoise sky. There was little horizon to see, as the massive, pointed mounds punctured the heavens so tenaciously they left just the celestial welkin above. But the powdery white sunlight was relentless in its efforts to kiss my cheeks and stroke the heads of the peaks like beloved children. Needled trees of varying greens and purples dotted the craggy sides of the intimidating formations and grew in clumps where there were pockets or dimples. Where the first mountains of the range burst from the ground raced a roaring, silvery river so wide it was impassable without a bridge or means of flight. It wound its way through the earthen growths like a snake in the grass while sending outward thinner, calmer streams from its core as veiny spies venturing up the mountainsides.

    Along the steep inclines, there were perfect rectangular doors spread sporadically over the surfaces that would have been seamless in texture with the rock and dirt of the mountains if the snow hadn't been so thick. From my vantage point at the valleyed entrance to the range, standing just inches from the riverbank, I could count well over one hundred doors. Of course, there were many more on the sides of the mountains I couldn't see, and miles upon miles of continuous range extending further into the kingdom that promised plenty more dwellings. It was striking, really, to gaze upon the mere cusp of such an impressive population while seeing only stillness, reminiscent of a deserted civilization.

    Of all the doors and dwellings, however, I was only interested in one. It sat isolated near the summit of the furthest mountain in my view, but, rather than a single rectangular door like the others I saw, it boasted a colossal entry made of brilliant purple aspex—an abundant mineral native to Montemba prized for its hardness and beautiful color—that sparkled blindingly in the sunshine. Several large windows of varying crude shapes punctuated the mountainside on either side of the door and blinked at me just as persistently, as they were framed by glittering aspex as well.

It was the palace of Montemba's reigning Elder, Du'ciact Et'Petrum Montem'tribus, more commonly known as Duke. He was notoriously serious, lacking in humor, and rigidly disciplined, but he was not without a soul, and for that, we shared a respectful friendship. Were he my Elder or I his, our relationship would not have been so amicable due to his penchant for military-enforced laws and my distaste for non-violent restriction, but we each had our own kingdoms to rule and, thus, were quite amiable. He was the only Elder I considered a friend apart from my mentor, Vi'den.

    I tilted my face up to the sky and breathed in deeply. The breeze wafted over my skin, and I bent at the knees and sprang into the air, clutching the winds with my inner fist. To fly on the winds was a medium of travel gifted to Elders upon initiation to the Council. Elders were the most deeply connected to the Grand Circle of our race, and our connection granted us the power to work with nature in ways other A'li-uud could not. Wind travel was the most commonly used power of the Elderhood, as it let us travel great distances in a negligible amount of time, sometimes as quickly as seconds or minutes.

    My feet landed on snow with a heavy crunch as the sparkling door appeared before me. I lifted my hand to bang the large, crystalline knocker, but, before I could, I was suddenly surrounded by seven swords with blades of glistening, violet aspex as long as my legs. They all pointed at me and were poised to strike. The hilts were held by tall, thick A'li-uud wearing pliable white furs and aggressive expressions. Their skin was so pale it was nearly translucent with only a hint of blue beneath the surface. In contrast to my sky-like hue, the warriors looked ghostly.

"This is the palace of Elder Du'ciact," said the nearest and most ferocious-faced warrior, lifting his weapon slightly to brush the edge of my jaw. "What business do you have here?"

With a look that could have withered the sun into a shadow, I replied haughtily, "I am an Elder. My business is not your concern."

"How do we know you're an Elder?" A slightly shorter, slightly fatter warrior barked.

"Unless I'm mistaken," I said coldly, turning to him, "only elders are capable of wind travel, which is how I made it to the door without your notice. I am Rexstrenu'us Et'Herba Campes'tribus, Elder of Campestria."

Six of the A'li-uud flicked their gazes to the first who had spoken to me. He glared at me for a breath, and then he lowered his sword and motioned for the others to do the same. As they obliged, he said rather begrudgingly, "My apologies, Fierce One."

"Wise One," I corrected him. "My kingdom is not one built of ferocity."

They exchanged looks of obvious disdain amongst themselves, but I chose not to pursue the topic further. My interest in conversation was only with Duke. The leader of the warriors allowed me entrance pressing his fingers to a smoothened chunk of aspex and guiding me inside after the door had groaned and swung back on its hinges. He bid two of his men to remain with me while he ordered the other four to resume their duties.

"I will inform Elder Du'ciact of your arrival," he said stiffly.

As he disappeared into the depths of the royal dwelling, I looked around in awe. I had been to Montemba as a child with my parents, but I had never been inside the Elder palace, and its differences from my own in the plains kingdom were striking. The ceiling, lined with ridges and indentations, began only a foot above the doorframe and soared several stories above my head at a steep incline, making me wonder if it was even a ceiling at all or perhaps simply the mountain hollowed for livability. The walls, as well, had the bumps and crevices of a mountainside, and they seemed to radiate a chill from the snow piled outside. The entrance room in which I stood was quite dim, and the sole source of light came from a gray stone fireplace which sat in the center of the space and extended all the way up to the ceiling. Flickers danced off of raw aspex chunks growing from the rock around and above me, which offered the illusion of light but provided none. The floor beneath my feet was uneven gray rock like that of the fireplace, and there were no rugs or mats to be seen for decoration or comfort's purposes. Two staircases, seemingly also constructed from the mountain's natural rock, brought a sense of symmetry to the room as there was one on either side of the space and they were identical to the naked eye in their rough, dark, unyielding composition. Most noticeably to me, however, was the utter lack of furniture. One solitary table long enough to seat six men comfortably—though it had no seating around it—was pushed up against the wall of the right staircase and served as the only piece of furniture in the room. I felt more as though I stood inside a functional military base rather than a home.

"Rex." Duke's voice rang through the vast room in echoes as he appeared from the shadows behind the fireplace, where I assumed there were plenty more rooms. "I did not know you were coming."

"Nor did I, until yesterday after I met with Vi'den," I admitted. Then, in a pointed tone which hid a note of good-natured teasing, I added, "He keeps no warriors on his premises, you know. It's quite a difference from Montemba."

The warrior leader, who had followed closely behind Duke, turned his chin upward in a haughty gesture of scorn. Duke, on the other hand, merely looked at me with grim sobriety and said, "Vi'den has too much faith in moral strength and goodness. He would be wiser to hope for the best and prepare for the worst as we do, particularly in these precarious times with the humans encroaching on our territory and learning of our existence."

Immediately, I wondered if the purpose of my visit would be for naught. Duke was well aware

I was in love with a human and I had taken great measures to ensure her safety from any vigilante A'li-uud. It surprised me to hear him make such a comment about humans and their potential threat to us. It had been he who came to my aid when another Elder attacked me for protecting a human, and, while Duke was prone to offensive action, he had supported my wishes to educate ourselves about the humans and their intentions before making any decisions about their fates.

"Is there somewhere we can talk?" I asked. Shooting a look to the warrior beside him, I added pointedly, "Privately?"

"Of course. This way," Duke replied, motioning with his hand for me to follow him.

We ventured behind the fireplace, leaving the warriors behind, and he took me back to the room he had been summoned from upon my arrival. It was just as sparse, rustic, and functional as the bit of the palace I had already seen and had the same mountainside walls and ceiling with a much smaller fireplace. A table identical to the one in the foyer sat squarely in the center of the room, but this one had six roughly-hewn chairs placed around it, each with a backrest that came to a sharp, spiked point. I imagined they were made of the wood from the purple and green needle trees which sprang freely throughout the Montemban range.

Spread across the table, there were plans and drawings, some featuring the entire kingdom of Montemba and others featuring solitary mountains. Circles and X-marks were scrawled in abundance on each map, and most had words written in tiny, cramped script beside them. As Duke gestured for me to take the seat directly across from his, I eyed at the plans with curiosity.

"Preparing for war?" I asked, only partially teasing.

Duke flattened his hand on some of the papers and spread them around further to allow me a better view. "I am always prepared for war," he said. "This is a defensive plan to prepare us for the inevitable human infiltration."

"Who's to say it's inevitable?"

"Whether it happens during our lifetime or the next, it is inevitable," he answered gravely.

My lips tightened into a thin line of disapproval, but I opted not to comment. Frankly, I had anticipated gaining Duke's support in my cause rather easily. With each passing minute, however, I was becoming less confident in the outcome. It seemed that his views on all matters relating to humans had intensified and gained more pessimistic ground since we had last seen one another.

"Anyway," he went on, sounding just as serious but a touch kinder, "how is Tabitha? I'm surprised she did not accompany you here."

The mention of Tabitha's name brought an image of her face to the forefront of my mind. I pictured her creamy skin, so cool to the touch in comparison to mine, and her rich, dark curls. The exact shape of her full, emotional lips was etched so deeply in my memory I could have sketched them with my eyes closed. My fingers twitched with desire to trace over her feminine curves and smooth jawline, and I could feel the pressure of her body curled up against my chest. *It didn't feel as though I'd only said goodbye to her that morning; it felt like it had been an eternity.*

"Tabitha is in space," I said. Duke's brow furrowed, and his eyes narrowed at me. "Actually, this is why I've come."

"You've sent her back to Earth?" He asked. I couldn't read the expression on his face, but it wasn't a pleasant one.

I shook my head. "No. Tabitha and I are on a mission. She is going to the human spaceships in our galaxy to warn them about our plans to destroy them."

"What?" Duke spat the word out like bitter fruit, and I could certainly read the expression on his face now, *fury*. "She'll be killed, and you'll be imprisoned for treason!"

"I won't," I said confidently with another shake of my head. "Tabitha is under no obligation to dedicate her loyalty to the laws of the Elderhood, and I am not intervening or sabotaging the plans put into motion by a Council vote. My only intention by coming to you, and going to some of the other Elders after I leave Montemba, is to persuade you to reconsider your vote for the destruction of the human ships so we can have an appeal."

He sat back in his chair and looked at me as though he had never seen me before. His skin, as pale as his warriors', seemed stark white even as the glow of the fireplace's flames licked his face. His ivory irises were almost indistinguishable from the sclera around them.

"Why?" He finally asked.

"They're innocent people, Duke." I leaned forward in earnest, balling my hands into fists of passion atop the table as I spoke. "They've done nothing to provoke such a heinous attack. The Grand Circle does not forgive senseless murder."

"You are willing to forsake the A'li-uud, your own race, for your love of a human?" He asked incredulously.

I quirked a brow at him as the corners of my mouth turned down with a distaste for the question. "That sounds like the kind of paranoid justification Torik would use."

"Torik lives in a kingdom of caves that rarely sees the sunlight and fights his own warriors to the brink of death for sport. He is hardly qualified as an Elder in many ways, but you cannot accuse him of being weak," Duke said sternly.

"Yes, I can. Unfounded fear is weakness, Duke, and Torik is riddled with it." I squinted slightly at him. "Besides, if you agree with him, why did you stop him from attacking me?"

"I never said I agree with him. However, I don't believe his fear is unfounded. We've spent over a thousand years observing the humans, and we have witnessed repeated acts of disrespect, violence, and destruction of their planet and their own kind. Humans are driven by power and greed. The threat they pose to our harmony is very real."

"We don't know their intentions!" I burst out, feeling so frustrated that my voice shot up by several decibels. "It would be no different than killing an A'li-uud for walking past your home because he *might* be planning on breaking into it!"

"A'li-uud and humans are completely different species. Our race doesn't engage in such petty behaviors," Duke said loftily. "At least, not in Montemba."

I allowed the jab to my leadership to whizz by without acknowledgment. "Do not dabble in semantics to rationalize your fears, Duke. To destroy the ships simply for crossing the boundaries of Andromeda would be nothing more than murder unless we had something to substantiate our suspicions, and you know it as well."

He looked at me carefully, considering my words, and then asked, "You truly believe you would feel this way independent of your love for Tabitha? As I recall, you voted for the destruction prior to meeting her. It wasn't until she found out this wheel was in motion that your opinion changed."

"I was hard-headed and narrow-minded," I admitted. "Yes, loving Tabitha has altered my perspective, but all for the better. It has opened my eyes and shown me just how far we've strayed from the peaceful path our forefathers wanted us to walk upon. Your father was an Elder. How do you suppose he would feel about this?"

Duke's face suddenly became dark as a heavy frown set on his lips, and his eyes were cast into shadow. For a moment, I wondered if I had overstepped my bounds, but I wasn't prepared to apologize because I genuinely wanted to know the answer to my question.

Finally, he looked away from me and stared at the dancing flames in the fireplace. "You know," he said slowly, his tone musing and contemplative, "there have been many times since I was made Elder that I have wondered what my father would have thought, either about things happening or my own personal behavior and choices. It seems, lately, that those times are growing more frequent." He breathed in deeply, keeping his eyes fixed to the fire. "My father was a peaceful, compassionate A'li-uud. He and I had very different views on Kingdom defense and other such things, but I always admired his respect for life—any life. It's something I've often wished I could emulate."

"You can," I said earnestly. "You have a chance now to stand up for life. It is respecting the Grand Circle to destroy lives when they are massacring our people. It is another matter entirely to destroy lives simply because they could."

I waited for Duke to respond or even just nod his head in acknowledgment. He did neither. He sat as still as if he were frozen, his eyes unmoving as they gazed into the crackling flames, and said nothing. Silence filled the space between us like thick smoke, and I patiently waited for him.

Finally, he turned his head slowly toward me, looked me squarely in the eye, and said solemnly, "You have my vote."

Chapter 2

Tabitha

"I can't believe how much nicer this ship is than the *Paragon*," Leanne whispered. "This must be the five-star part of the fleet."

Despite being preoccupied with nerves and anticipation, I couldn't help but agree with her. We were only standing in the loading bay, one of the grungiest areas of any spaceship, but it was as bright and cheerful as a sunny morning in the country. The walls were gunmetal gray like the entire ship's construction, of course, but thousands of magazine clippings featuring flowers and beautiful landscapes and smiling faces had been taped over the metal in massive floor-to-ceiling collages. Rather than the eye-aching, blue-white fluorescent lights standard to loading bays, overhead lamps bathed us in a warm, comfortable, golden glow reminiscent of Earth's afternoon sunshine. Colorful floor mats of neon pink and electric blue and venom green dotted the otherwise dull floor. If it weren't for the tense and slightly hostile atmosphere, it would have been like standing in a nursery.

We had blasted off into space from the A'li-uud planet of Albaterra that morning, but time lost all meaning in space, and it felt like it had been weeks since we'd started our mission. I was tired, and I was hungry, but, most of all, I missed Rex so much that my chest felt tight and weighted. Leanne had attributed the symptoms to space travel, citing my two-month hiatus on Albaterra as the culprit for my discomfort, *but I knew better. I was terrified for his safety in my absence, though there wasn't much I could have done for him if I'd stayed.* The responsibility of getting the vote to destroy human ships reversed was his and his alone. Yet, I'd been witness to the attack on Rex by the stout cave Elder called Torik, and I feared his ventures around Albaterra would place him back in the same predicament—*or worse.*

Ca-es'a understood. He was Rex's most faithful warrior, and he'd been named the captain of the small A'li-uud spacecraft we were taking to intercept the human ships. We had only been in space for about an hour when he'd noticed the preoccupation in my eyes and said, "There is nothing we can do for him out here. We must do our job and return home."

"I know," I'd whispered. He'd then laid a hand on my shoulder to soothe my worries, and I'd looked into his star-white eyes in search of reassurance. *We were bonded by our love for Rex.*

Now, the captain of my little ship and my personal protector was sitting on the ground with his back pressed against a mishmash of multi-colored tulip pictures and a pistol pointed at his head. He was near enough to me that I could clearly make out the expression on his face, and it was one of well-managed fury. His eyes stared unblinkingly at his captor, his navy blue skin was taut with the bulge of flexed muscles, and his jaw was set so sharply it could have cut glass. I knew that were it not for his orders and his promise to Rex to keep me safe, he would have ripped the head right off the gun-wielding human's body. A'li-uud warriors were fierce, skilled fighters. *I had learned that after being attacked by one myself.*

The remaining seven A'li-uud members of my crew were lined up against the same wall as Ca-es'a, though they'd been placed a short distance away and were being detained by three humans with stun guns. They, too, looked enraged, but they kept their tempers in check with restraint equal to Ca-es'a.

"So," someone said behind me. I turned to see the tall lumberjack-like man with a dark brown beard who had been the first person I'd interacted with upon exiting my ship. "You say you weren't kidnapped by these things?"

"They're A'li-uud," I said heatedly, glaring at him in disgust. "And, no. They're helping me."

His eyes drifted to Ca-es'a and the other blue-skinned beings with a wary expression on his slightly lined face. "What are they, aliens?"

"Actually, we're technically the aliens here. We're in *their* galaxy," I replied, emphasizing the ownership in favor of the A'li-uud.

"Yeah, whatever," he grumbled. He crossed his arms over his heather gray jumpsuit, covering the small emblem of a geometric pentagon on his left breast. I knew the symbol to be the official logo of the United States' federal branch dedicated to space exploration as I myself had owned several jumpsuits with the very same logo before my ship, the *Paragon*, had crashed in Rex's kingdom. With an uncomfortable grunt, he scuffed the toe of his black, shin-high boot against the floor and shot another look at the A'li-uud against the wall as he asked, "So, are they dangerous?"

"No more than we are," I snapped. I was rapidly growing frustrated and unable to hold my temper back. I had gone into space and left Rex behind to fend for himself without some of his best warriors so that I could warn the crews of the three humans ships about the possible danger to them.

While I knew it was the right thing to do, I was starting to wonder if it was even worth it. Ever since we'd boarded the *Quintessence* and disembarked from our little spacecraft, we'd been met with nothing but suspicion. It was logical, I supposed, as the A'li-uud were the first aliens humans had ever encountered, to my knowledge, but I felt an unreasonable amount of irritation about the hassle.

Trying to remain calm, I looked at the air-sealed door I knew would lead into the main part of the ship and asked, "Can I speak to your captain, please?"

"Oh, don't worry about that. He's on his way down now." The guy made a horrible snarling noise in his throat, and then spat onto the ground, and Leanne stared at him with utter revulsion. He didn't seem to notice. "The captain's obsessed with aliens. Been hoping we'd run into other life forms since we left Earth."

"Well, I expect he'll be happy to see us, then," I replied wryly, turning my back on him pointedly.

As I turned, Ca-es'a met my gaze. I tried to apologize to him with my eyes, but I wasn't sure if A'li-uud communicated that way, especially with humans. I felt horrible guilt as I looked at him and the others. Even though it wasn't me or people I knew holding them at gunpoint, I still felt responsible because they were on this mission to help me—*or to help Rex, at least*—and because it was my race treating them so terribly. I couldn't help but hope the A'li-uud wouldn't associate me with the experience, and the way Ca-es'a's face softened as we looked at each other gave me hope they wouldn't.

    I didn't have to wait long for the captain. Only a minute later the door slid open, and he stepped into the loading bay. Despite never having met him, I recognized him at once as captain because his gray jumpsuit was trimmed with gold around the collar and wristbands. Even in his uniform, I could see he was an eccentric man. His eyes were just a little too large for his head and protruded rather like a frog's, giving him a goggled appearance. He had a mouth that stretched from cheek to cheek in a goofy grin and thick, flat lips. He was neither slender nor fat, just doughy, and he walked with a bounce in his step which reminded me of a happy child with a balloon in one hand and a lollipop in the other. When he saw me, all of his exaggerated features became all the more pronounced, and he bopped over to us with his hand extended.

"Ronald White," he said jovially, shaking my hand energetically. "Captain of the *Quintessence*. It's a pleasure to meet you."

"Thank you," I replied with a cordial inclination of my head. "I'm Tabitha Bartel. I used to be the chef aboard the *Paragon*."

"Yes, you'll have to tell me all about the *Paragon* and your ordeal. There's been quite a lot of chatter amongst the fleet as to your whereabouts. Some had been convinced you'd been hijacked by alien pirates." As he spoke, his frog eyes slid to the A'li-uud, who were still held against the wall at gunpoint. He was practically vibrating with excitement.

I followed his gaze to the blue-skinned members of my crew and asked a little icily, "Could you perhaps call your men off? The A'li-uud are here to help, not harm."

"Of course, of course!" Captain White nodded enthusiastically and called, "Turbot, stand down!" Then, turning to me, he murmured, "You have to understand, we've never met an alien life force before, and to have so many board our ship in the company of humans, well, it can be a cause of alarm for some."

My instinct was to scoff, but deep down I knew he was right, so I merely said, "I understand.

You have my word they will be nothing but peaceful and gracious."

"Do they speak English?" He asked, watching his men lower their weapons rather dubiously.

"Yes," I said. "They speak whatever language is spoken to them. Amongst themselves, they speak their own language, though."

"Really!" His eyes lit up, and he clasped his hands over his chest with excitement. "I would love to hear it!"

"I'm sure they wouldn't mind, Captain, but we came aboard for something very important," I told him. He looked back at me reluctantly, and I peered at him with earnest. "I'd appreciate it if we could go somewhere more exclusive to talk."

Ca-es'a and the other A'li-uud were getting to their feet slowly, and I could feel their eyes on me as Captain White replied cheerfully, "Well, certainly. I'd be glad for your friends to join us if it suits you."

I lifted a hand and waved Ca-es'a over. He clacked something to the other aliens in their native tongue, and Captain White let out a small giggle of thrill. Then, he led me, Leanne, and the rest of my crew out of the loading bay and into the main stretch of the ship, leaving the members of his crew behind with suspicious glares and avid curiosity on their faces.

We were led to the ship's control center, where there were five other human crewmembers manning their respective stations. Upon seeing Ca-es'a, who was the first A'li-uud to enter, they all stiffened, and the only female screamed. Captain White brandished his hands haphazardly about and cried, "Don't worry, don't worry! They are our guests."

"Are they real?" Asked the lanky Middle Eastern man standing over a glowing panel of buttons and knobs. He sounded awed rather than frightened, though his stance told me he was on his guard.

"Of course they're real," Captain White responded rather scornfully. "And they are to be treated with the same respect as any other guest."

Ca-es'a was standing unnaturally close to me, which made me feel more alert than I ordinarily would have. It was almost as if he anticipated an attack on me from my own kind, something I hadn't even considered as a possibility. I could feel the warmth from his skin radiating against mine, and his fingertips repeatedly brushed the small of my back as we filed in as though he was prepared to throw me down to the ground if needed. *While it made me feel a sense of anxiety toward my own people, it also gave me reassurance I was safe in his care.*

  The captain took a seat in a chair which could only be for the ship's captain. It had a very tall backrest and was well-cushioned. And of course, it had been mounted in the very center of the room. As he sat, it swiveled slightly, and I realized it could turn in a full circle so he could see any part of the room at any time without having to stand. Frankly, I was reminded of old episodes of *Star Trek* my mother used to watch when my father worked late.

"Captain, we're here because you're in possible danger," I said bluntly. "The A'li-uud Elders discovered our fleet had crossed into their galaxy, Andromeda, a little more than two months ago, and they voted to destroy our ships to eliminate any potential threat we might pose to them."

"You must tell me about these A'li-uud," Captain White replied eagerly, leaning forward in his chair, forming a steeple with his fingers beneath his chin. His eyes continuously roved between Ca-es'a and me, who I could feel standing rigidly behind me.

"I'm sorry, Captain, but we don't have time," I said. "One of the Elders is working now to get the vote appealed at my request, but there's a chance another missile could be released before he's able to convince everyone."

The *Quintessence* crew in the room exchanged worried looks with each other. The woman, a petite blonde with a bob and doe-like eyes, chimed in, "Captain, if I may, I think we need to take this warning seriously. A member of our fleet wouldn't take these measures if the threat wasn't real."

Captain White's pudgy lips turned down in a frown. "I thought you said they are a peaceful race."

"They are," I explained, "but their initial reaction to finding our ships in their galaxy was to protect their kind. They shot the *Paragon* because we were so close to Albaterra—"

"Is that their planet?" He asked excitedly. "Albaterra?"

"Yes, and—"

"You have been there since the *Paragon* disappeared from our radars?"

"Yes, Captain, but we must—"

"What is it like?"

I was frustrated by his constant interruptions, and I was even more frustrated by his lack of concern for the looming danger to his ship and his crew. Ca-es'a either sensed my frustration or had grown irritated himself because, suddenly, his low, oddly-accented voice brimmed from behind me.

"Albaterra is a place of peace and harmony," he intoned. I turned around to look at him and saw his white eyes staring intently at Captain White. His lips barely moved as he spoke. "We, as a race, respect nature in its rawest form, its magic and its ability to create and destroy. But do not let this fool you. The A'li-uud are fierce warriors and highly protective of our lands and our people. What Tabitha tells you is true, and our Elders will not hesitate to destroy you if Rex does not appeal to them in time."

I could see Captain White burning with questions. His entire face had lit up like Times Square on New Year's Eve, and he was sitting so near the edge of his seat he was close to falling off. He was not a foolish man, though, and it was clear he took his captaincy seriously because he whirled the chair around to face the Middle Eastern man and asked, "Is the rest of the fleet in range?"

"We can make contact with the *Criterion*," the man replied, pressing buttons at such rapid-fire speed that his fingers looked like a blur. "The *Epitome* is on our radar but out of communication range."

Captain White turned back to us. "I'm not willing to put my crew in harm's way for the sake of my curiosities, as much as I would love to learn more about you"—he inclined his head to Ca-es'a—"so I will heed the warning. We will pass along your information to the *Criterion*, but I'm afraid you'll have to take your ship to the *Epitome* and tell them these things yourself, as I intend to get my ship out of the galaxy as quickly as possible."

"I understand," I said in a whoosh of breath. I was thankful he had internalized what I'd told him. "Thank you."

"When things get sorted out, however," he added with a broad smile, "I would love the opportunity to visit this planet Albaterra and spend some time with these A'li-uud. I would consider it a great personal favor."

I smiled tightly and said, "I'll see what I can do."

Chapter 3

Rex

Convincing Duke to change his vote had been more difficult than I'd anticipated, and, as I left his palace, I had a hard knot in my gut of concern that persuading those with whom I didn't have a friendship would be impossible. As Duke showed me out, he seemed to sense my worry and clapped a hand on my back.

"Go to Maquaria next," he advised. "Ma'ris has been opposed to the violence from the start. And do not bother with Torik. He would watch his own warrior flayed alive simply to stave off boredom."

I agreed completely and thanked him for hearing me out. His guards eyed me in disgruntled docility with their hands twitching beside their weapons, but I ignored them and turned my face up to the sky. The moment the wind brushed my cheek, I bent at the knees and jumped.

Maquaria was Albaterra's only underwater Kingdom, and it was one of the few to which I had never ventured. My father had told me many years ago it was an unnaturally tranquil place as far as the A'li-uud who inhabited it, but that it held much greater organic dangers than any other kingdom on the planet. *I had always been curious about what he meant, and now I would get my chance to find out for myself.*

When I landed, I was surprised to find myself on hard, dry ground. Thick clumps of shin-high, brilliantly green grass surrounded me on all sides and licked my legs with the help of the cool, pungent breeze. I noticed the grass was coarser than the prairie grasses I was accustomed to in my home Kingdom of Campestria and that the blades felt like they were covered in a strange, sticky dust.

Tall trees with spiny trunks and blanket-sized leaves leaned in graceful arches toward the ground as if whispering secrets to the soil. The air smelled strongly of fruit and fish, though I could see neither. I could, however, hear the telltale roar of water nearby and began stomping my way through the grass toward the sounds.

    Within minutes, I had cleared my way through the brush and was standing on a beach. To my left, there were large, rocky cliffs, while my right was nothing but vast, limitless ocean. Beneath my feet, there was sand, and it was so soft I could have comfortably taken a nap atop it. *I couldn't help but notice that the sand was the same alabaster color as Tabitha's skin, and I felt a pang of longing for her.* I looked around in confusion, searching for any sign of A'li-uud civilization. It dawned on me that perhaps I was supposed to just start walking into the water.

Before I could, however, I caught movement out of the corner of my eye. I turned my head and saw two well-toned but very lanky A'li-uud emerging from a thin crevice in the cliffs. They wore strands of underwater weeds as bottoms and nothing on their chests—a popular practice for those of us in the warmer Albaterran climates—and they held staves decorated with shells which came to sharp points at the tips. In contrast to my greeting by the warriors in Montemba, these warriors simply looked at me as they took their places on either side of the crevice.

I approached them cautiously, my hands hanging limply by my sides to show no threat. They were both alert, but neither seemed inclined to go on the defensive. When I was within earshot of them, I called, "I am Elder Rexstrenu'us of Campestria. I have come to speak with Ma'ris."

They didn't respond, which I found unnerving, but I continued approaching them until I was just a few feet away. Their staves could have easily pierced my heart from where they stood.

Finally, when neither spoke to me, I asked, "How do I enter Maquaria?"

"Through the cliffs." Both A'li-uud had incredibly bold cerulean skin, but the one with a slightly more intense hue was the one to answer.

"Thank you," I said, still rather unnerved. I didn't know if they intended to follow me or, worse, to attack me when I tried to pass through them into the crevice, so I stepped carefully inside, ready to defend myself if necessary.

The crevice was the opening to what seemed to be a long, narrow corridor. It would have been completely black and practically unnavigable if there hadn't been large shells mounted on the walls on either side with small, pleasant flames burning within them. The air was moist and thick and smelled even more strongly of fish than it had in the openness of the beach, and I could hear dripping water echoing throughout the tight space. A quick glance overhead showed me thick stalactites growing down from the ceiling which seemed to shimmer despite the poor lighting.

    I walked carefully and methodically, as the ground was doused in shadows and I couldn't see where I was stepping. The path was uneven and bumpy, even a little rocky, and I stumbled several times. When it felt like I had been walking for nearly twenty minutes, I turned around to see how far I had come, and I couldn't even see the slightest pinprick of light from the crevice opening. Neither guard had followed me.

 Eventually, I realized that the corridor was slowly descending into the earth as my steps became more unstable and uncertain, and my balance seemed to be tugged from my core. I extended my arms out to my sides so I could graze my palms over the walls to keep myself from tripping. Just as I was beginning to wonder if the guards had tricked me into actually getting lost in some kind of dungeon or criminal keep, the corridor suddenly came to a stop, and I was looking at a bumpy, ridged wall. It prevented me from going any further, and I would have been forced to turn around if not for the pool of water lapping at my feet. I looked down and realized there was a staircase leading into the depths of the water.

    Nervously, I lowered myself onto the first step. To my surprise, my foot did not become wet; in fact, as I tested by continuing onto the next stair, I realized I wasn't stepping into the water at all. There was certainly a pool, but the staircase and the space around it seemed to be protected by a very clear, nearly imperceptible material. Water swirled around the staircase on both sides but never did it break over the steps, and I descended down the remainder of the staircase with confidence.

When I reached the bottom, I discovered I was essentially standing in a tube of the clear material, completely dry and able to see the treasures of the ocean on every side of me. Below, the shallow floor gradually dropped into oblivion, decorated by swaying, feathery plants and rocks of every color. Fish of all shapes swam around me, some alone and some in groups, and I spotted something large and shadowy in the distance swimming very slowly. The sound inside the tube was almost complete silence; save for a slight shushing noise which was actually quite relaxing.

What I found most surprising was how bright everything seemed, as though the underwater world had its own sun.

I resumed walking through the tube, which did not remain straight but made unpredictable twists and turns and even presented some unexpected forks. It seemed that, given the tube's clear construction, I would have been able to see a city or some roaming guards in front of me within a mile's distance, but all I saw was the stretch of underwater ocean and its animal inhabitants. With no indication which direction I should go to get to Maquaria or Ma'ris, I let my instinct guide me and wound my way unknowingly through the tube.

Another fork appeared in front of me, and I took the left path. Within just moments, I rounded a corner and saw two A'li-uud guards dressed exactly as the two on the beach had been. They stood on either side of a grand golden door with so many carvings in it that it seemed almost like a puzzle. When they saw me, they looked at one another rather knowingly.

"I am Elder Rexstrenu'us of Campestria," I announced without preface. "I am here to see—"

"We know who you are," the taller of the two interrupted. "Elder Ma'ris is expecting you."

Startled, I watched as he opened the door pressing a lovely pink shell to its center. As it opened slowly, I was greeted by the sight of the grandest city I had ever seen. Tall castle-like buildings made of the same gold as the door towered over streets of water-smoothed stone, which were lined with thin golden lampposts topped with large golden shells which held balls of pale purple fire in their centers. Outposts and kiosks of green and pink and royal blue coral stood peacefully along the sides of the streets with everything inside from dried fish hanging from their ceilings in bunches to beautifully-crafted, shiny shell dishware laid out neatly on shelves of bone. The A'li-uud milling about had skin in varying shades of cerulean and turquoise, and they wore clothes of seaweed strands just as the guards did. The entire city seemed to be encapsulated by the same clear tubing I had been walking through, and sea creatures swam around and above the golden peaks with the same leisurely meanderings as the A'li-uud within.

"Welcome to Maquaria," the guard said. There was a look of slight amusement on his face as he observed my awed expression.

"Thank you," I murmured absent-mindedly, striding slowly past him onto the stone street.

I realized after a moment I didn't have the slightest idea where to find Ma'ris, and I was about to turn around and ask the guard when I spotted a row of warriors standing rigidly on alternating steps of an exquisite golden staircase. The staircase led to the largest of all the castles within sight, and I knew at once it was the Maquaria's Elder palace.

    Just like the other guards I had encountered, the warriors on the stairs didn't speak or acknowledge me as I slowly walked up toward the palace. Their eyes followed me as I moved, but none seemed inclined to question or stop me, so I brazenly approached the massive double doors which served as entrance and came to a stop before them. A guard stood on either side.

"You wish to see Elder Ma'ris?" The one on my right inquired.

"Yes," I answered.

"Come," he said, pressing a shell to one of the doors just as the guard outside the city had. "He has been anticipating your arrival."

I didn't know how the warrior knew who I was—although my deep blue skin tone and goat-skin pants may have been an indication of where I was from, at the least—but I followed him in without question. The interior of the castle was as breathtaking as the exterior with just as much gold and multi-colored coral accents on the arches and trim that gave the space a very cheerful, relaxing appearance. There was no fireplace, which I initially found surprising before remembering we were underwater, but there were large seashell lamps hanging from the ceiling, mounted on the walls with the same purple flames in them as the streetlights outside. There was also no furniture like the Elder palace of Montemba, but the architecture of the entrance hall was so intricate and eye-catching that the room didn't feel empty at all.

"Welcome, young Rexstrenu'us." Ma'ris's warbling voice filled the entrance hall before I saw him, and, when he strolled in, his arms were extended out to the side in a grand gesture of greeting.

"Hello, Ma'ris," I replied pleasantly. "I heard you were expecting me."

"Vi'den reached out and told me you would be arriving. He did not say when, however, so I merely told my guards to look out for a young Campestrian A'li-uud," Ma'ris explained.

If any of the other Elders had continuously pointed out my youth, I would have become angry and offended. To hear it from Ma'ris, though, was not a jab at my credibility or qualifications; he was the oldest Elder. In his eyes, everyone was young, even Vi'den, who was rather ancient himself. The greatest difference in age between Ma'ris and Vi'den could be seen in their faces; where Vi'den had slight lines near his eyes and the corners of his mouth, Ma'ris had divots so deep they had their own shadows. His skin was no longer smoothly blue and had been marred by dark navy marks similar to the brown age spots humans developed as they grew older. His voice and manner of speaking was also garbled and sounded like he constantly had a mouthful of bubbles, but I wasn't sure if that could be attributed more to his living underwater for so long.

"I don't suppose Vi'den told you the reason for my visit?" I asked hopefully. It would save precious time if Ma'ris knew and already had his mind made up.

Alas, that was not the case. "He did not," he said solemnly. "Come, and you can explain it all to me."

He led me into a dining room so large it could have been a ballroom instead. Strikingly realistic murals of previous Maquarian Elders were painted on the wide panels of the walls and trimmed with more gold, giving the room some additional color it otherwise would have lacked. The table was offset to the southern side of the space, and it was so long it stretched well over half of the room's length. It could have seated at least thirty A'li-uud on either side. Ma'ris took the lone chair at the head of the table and motioned for me to sit in the seat to his right. I obliged.

"Now," he burbled kindly, "why have you come to my quaint little water-kingdom?"

The last thing I would have called Maquaria was "quaint," but I was in a race against the clock to speak to as many Elders as possible and didn't have time to correct him. "I am here to ask for your support in reversing the vote to destroy the human ships which have breached our galaxy's borders."

His eyebrows lifted toward his scalp with surprise, and he said, "You were the one who voted in favor of the humans' destruction, were you not?"

"Yes, and I've realized the error of my decision," I said. Then, hastily, I added, "And I know you're going to say it's because I love a human, but it's not. The A'li-uud race has always been one to shed as little blood as possible while maintaining our existence and our planet, and to destroy the ships without reason would go against everything we stand for."

Ma'ris was looking at me with a rather disappointed expression on his face, and I stopped talking as I tried to understand what it meant. "I am surprised at you, Rexstrenu'us," he gurgled. I stared, unsure of what he meant. "You have always been a sensitive man, perhaps a little too much so. On occasion, I have found you naïve." I continued to stare, but he went on as though he didn't notice. "To hear you deny the impact of love, however, is ignorance I would have never expected from you."

"I don't mean to deny the impact of love," I replied, a little taken aback by his words. "I'm just saying that my views aren't solely based on love."

"But they are," he said chidingly. "Your love for the human opened your mind to the possibility of regret for the bloodshed, and your love for your people solidified it." He pressed his palms together with a small smile on his aged face and explained,

"To love one is not to destroy another, Rexstrenu'us. Some Elders would argue that to kill the humans is to defend and therefore love, the A'li-uud, but it is not. It is an act of hatred and prejudice. To love our race is to uphold the values and the ways of the Grand Circle, and we must not make decisions out of fear and loathing if we truly love our kind."

His eloquent words left me speechless. It was exactly the way I felt, and, for the first time, I admitted to myself I had been able to accept that because I loved Tabitha. She had opened my mind, just as Ma'ris had said, and allowed me to be a true A'li-uud leader.

"You need not waste valuable time trying to persuade me to your side," Ma'ris continued. "I never was an advocate for the destruction anyway. You have my support."

Chapter 4

Tabitha

I stared out of the giant, curved window which occupied an entire wall of the command center with my belly in knots. It had come as a welcome surprise that the *Quintessence*, overall, was open to my warning and offered to inform the *Criterion* for me. That left just one ship, the *Epitome*, for us to visit and warn before we could return to Albaterra and I could make sure Rex was okay.

There was no reason for me to believe he wouldn't be okay, of course. He was a good fighter, a respected Elder, and very smart; he wouldn't put himself in a situation which could end up in injury or worse. My concern lay with those like Torik because that was out of Rex's control, and I was certain that, if some kind of unfortunate circumstances befell him, it would be because Torik or another hateful A'li-uud took it upon himself to deliver skewed justice. I was also very nervous that Rex wouldn't speak to enough Elders in time before another missile was launched, and being in space when that happened—or even being aboard the *Epitome* at the time—could mean the end of my days.

"Is this the *Epitome*?" Ca-es'a asked suddenly.

I blinked rapidly, realizing I'd become lost in my thoughts, and my eyes focused on the vision outside of our spacecraft window. Ahead of us, there was a very large, very fast ship. I could see Albaterra below it, and it almost looked as though the ship was either hovering over the planet or zooming around it like a thief casing a bank. It was like an enormous disc, ovular in shape and rather flat, with three symmetrically-placed barrels mounted on its rear.

"I think so," I said uncertainly. "It's either the *Epitome* or the *Criterion* because the *Quintessence* is long behind us."

Leanne, who had been lingering in the room out of boredom, crossed the space to the window and pressed her nose against it. Her eyes squinted into slits.

"That's the *Epitome*," she said finally, stepping back from the window and looking between Ca-es'a and me.

"How do you know?" I asked, going to the window beside her and looking out at closer range.

She pointed, though the gesture was essentially useless because, from this distance, her finger was almost the same size as the ship. "Look at the furthest cylinder on the right. There's an E."

I got so close to the window that the tip of my nose crunched against it just as hers had, and I imitated her by squeezing my eyes into thin lines. I couldn't see anything resembling a letter, much less specifically an E. It didn't surprise me she could see it, though, because, being a seamstress, her eyesight was as stellar as an A'li-uud's. Her entire business was based on the minute details of tiny stitches and seed-like beads and the intricate weaving of lace.

"Well, I don't see it, but I believe you," I told her. She grinned, and I turned around to Ca-es'a. "Let's catch up with it."

Honestly, I should have been grateful for only having one ship left to advise, but I wasn't. Knowing the only thing that separated me from Rex was passing a message to a single ship made it feel like time had slowed and the moment I could see him again was actually much further away than it had been when we'd first blasted off into space. As Ca-es'a started to steer our little spacecraft toward the giant disc, I swung my eyes from our destination and instead focused on Albaterra, trying to imagine what Rex was doing at that very moment.

The A'li-uud ship we were aboard was extraordinarily fast, and we gained on the *Epitome* at rapid-fire speed. It didn't take more than five minutes to cross half of the space between us, and, within another five minutes, we were right up alongside it. We were so close, in fact, I could even see people passing by the windows and going about their day. I was certain the *Epitome* had picked us up on its radar as the *Quintessence* had, but, from the outside, everything seemed calm and normal.

"Come in! Come in!" A crackling voice suddenly burst through the speakers in the command center, and I whirled around to look at them as though they would reveal the source of the words. "This is Lieutenant Maylor of the *Epitome*. We are armed, and we will shoot. State your purpose."

Ca-es'a moved for the telecom, but I leaped forward and snatched it away from him. It was remarkably similar to the types of microphones radio DJs used and easy for me to swing out of his reach.

"You don't sound like you speak English natively," I said to him apologetically. "I think I should talk."

"As you wish," Ca-es'a replied.

I pressed the small red button on the base of the telecom and placed it near my mouth. "Lieutenant Maylor, my name is Tabitha Bartel. I am the chef of the *Paragon*, a ship in your fleet. Requesting permission to board."

There was silence in the speakers for nearly a minute, and then the same voice flooded the room again.

"The *Paragon* went missing two months ago. Where did you acquire your vessel?"

I scrunched my eyebrows together in confusion and looked around. Leanne waved her hands around and silently mouthed, "The ship."

"Oh, right," I said. I pressed the button down again. "The *Paragon* crashed the nearest planet, and alien life forms provided us this spacecraft to reach the rest of our fleet. Again, we are requesting permission to board."

More silence took over, and my heart was pounding in my ears. I wasn't nervous about their response, but I wanted it to be over with. I could see the multi-colored atmosphere of Albaterra below us; *it was so close that I felt like I could simply jump from the ship and land in Campestria.*

I jumped when the voice split the air again. "Permission granted. We are preparing for your boarding in the portside loading bay."

Ca-es'a nodded once, signaling he understood, and I thanked Lieutenant Maylor before placing the telecom back on one of the surfaces. Leanne no longer looked bored; on the contrary, she wore an expression of obvious excitement. I quirked a brow of curiosity at her.

"Why do you seem so thrilled?" I asked.

Her lips split into a Cheshire cat smile, and she said gleefully, "I met a guy during training who was assigned to the *Epitome*, and you know how those guys can get when they haven't felt a woman's touch for months on end."

"Leanne, I'm sure there are women on board the *Epitome*."

She immediately frowned and shot me an unappreciative look. "Well, you don't have to ruin it for me!"

"Sorry," I said with a laugh. I could always trust Leanne to deliver a bout of superficial humor to any situation.

We pulled into the loading bay after about a half hour, and I noticed it seemed to be much more similar to the *Paragon's*, as opposed to the

Quintessence's homier appearance. Stark metal walls and floors were the only sources of decoration if it could be called that, and every item within the bay was one of functional purpose. It looked like a proper military ship, or, at least, the bay did.

When our craft was finally docked, and everything was turned off, I looked at Ca-es'a. "Do you think you should maybe stay here this time? I don't want to subject you to being held up at gunpoint again."

"I was tasked by my Elder to protect you," he said seriously, "and that is what I intend to do."

"You can't protect me very well when you're being forced to sit against a wall," I pointed out.

Ca-es'a's expression soured, not at my statement but at the memory, and he didn't seem to have an immediate answer for me. Leanne, however, piped up, "Oh, let them come, Tabitha. If they don't show themselves right away, there will really be questions when the *Epitome* crew finds them in here."

She had a point, though I didn't want to admit it, so I nodded reluctantly. "Let's go, then."

I stepped out of the small A'li-uud spacecraft first, and I was instantly met with scurrying crewmembers who did everything from outright ignoring me to shaking my hand. Several physically stopped in their tracks and peered into my eyes as though to make sure I was truly human or to reassure themselves that I wasn't sick or hurt. I just smiled with as friendly a smile as I could and allowed myself to be led a short distance from my spacecraft before stopping and waiting for the others to disembark.

Leanne was next, and she was greeted with similar responses. When Ca-es'a stepped out after her, however, there was an immediate change in the climate of the loading bay. I hadn't warned the *Quintessence* before boarding I had aliens with me or procured the ship from them, and, thus, they had been panicked upon seeing the A'li-uud. It was clear that the crew of the *Epitome*, however, had heard of the forewarning I had offered Lieutenant Maylor, and they simply allowed Ca-es'a to pass them and take his place behind me. *I noticed they either shot him alarmed, suspicious glances or pretended he didn't exist, but I figured that both were preferable to threatening him with firearms, so I didn't address it.*

The remainder of my crew exited our small ship one-by-one and joined Leanne, Ca-es'a, and myself off to the side. The *Epitome* mechanics and technologists started performing numerous routines on the ship, but one man broke away from the group and approached us.

"The captain is waiting for you," he said. His voice was quite possibly the dullest, most monotonous voice I had ever heard in my life, and his face was equally lacking in excitement. "I'll take you."

"Thank you," I said, but the words hadn't even fully left my mouth before he turned around and started walking toward the only door in the bay. I glanced behind me to the others and made a small gesture with my hand, motioning for them to follow.

The man led us through the door into a corridor lined on both sides with various computers and control panels, all of which glowed a bright, bold blue color. It was identical to the corridor the *Paragon* had had leading up to the loading bay, and I wondered if the two ships were twins. When we stepped out of the corridor through another door and entered another hall that split into several different directions, I realized it was, in fact, exactly the same as the *Paragon*. For some reason, I was instantly hit with a confusing mix of comfort at being somewhere familiar and horror at being somewhere that reminded me so fiercely of the place I'd been when I'd nearly died over two months ago.

We wound through the ship until we finally reached the main portion where the crew worked and lived. I could have navigated us without the man's help, given the mirror layout of the *Epitome* to the *Paragon*, but I didn't want to be rude by dismissing him. I knew it would alarm any passersby who happened to see eight A'li-uud wandering their ship without the escort of a fellow crewmember. He directed us all the way to the command center, where, rather than just entering, he pressed a button to the right of the door I knew to be a bell.

The door slid open, presumably because there was a button inside that someone had pressed, and he led us in. This command center was exactly the same as the *Paragon's* and not too different from the *Quintessence,* though perhaps a touch more neutral and boring in its style. The crewmembers within the room all had their eyes trained on us as we entered, but I was pleased to see that nobody looked frightened or surprised. There was, however, more than one faces that looked rather angry, which caught me off-guard.

"Captain, I've brought the chef and her crew," the dull man said.

"Thank you, Pierce." This came from the man sitting in the tall-backed, swiveling chair in the center of the room, which looked exactly like the one from the *Quintessence*. He had thin, white hair with very faint streaks of gray, and it was slicked back so much I could see his scalp through the strands. His gray jumpsuit fit his unexpectedly thick, muscular body a little too snugly. His face was well-lined and noticeably tanner than one might expect for someone who'd spent months in space. He had sharp, rather unfriendly blue eyes that darted critically between myself and each member of my crew. "Return to your post."

The dull man nodded and left immediately as bid. Despite his complete lack of personality, it felt like he took all kindness out of the room with him when he disappeared. There was a strict, militant feeling in the air, utterly devoid of a sense of humor and completely opposite from Captain White's command center. *In a strange way, though, I could almost feel Ca-es'a relaxing slightly, as though the rigidity was comfortably familiar to him, though I couldn't imagine that being true as Rex was far from rigid.*

"Who is the chef?" The captain asked. He had an odd, barking way of talking which reminded me of my dad telling my brother how to mow the lawn properly. It made me inclined to shrink down and hide behind Leanne or Ca-es'a, but I stepped forward against my instinct.

"I am," I said. "Tabitha Bartel of the *Paragon*."

"And these other humans? Are they *Paragon* crew as well?" He asked, brandishing a careless hand at the other three humans behind me.

"Yes, Captain," I told him.

Leanne stepped forward beside me. "Leanne Terry. I am the seamstress. Well, I was before we crashed—"

"We've got a chef and a seamstress heading up an impromptu space expedition," the captain commented sardonically. As he spoke, he looked over his shoulder at a man with a shaved head and a sharp face who cracked a cynical, rather degrading smile. When he turned back, he motioned to three crewmembers standing off to the side with pistols on their hips and stun guns in their hands. "Take the blue freaks to the cells. Leave the others."

"Wait, what?" I cried, alarmed. The three men stepped forward with their stun guns drawn and their free hands on their pistols, moving toward us quickly and unrelentingly.

"Don't worry," the captain said icily. "We'll let you say goodbye."

I stared in horror as the A'li-uud were forcibly pushed out of the room, and, just before the door closed Ca-es'a's eyes met mine.

Chapter 5

Rex

Frankly, I wanted to spend more time in Maquaria. It was so beautiful and so unique I found myself awe-struck again as I departed from Ma'ris's palace. There was so much gold and rich color it had the appearance of a luxurious, elite city, but there wasn't even the slightest hint of pretension or division in the atmosphere. If anything, I felt as though I could have sat down with any one of the A'li-uud I saw casually strolling the stone streets for a meal and been as comfortable as though I'd sat down with my own family. Maquaria was, in short, all-inclusive and a hub of acceptance.

I didn't have time, though. With Ma'ris giving me his support, I now had four votes including my own. To gain a majority, I would need six, which meant that I needed to appeal to two more Elders at least. Duke and Ma'ris had been, for all intents and purposes, shoo-ins. The others would take more insistent persuasion, and there was a much greater chance of rejection.

As I left the city and wound my way back through the clear tunnels, I was too distracted with the weight of carefully choosing the next Elder I would target to appreciate the beauty of the water and the sea creatures swirling all around me. I was so lost in my head, in fact, I arrived back to the dim, narrow, rock-walled corridor in what felt like a fraction of the time it had taken me to locate Maquaria. When I finally stepped back through the crevice, and white sunlight kissed my skin again, I had made a decision. *I would go to Kharid of Dhal'at.*

Dhal'at was the kingdom of deserts, a broad expanse of land covered mostly in the sand with very little water to be found. I had been there a handful of times as a warrior because Dhal'at, and Campestria had an active trade market. Hicorn, wild plains goats the people of my kingdom used for everything from clothes to weapons to food, were rampant in Campestria, and Dhal'atians had discovered that hicorn was an ideal food source for their angui farms. Angui were fast-moving sand snakes with fangs so venomous they could take down an A'li-uud warrior with one strike, and he'd be dead within the minute. Dhal'atians used angui for food and milked them for their venom to make their weapons more dangerous. Campestria and Dhal'at had struck a deal that provided Dhal'at with hicorn to feed their angui in exchange for a portion of the angui venom. My own scimitar was tipped with angui venom, though I only used it for battle because the venom would have rendered any hunting prey inedible.

    I lifted my chin and jumped on the winds. It would be a slightly longer journey than my trip to Montemba or Maquaria because Dhal'at was on the opposite side of the planet, and I would have to travel over three other kingdoms to reach it. Nevertheless, I used the time in flight to focus intently on crafting an argument to present to Kharid.

Suddenly, I was slammed in the side, and my ribs erupted in pain. Nothing of the sort had ever happened before during wind travel. I was struck again, this time in the neck, and I fell from the winds. As I plummeted toward the ground at an alarming speed, arms curled around my waist from behind. I realized I had been caught mid-fall and was, once again, being swept along by means of wind travel. Then, with a hard thud, my feet collided with the ground, the arms released me, and I fell forward onto my hands and knees.

A boot swung out of nowhere and hooked beneath my torso, crashing into my stomach with such force that my breath was ripped from me. I rolled involuntarily onto my back, and, when I looked up through hazy, dazed vision, I saw the ugly face of Torik leering down at me.

"Got ya," he sneered.

His fist smashed into my nose with unforgiving force, and I cried out in pain. I hadn't been made an Elder because of my status. However, I was a skilled warrior, and I was smart. Rather than pressing a hand to my nose as my body begged me to do, I rolled over again and hopped to my feet in one swift, rather painful leap. As I stared at Torik and started to take in the dank, dusty, muddy environment of my surroundings, I realized I had flown over Skulona, the cave kingdom ruled by Torik, who had intercepted me and brought me back to the ground.

"You know," he said maliciously, his face contorted in a hideous mix of rage and sadistic glee, "I've never liked you. Ever since you joined the Elderhood, you've been nothing but problems for me."

"You're so arrogant you've convinced yourself of that," I shot back. "The whole point of the Elder Council is to examine all sides of an argument and have multiple points of view, but anyone who disagrees with you must be out to get you, right?"

"That's right," he growled. His stumpy body was swaying back and forth like he was itching to pounce on me, and his hands were curled into fists at his sides.

I stared at him, feeling more hatred for the evil A'li-uud than I ever had before. "You, and all like you, are the reason our race has taken such a drastic change. If it weren't for your bloodthirsty ways of thinking, we would still be the respectable followers of the Grand Circle as our forefathers deemed."

"Our forefathers were fools," he spat, bits of saliva flying from his mouth with each word. "What they wanted was weak and easily compromised. Humans are nothing but idiots, and, thanks to the bleeding hearts of the Councils before us, we're gonna end up slaves to the mindless beasts unless we stop all our hand-shaking and do something about it."

"You're ignorant." The statement was not an accusation or a personal attack; it was simply the truth. *Of course, Torik didn't see it that way.*

"I'm sure Vi'den did his whole peace-loving number on you when he was your mentor," he went on, his voice a low snarl. "He'll get his eventually. But you're younger, stronger. You're actually a good warrior, and that makes you more dangerous. I'm not going to be licking human boots because you're too stupid to destroy them from the start. And now that you've committed the ultimate sin against our race by falling in love with one of those vermin, I have a reason to get you out of the way."

He leaped toward me without warning, and his fists made contact with my skull. I heard a horrible crack in my ears and stumbled back, though I didn't fall. As he lunged to attack me again, I seized his wrist and twisted, sending him tumbling into the air until he landed squarely on his back. He scrambled to his feet without missing a beat and darted toward me again. We grappled with each other, both of us unyielding to the other.

My fingers clawed into his beefy upper arms as his strained to reach my throat. I counted to three in my head, then I swept my left foot out and curled it around his ankle before kicking back, sending him back onto the ground again.

"You can't win against me," he said, grinning up at me with disgusting smugness. His chubby face was paler than usual, and I knew it was from the adrenaline of the fight. "I battle better warriors than you every day."

"So I've heard," I replied dryly. "It takes a special kind of leader to care so little about his people that he maims them for fun doesn't it?"

He jumped to his feet again, and the grin spread. "Yes, it does. I heard you beat up your best warrior pretty bad a little while ago. Pugna'ta, wasn't it? I don't know if you know this, but she participates in my cave battles from time to time. She's done some good damage, too."

I knew he was hoping to get a rise out of me, to see me become infuriated one of my warriors would have anything to do with him, but the information was meaningless to me. Pugna'ta was one of my best warriors, certainly, but she had crossed a line when she'd attacked Tabitha at my house. I no longer cared at all about her. It didn't even matter to me if Pugna'ta defected to Torik's army.

"So, what did you bring me to ground for, Torik?" I asked. Time was ticking, and I needed to get to Kharid. "To kill me?"

"If you're lucky," he said silkily. Then, with another great leap, he was on top of me.

His fist barreled into my temple again, and I saw wavy lines before my eyes. He wasn't lying about being difficult—or impossible—to beat; Torik was perhaps the best hand-to-hand fighter in all of Albaterra. He struck hard, and he was willing to die rather than admit defeat. I covered my head as he swung again, this time battering the forearm that covered my skull, and I used the opportunity to jab my other hand into his neck. He made a horrible gagging sound and stumbled back slightly. I could see an indentation where my knuckles had met his skin. I was taller than he was, so I grabbed his hair and shoved his head down as I lifted my knee up. There was a sharp, appalling crack as they collided.

  When I released him, I threw him back, and he nearly tripped and fell onto his rear. He glared furiously at me through distorted vision, and then he asked in a voice eviler than any I'd ever heard, "What's going to happen to your pretty little human when you're dead? Who's going to protect her then?"

"She is none of your concern," I hissed dangerously.

"I think she'd make a great guest for a cave battle, don't you? It would be so satisfying to watch my warriors tear her fingers from her soft little hands one by one. Then they could move to her toes, then her arms, and then her legs, until all that's left is her head and her torso. Everything I'd need her for is on her head and her torso, you know, and she has such an attractive figure—"

With a roar I didn't even recognize, I sprang forward and tackled him to the ground. Dust exploded into the air around us as the impact split a crack through the dried mud, and my nostrils were filled with the putrid odor. I barely noticed, though. Torik's throat was in my hands, exactly like Pugna'ta's had been, and I was squeezing with such vehemence I was sure his head was going to pop right off of his neck. He made a strange, squeaking, strangled sound, but, rather than clawing at my hands, he swung both fists inward, slamming them into my cheekbones. I released him at once, yelling with pain and cradling my face. He jerked out from under me to thrust me into the ground the same way I had done to him.

Each of his legs was on either side of my hips, and he was swinging fist after fist into my face. One crashed into my nose so hard I was sure it was going to just crumble away into nothingness. Another split the side of my head open from the sheer impact. Over and over again, he punched until the only thing I could taste and smell was blood. My vision was so compromised it was as though I was looking through thin, white fabric, and I was in so much pain I couldn't even feel the strikes anymore. I did, however, feel the broken bones in my face and the lacerations in my skin. I wondered if being burned alive would perhaps be a less painful alternative to this beating.

    When he didn't stop, I realized he actually did intend to kill me, and he wanted to do it with his bare hands. I was so weakened from his assault that I almost didn't care if he did, but then Tabitha's face flashed in the front of my mind. *It was as though she had actually stepped into my mind; I could see her so clearly.* Her dark brown curls hung around her face, framing her lovely cheekbones, and her pale, creamy skin practically glowed with life. There was a smile on her lips that was shaped with pride hinted at flirtation. *As I saw her eyes pressing into me with more love than I had ever known, I was filled with a final burst of strength, and I knew I couldn't let Torik kill me because I had to see her again.* With a booming roar of pain, I heaved forward.

Torik fell off of me, and his expression was one of such surprise it was almost comical. We both got to our feet without hesitation, but I wound my arm back and thrust it forward with full force. My knuckles crashed into the snubbed end of his nose and drove upwards until it looked like he had a snout and the bridge of his nose seemed to disappear between his eyes. Immediately, he fell to his knees, bellowing in agony. *I knew that, if I ever was going to have a chance to kill him, to make sure he could never come after me again, now would be the time.* He was kneeling before me with his hands pressed to his face, completely vulnerable to any attack.

I didn't want to kill him, though. My entire mission was about peace and returning to our roots as A'li-uud. To kill another member of our race was the greatest crime of all. Whether he deserved it or not, I knew I would have to live with the knowledge that I'd killed another A'li-uud in his moment of weakness, and that simply wasn't something I could do.

The wind kissed my cheeks, soothing my wounds and licking at my blood. I lifted my chin and closed my eyes, and then, before he could rise and attack me once more, I jumped. The breeze caught me like an old friend, and I was flying. The last thing I saw before I was enveloped entirely by the power of wind travel was Torik still kneeling on the ground, clutching his face, rocking back and forth.

Chapter 6

Tabitha

"What are you doing?" I cried, whirling around to face the militant captain. "Why are you taking them away?"

"We know nothing about them," he replied coolly. He looked wholly unconcerned by my panicked demeanor. If anything, he had a hint of amusement lingering beneath the stern, unforgiving expression he wore.

"You know I trust them. Isn't that enough?" I demanded.

He studied me for a second before answering. "We don't know anything about you, either. So, while we become acquainted, you'll have to excuse me for keeping my crew safe from the aliens you've brought onboard my ship."

I was so angry I was seething. I could actually feel fury bubbling in my stomach like a caustic potion, and it was so intense I felt a strong desire to vomit. Leanne beside me was as still as a block of ice, which was unusual for her because she was so often bouncing around or fluttering her hands while chattering incessantly. Right now, though, she seemed to have internalized the seriousness of the situation as much as I had, and I felt a strong burst of gratitude shoot through me for her presence next to me.

"Now," the captain said, leaning back in his chair a little too comfortably for the circumstances, "who are you?"

"Tabitha Bartel," I said through barely moving lips.

"The chef from the *Paragon*," he added with a roll of his eyes. It wasn't a question, so I didn't respond. "What happened to the *Paragon*? It went off the radar over two months ago."

"We were hit by an alien missile," I answered. My voice was cold and tight, almost as if I'd been standing in tundra for an hour before having the conversation. "Our ship went down on the planet Albaterra, and those of us who survived the crash have been living there ever since."

Leanne made a small scoffing noise in the back of her throat, clearly indicating her disdain for the underground dungeons she and the others had been kept in during that time, but I shot her a sharp look before turning my attention back to the captain. He had quirked an eyebrow, and he had lifted a solitary finger into the air.

"You mean to tell me that *those* creatures essentially bombed your ship, killing, however, many members of your crew, and you're upset that I'm having them confined for now?" He asked, pointing the finger to the door behind me where the A'li-uud had been taken.

"They attacked because we were too close to their planet," I said heatedly. "You know Earth would do the exact same thing."

"Ah, and there's the rub," he said. A rather evil grin spread across his face. "I know what humans can do. I *don't* know what *they* can do."

What I was finding most difficult to stomach about this captain was his strange, almost sadistic way of thinking and communicating. He seemed to glean some kind of personal pleasure in my anger, and his eyes lit up with a thrill when he talked about the A'li-uud, but the thrill was of a completely different breed than the kind Captain White had displayed on the *Quintessence*. *It was more along the lines of the thrill a mad scientist would get while performing horrible acts of human experimentation, or even the thrill of the psychotic serial killer in a horror movie. Frankly, I found it utterly disturbing.*

"I told you who I am," I said suddenly, trying to keep my voice calm and even. "Who are you?"

"Captain Otto Powell," he replied. He sounded rather bored.

"It's nice to meet you," I said with false politeness.

He grinned again, this time with obvious amusement, and shook his head. "No, it isn't. It's never nice to meet me. I'm not a nice person to meet." His eyes were sparkling maliciously as he spoke, and several of his crewmembers in the command center chuckled appreciatively at his words. "Did your captain survive the crash?"

"Yes," Leanne answered, her voice loud and abrasive. It was obvious to me she was made just as uncomfortable by this Captain Powell as I was.

"Why didn't you bring him on this little mission of yours?" He asked. "Which, by the way, we'll get to discussing in a moment."

"Rex assembled my crew," I told him without thinking.

Immediately, his eyes lit up with unnatural glee. He leaned back in his chair, swiveling around to face his crewmembers, and crowd, "Did you hear that? The alien's name is *Rex*."

I stiffened, feeling strangely offended, and snapped, "Actually, his name is Rexstrenu'us, and he's an A'li-uud, not an alien. He's also a Tribe Elder, so he deserves a little respect."

Captain Powell turned back around with slow, deliberate movement. When he was facing me again, his eyes bore into mine like drills, and there was no longer even a flicker of amusement on his harsh features. "I don't give a damn about the social hierarchy of aliens, and, if you speak to me like that again, you're not going to make it off this ship. Am I understood?"

My mouth flew open to retort back with venom, but Leanne nudged me in the small of my back, silently warning me to check my temper. Closing my mouth again, I glared furiously at him but nodded reluctantly.

"Good," he said. "Now, tell me the reason you brought those freaks onto my ship."

I bristled, but I held my tongue about his slander. "The A'li-uud destroyed the *Paragon* when we got too close to their planet. Their Elder Council agreed to destroy all of the human ships in their galaxy, which is where you are right now. I've come to warn you to get out of Andromeda as quickly as you can. Rex is already working to overturn the vote, but I thought it best to also reach out to the other ships in the *Paragon's* fleet to forewarn everyone in case the vote doesn't get repealed in time—or at all."

"And you thought it best to bring the very people planning on massacring my crew onboard?" Captain Powell's voice was filled with incredulity.

"Like I said," I replied icily, "I didn't assemble the crew. And the A'li-uud are not a warring race by nature; they are simply acting on what they think is best to preserve their existence."

He watched me in silence for a long moment, and I shifted my weight from foot to foot uncomfortably. The other *Epitome* crewmembers in the command center were watching him closely, and they seemed to be ready to spring into action the moment he cast an order. As the seconds wore on without any kind of response from Captain Powell, I started to get a sick feeling in my stomach, and it was only made sicker when he finally spoke again.

"Lieutenant, see that the aliens are properly confined to their cells and have Officer Griggs report to me," he said. He didn't look away from me as he made his command.

The bald man he had addressed earlier stepped out from his station with a sharp nod. "Yes, Sir," he said compliantly. He sounded just as militant and cruel as the captain, and I knew I couldn't rely on him to help ease Powell's demeanor. As he brushed past me and exited the room, I saw Leanne turn her head to watch him out of the corner of my vision, and it struck me that this may have been the man she'd told me about meeting during training. I hoped I was wrong.

"Actually, Captain," I said boldly, sounding much more confident than I actually felt, "our only purpose was to warn you. Now that we have done so, I would like to take my crew and get out of your hair."

His mouth curled up in a sinister smile, and he shook his head so slowly it was almost painstaking to watch. "Oh, no," he said. "No, you're not going anywhere."

"What do you mean?" I asked. My mouth had gone dry, and it was difficult to force my tongue to say the words. I could feel Leanne tensing up beside me.

"You're a foolish girl," Captain Powell explained. "You seem to trust these blue-skins, despite having been given every reason not to, and you came here under the assumption I would be so stupid too. Fortunately for you, I'm not. I'm also not allowing you to go back to whatever planet those creatures are from to be turned into alien food or some horrible experiment." His eyes flashed wickedly. "Consider me your fairy godfather, Miss Bartel, because I'm not going to let you get yourself killed."

"They won't hurt me!" I cried. A flush of panic washed over my cheeks, and the room suddenly felt too warm. "I've been living there for two months, and they haven't touched a hair on my head!"

That wasn't entirely true. One of Rex's warriors, Pugna'ta, had attacked me while I was staying in Rex's palace. I still had three raised, pink scratches on each of my cheeks from her nails raking across my face. It had been a violent assault, and she would have killed me if Rex hadn't returned home in time. A second occurrence was when the Elder Torik who tried to attack me after learning Rex was protecting me, but he hadn't managed to get to me before Rex, and another Elder interfered. *Nevertheless, I felt safe with the A'li-uud, much safer than I did with Captain Powell.*

His eyes grazed the scratches on my cheeks, and he asked, "I suppose you got those falling down, did you?"

My jaw set stubbornly, and I tossed my head like a defiant teenager. "That's not your concern."

"Actually, it is," he said. "As a captain in this fleet, it's my duty to ensure the safety of my crew. When another captain in the fleet is unable to ensure the safety of *his* crew, it's my duty to take over. It seems your captain is unable to perform as such, which means you are now my responsibility."

"I don't need—"

"I may not be the kind of guy you want to have tea and crumpets with, Miss Bartel, but I'm a good captain, and I take that seriously," he continued. "You will not be returning to that planet."

"You're keeping me here against my will," I hissed. "That's kidnapping."

He chuckled. "No, that's my job."

I was breathing so hard I sounded like a bull ready to charge. Everything from rage to panic was coursing through me so fast I could hardly keep up, but at the forefront of my mind, there was the horrible thought I would never see Rex again. *If Captain Powell kept me on board and refused to allow me to return to Albaterra, I would either die in the explosion when the Epitome was destroyed, or I would be brought back to Earth, unable to get to Albaterra again until the next mission—or, possibly, never.* It was a horrendous thought, and it brought pain to my gut as viscerally as if I'd been punched.

The door behind me opened again, and the bald man reentered the room with a grizzly-bearded man in tow. "Officer Griggs, Sir," the lieutenant said before taking his post again.

"Ah, Officer Griggs!" Captain Powell said, his tone repulsively jovial. He rose from his chair with his arms outstretched as if greeting an old friend. Officer Griggs nodded in greeting, though he didn't speak, and the captain seemed to accept that as a proper response. "There are some new people I'd like you to meet."

He introduced me, Leanne, and the other two humans of my crew. Griggs didn't seem to respond in any way as he heard our names, not even to make eye contact with any of us. He reminded me of an old bear with his scraggly, neck-length beard and little black eyes, and his nose even seemed longer and bigger than average. After we had all been introduced, Captain Powell looked to us and motioned to Griggs.

"This is Waylon Griggs, Chief Security Officer for the *Epitome*," he told us, clapping Griggs on the back with pride. "He served twenty-seven years in the army, and there's a rumor going around that he built a cabin in the mountains after retiring with his bare hands and ate a diet of raw cougar, though he won't confirm that either way." Powell chuckled appreciatively, and Griggs remained as blank-faced as ever.

"Anyway," Powell went on, addressing all of us together now, "our guests have brought onboard some guests of their own. I have just been informed that these aliens intend to destroy us all, and I think it's so convenient Miss Bartel here has provided us with a representative sampling of their population. Isn't that convenient, Griggs?"

Officer Griggs nodded once again, though, this time, he made a small grunt as he did it. He was completely emotionless, and I didn't know if that was a good or bad thing, though I thought I preferred it to the evil glee Powell was displaying.

Suddenly, as though reading my mind about his behavior, the captain's face transformed. His expression became ugly and twisted, and his eyes flashed aggressively. He looked at me, but he spoke to Griggs as he said, "I want them killed. All of them."

"No!" I cried, jumping forward. Leanne's hands closed around my forearms, and she wrenched me back before I could reach the captain, who was watching me with searing interest. "They haven't done anything to you! That's murder!"

"Actually, Miss Bartel, our government recognizes murder only as the killing of one human by another human," Captain Powell corrected. "Those creatures—A'li-uud, I believe you called them—are not human, and, thus, killing them would not constitute murder. In fact, I'm quite certain killing them would be considered an act of international security."

"Just let us go," I whimpered, feeling angry tears starting to prickle in my eyes. "It doesn't affect you if I go back with them and they hurt me. Let me take that chance. Just let us go."

"There is one thing in this universe that matters to me, and that is my duty," Captain Powell said coldly. "I have a duty to protect you, no matter how stupid you are. I've already said once you're not going anywhere. Don't make me say it again."

"So you're willing to take innocent lives?" I asked, my voice a near whisper.

"To protect my crew, yes," he said. "And, if I recall correctly, that's exactly what they intended to do to us."

My limbs were weak and shaking, and I felt like I was trying to stand on jelly. Leanne's hands were still wrapped around my forearms, but I couldn't feel them anymore. My skin was rapidly changing between too hot and too cold, and I could hear my heart pumping so hard it sounded like it was located in my ears rather than my chest.

"You can't do this," I whispered.

Captain Powell looked at Griggs. "Don't make it bloody. The government is going to want to examine their bodies and find out as much about them as they can."

"We don't know what they're capable of," Griggs said, finally speaking. His voice was as bear-like as the rest of him, growling and coarse. "It'll take a day of planning to make sure my boys don't get hurt in the process."

"Fine," Powell agreed. "Just keep me informed."

"Yes, Sir."

I watched Griggs leave the command center as though in slow motion, and I realized he was going to plot the deaths of my friends.

Chapter 7

Rex

When I had left Maquaria, I had intended to go to Dhal'at to present my case to Kharid. After the fight and attempted murder at Torik's hands, however, I changed course and headed to Finiba instead.

The Kingdom of rolling hills had always been my favorite, with its lush green mounds, clear babbling rivers and serene whispers in the breeze, and it was made all the better being the kingdom ruled by Vi'den. While Duke was the Elder, I would most consider my friend, Vi'den was the Elder I trusted above all others. He had mentored me in the early years of my Elderhood, and he was the embodiment of everything an A'li-uud Elder was supposed to be; wise, compassionate, just, and good. *I respected him as much as I admired him.*

I landed just in front of Vi'den's palace, which was the least palace-like of any Elder palace I had seen. It was embedded in the side of one of the hills, with just a door and a window in the front and the head of a chimney poking out of the ground above. The landscaping around the front of the home was lovely with its garden of red and yellow flowers, but it seemed much too quaint a house for someone of Vi'den's importance to live. Nevertheless, I had been there many times, and I had come to love it.

  Just moments after I knocked on the door, Vi'den appeared in the threshold. He was one of the few A'li-uud who wore clothes that covered his full body; usually, robes and today was no different. Long robes of purple and silver spilled from his shoulders in swaths, coming to rest in a gentle pool around his feet. The arms were flared and covered his hands until he lifted them to press his fingertips to my face. I flinched immediately in pain. I hadn't seen myself since the fight, but if I looked anything like I felt, then I must have looked an utter mess.

"What has happened to you?" He murmured. There was a note of sorrow in his tone, but there was an absence of surprise, and I knew he had expected something like this to happen on my travels but had hoped it would not.

"Torik," I said bitterly, pulling my face back to prevent him from touching my wounds further. "That's why I'm here."

"Come in." He stepped back to allow me entrance, and I walked through the doorway into a small but comfortable living space. Just yesterday,

I had brought Tabitha here under the same conditions, except she had been the one injured.

I dropped onto the same chair in which Tabitha had sat and drew comfort in knowing I was touching something she had touched. *I missed her desperately.* "He brought me to ground as I was flying over Skulona," I explained. "I don't know how he knew I would be flying that way, or that it was me, but he did."

Vi'den was padding around shelves of remedies quietly. Part of me wanted him to speak, to say something in my defense or to Torik's detriment, but he remained stoically tight-lipped as he pulled pots and pouches into his hands.

Finally, he turned around and approached me, placing the variety of items onto the tabletop behind me and holding onto just one pouch. As he opened it, I was struck by a very strong, almost acrid odor, but I didn't complain and allowed him to press the powder to the oozing lacerations on my skin.

"I am not going to heal these yet," he said quietly. "I am just applying something for pain relief and disinfectant."

A little affronted, I asked, "Why aren't you healing them?"

"The Council needs to see your wounds," Vi'den said. His tone was somber, and his expression was grave. "It is a grave offense to attack an Elder, and you need the proof."

"Vi'den," I said pointedly. "It wasn't just an attack. He was trying to kill me."

For the briefest of moments, Vi'den's movements paused. When he resumed, he murmured, "Are you certain?"

"Yes, and he also threatened Tabitha's life and well-being."

"We must call the Council together at once." Vi'den spoke in a voice so low it was almost imperceptible, but I could hear the urgency in his tone. "To attempt to murder an Elder is the greatest crime short of succeeding, and for the perpetrator to be another Elder is simply unforgivable. Immediate action must be taken."

I shook my head. "I need to get the votes to ensure the safety of Tabitha and the other humans. I can't waste time in a trial."

"It is not a wasting of time," Vi'den said sharply, his eyes boring into mine. "We are nothing if the Elderhood is not strong. I understand your plight, Rex, but it is your duty to prioritize." I looked down, slightly ashamed and not altogether convinced. In a slightly softer tone, Vi'den added, "Besides, all of the Council members will be in one location. It will be easier for you to resume your persuasions after the trial is over."

***

Just two hours later, I was sitting in my seat beside Duke in the chamber of P'otes-tat Ulti, the Elders' city. Upon seeing me, Duke's eyes had widened, and he'd emitted a ferocious growl from the back of his throat, but I dismissed all questions with a wave of my hand and shake of my head before he could ask them. *He would learn soon enough what had happened.*

The other Elders were sitting in their seats as well, all except Torik, whose chair remained noticeably empty. Without his presence, the chamber was actually eerily quiet, yet it did not feel peaceful. On the contrary, the air was thick with tension, curiosity, and anticipation. Vi'den sat directly across from me, as always. I could see him clearly, which was unusual because the stone fire pit in the center of the Elder circle was usually filled with tall, crackling flames which sent billows of gray-white smoke up to the tower-high ceiling. Today, however, the pit was covered by a stone slab I had become familiar with during my last foray in P'otes-tat Ulti when I'd been tried for treason after it had been made known I was hiding Tabitha.

Vi'den looked more serious than I had ever seen him, and I could make out the shadow of sorrow on his down-turned lips. He took the offense of an Elder attempting to kill another Elder hard, just as hard as I would have taken it if it had been Tabitha trying to murder me rather than Torik. Vi'den's heart was swollen with love for the Elderhood and the A'li-uud, and it was easy for me to see the pain this trial caused him.

The other Elders, in contrast, wore expressions of wonderment and anxious worry. They had not been informed of the reason for the trial; they had merely been called to the Forum with the understanding there was a charge to be answered. Several of them shot repeated looks to Torik's empty seat, though none seemed sorry to find him absent. Others merely remained still and calm as they waited stiffly for the trial to begin.

Within moments, the door which led to the waiting chamber opened. Torik entered first, and behind him walked two stony-faced A'li-uud with weapons drawn in one hand and Torik's arms in the other. Realization dawned on many of the faces around the circle, and I felt Duke's gaze shoot over to me in surprise, but I didn't look his way. I was focused on watching Torik, who was visibly seething. His muscles flexed with each step he took. I wondered if he was refraining from assaulting the A'li-uud guiding him, but, of course, his hands were tied tightly behind his back and he would have been unable to strike them even if he'd wanted.

They brought him to the center of the room, helping him step up onto the stone slab. The moment he was atop it, his hateful eyes met mine, and we stared at one another with an equal measure of loathing. Then, he turned around and faced Vi'den, who stood up slowly from his seat. For a moment, I thought he was going to cry.

"I am sorry to address the Council today," Vi'den said soberly. He looked around the room as he spoke, and his face seemed to implore each Elder he looked at to understand his pain. "Never in my long Elderhood have I had to address this charge, and I had hoped I never would. Unfortunately, that wish was not to be fulfilled, as, today, we bring one of our own before us to answer the charge of attempted murder on a brother Elder."

There was a collective intake of breath around the room, excluding my own and Vi'den's. Duke went rigid in his seat, and I could see his fingers gripping the arms of his chair with such force that his already pale knuckles became as white as the snow that blanketed his kingdom. Ma'ris, who sat beside Vi'den, seemed as sorrowful as Vi'den but with significantly greater resolve. I found myself wondering if he had attended a trial of this nature in one of his previous Councils.

"Torik Et'Spaela Skul'tribus," Vi'den continued. His sad voice rang through the chamber in echoes. "You have been brought before the Council today to answer to the charge of attempted murder on Elder Rexstrenu'us Et'Herba Cam-pes'tribus. How do you plead?"

Rather than speaking, Torik made an animalistic growling sound and spat onto the floor. Vi'den didn't bat an eye; *his expression, however, became a little stonier.*

"If you choose not to respond to the charge, a plea of guilty will be entered for you," Vi'den advised coolly.

"Fine," Torik snarled. "Guilty. But I had a good reason."

"There is no good reason to take the life of another," Ma'ris warbled angrily.

"I didn't *take the life of another*," Torik snapped. He jerked his shoulder backward toward me. "He's sitting right there."

All eyes turned to me, including Torik's, who turned around on the slab to face me. I looked blankly back at him without meeting the gazes of the other Elders, though I could feel them studying the injuries on my face.

"You have the right to an explanation," Vi'den said loudly, causing everyone to turn and look to him again. "Proceed."

"It's simple. He cares more about the humans than about the A'li-uud," Torik said nastily. "He fell in love with that simpleton human, and he's letting her tell him what we should do. I'm not the one who should be on trial here. He is. He's putting all of us in danger."

There was a moment of such silence I could've heard a water droplet fall an inch to the floor. Then, Vi'den asked, "Is that your explanation?"

"You make it sound like it's not good enough." Torik was growing angrier by the moment. I couldn't see his face, but I was sure it was contorted in rage as it usually was when he was irate. "The endangerment of our race should be the only explanation."

"Rex already went on trial for treason, and he was cleared," Duke interjected.

"He was cleared for acting without the Council's approval," Torik barked, twisting around to look at Duke. "I did the same thing. Are you gonna clear me?"

"Not likely," Duke hissed. I finally looked over at him and saw his eyes flashing, though I couldn't be sure if it was out of defensiveness for me or anger at Torik's aggressiveness.

"Then you're as much of a traitor as he is," Torik said sourly. "And I don't have time for traitors."

Vi'den clapped his hands once, a sound that traveled up to the ceiling and reverberated back down with such noise it hurt my ears. "Guards, please have Torik step down while we call our witness and victim before the Council."

The two A'li-uud who had ushered Torik in stepped forward, and each seized a beefy arm.

They wrenched him from the slab rather roughly, and he stumbled, cursing at them under his breath. Once he was pulled to the side, Vi'den looked at me from across the circle.

"Elder Rexstrenu'us Et'Herba Campes'tribus, you are called before the Council to recount your recollection of the events," he said.

I stood and made my way up onto the slab in the center of the room where Torik had just been. The ceiling, which was made of glass, allowed a thick stream of sunlight into the chamber, which spilled down onto my head and bathed me in white light. I knew everyone could see my injuries clearly now, and I heard some mumblings amongst the other Elders as they took in the sight.

"Proceed," Vi'den said to me. He spoke much more kindly than he had to Torik.

I thought back to mere hours before and then began. "I was leaving Maquaria and traveling to Dhal'at by wind travel. To get to Dhal'at from Maquaria, I flew over Skulona. In mid-flight, I was suddenly hit by something and lost the wind. When I started to fall, I was caught and brought to ground. That was when I realized it was Torik who had intercepted me."

As I spoke, my gaze drifted over to him. Where he stood against the wall, he was bathed in shadows, but I could still make out the evil glare of rage on his face. It only served to fuel my passion as I told the story.

"He assaulted me and told me he'd always felt I was in conflict with him. I asked him if he intended to kill me, to which he responded, 'If you're lucky.' We then began to fight. I will admit I was not fighting only in self-defense; it is not a secret Torik, and I have never gotten along, and there are many distasteful feelings between us. However, it became clear he was fighting to kill."

I felt rage bubble up inside of me as I remembered the next part, and my anger was evident in my voice, which shook with intensity.

"He started making threats toward Tabitha, the human I am in love with, going so far as to say he would bring her into one of his cave battles when I was gone and have her dismembered before he'd use her torso for his own personal desires." I let out a deep, ragged breath and closed my eyes, trying to calm myself. A full minute passed in silence as the Elders waited for me to continue, but I wasn't willing to speak until I was completely in control of myself again. When I was, I finished. "I went on the offensive, attacked him, and escaped by wind travel. I went directly to Vi'den afterward."

Vi'den inclined his head as I locked eyes with him, and I could see approval on his face—though I didn't know what exactly he was approving. I imagined it was for my honest testimony. After several long moments had passed, Vi'den asked, "Is that your full statement?"

"It is," I answered.

"Thank you. Please take your seat," he said, motioning with his hand to my chair.

I stepped down from the slab as the guards brought Torik back to the center of the circle. The expression of approval on Vi'den's face faded into stern antipathy as he looked upon the stumpy A'li-uud, whose shoulders were rising and falling with visible anger. Before addressing him, Vi'den looked around the circle at the Council.

"It is my personal feeling we have heard all we need to hear. The act of an Elder attacking another with the intent to kill is a grievous, unforgivable one, and I am of the opinion it needs to be punished regardless of reason. If anyone has further questions they would like to ask Torik or needs time to settle their opinions, please speak now."

Nobody moved. Nobody spoke. Nobody even blinked. The room was completely still, with the exception of Torik's heaving shoulders, and Vi'den nodded once.

"Torik Et'Spaela Skul'tribus, you have been found guilty by the Council on this day for attempted murder against another Elder," he said fiercely. "All in favor of stripping the charged off his Elderhood?"

There was a series of murmured agreements.

"It is so. All in favor of a life sentence of imprisonment?"

Again, I heard agreement from every mouth, including my own.

"It is so." Vi'den's eyes flared with fire as he looked upon Torik and said, "Torik Et'Spaela Skul'tribus has been stripped of his Elder status and will serve the remainder of his life in the dungeons of P'otes-tat Ulti. Guards, remove him."

As the guards stepped up to take him from the slab again, Torik threw his shoulder into the chest of the nearest and shouted, "You're all fools, all of you! Because of his stupidity, you're going to get us all killed—or, worse, enslaved—by those beasts!" The guard he had shoved yanked him violently from the slab, and Torik fell onto the stone floor. As he was wrenched to his feet, his eyes turned to me, and he roared, "You better hope that human of yours kills you, traitor, or else I will!"

Chapter 8

Tabitha

Leanne and I, as well as our other two human crew members, were shown to a room with four bunks. As the *Epitome* was identical to the *Paragon*, I knew the room to be a stowaway for anyone who happened to commit a grievance onboard during a mission. It locked from the outside and, in normal criminal circumstances, the door would only be opened to deliver meals. A bathroom was set at the back of the room with a very small shower, a toilet, and a sink. There wasn't even a mirror.

We weren't considered criminals, though, and the door was left unlocked for us to come and go as we pleased. Captain Powell warned us that any misconduct on our way back to Earth would result in lockdown, but, for now, we were permitted to walk the halls of the ship like any other crewmember. I had a horrible feeling that the reason he wasn't keeping us locked in, however, was because he was hoping one of us would do something regrettable he could punish us for.

He wasn't wrong. The moment we were left alone in the room, I turned to Leanne and said, "We have to save them."

"How are we supposed to do that?" She asked dubiously, her eyes darting to the door's thick-paned rectangular window. We both knew the doors on the ship were essentially soundproof, and it would have been impossible for anyone to hear our conversation, but I understood her paranoia.

"I don't know," I replied miserably. I bit down on my lower lip as I thought about it. "But we can't let them die because Powell is in some kind of sick power trip."

She looked at me reluctantly, and I knew she wasn't keen on the idea of putting herself at risk to rescue the very people who had kept her imprisoned for two months. *Nevertheless, Leanne was not a heartless or cowardly person, and I knew she would do what was right, especially if I was the one who asked her to do it.*

"We know we have a day to figure this out and execute a plan," I said slowly.

"That's not much time."

"It's going to have to be enough," I replied. "Leanne, I can't let them die because of me. It was my mission that brought them here in the first place."

"On Rex's command, though," she interjected. I could tell she was debating with herself whether she should try to talk me out of rescuing them or going along with whatever plan I concocted. "It's not your fault."

"Yes, it is," I said firmly.

She went quiet. The two men in the room were watching us but keeping their mouths shut, and I was grateful for that. I didn't know if they could be trusted to help or to at least not tell the *Epitome* crew, but I didn't have time to find out one way or the other. I leaned back against the wall and looked at the bottom of the bunk above me. My entire body was riddled with fear, but there was something else there too, and I recognized it as steely determination. *I knew I would have to try to save them. Ca-es'a had done everything in his power to protect me, both on Albaterra and on this mission, and I wasn't going to let him die.*

"We need to find out where they are, I guess," Leanne murmured thoughtfully, interrupting the silence.

I was immediately flooded with gratitude for my friend, but I didn't let the sentiment rule me. Instead, I said, "I know where they are. There's a brig near the loading bay."

"How do you know that?" She asked, looking at me in amazement.

"I was the chef. I delivered food all over the ship," I answered with a shrug.

"But nobody got into trouble on the *Paragon*."

"No, but they still used that room," I explained. "I had to bring dinner there for a couple of guys sometimes when they were putting things in there for storage or cleaning."

"So you know where it is, then?"

I nodded. "It's the furthest room from the main part of the ship. If the *Epitome's* brig is like the *Paragon's*, it will have twelve cells, six on either side of an aisle. I'm pretty sure they would put one A'li-uud to a cell since they aren't very big unless they've used some of the cells for extra parts or something."

"Okay, so we know where they are," Leanne said. She twisted her fingers together in her lap. "How do we get them out? And what do we do once they're free?"

"We have to get the cell keys," I said. My voice sounded knowledgeable and confident, but my insides quaked at the thought. I had no idea how we were supposed to secure the keys, get to the brig, and unlock all the cells without getting caught. "Then, we make a break for it."

"You mean, get on the spacecraft and get off the *Epitome*?"

I nodded again. Hearing the words out loud made the idea sound even crazier than it had in my head, but I knew there was no other way. "Then, we can go back to Albaterra."

She looked at me hard, now, and much more seriously than she usually did. "What are we supposed to do after that?" she asked. She almost sounded like she was about to give me a lecture. "Just live on Albaterra?"

"Maybe. I don't know." I sighed a shaky breath. "Maybe some of the A'li-uud can take the *Paragon* survivors back to Earth."

Her lips tightened, and she laughed derisively. "Somehow, I don't see that happening."

"We'll worry about it then," I said dismissively, waving a hand around as though to clear the idea from the air. "We need to worry about our crewmembers right now."

Leanne just looked at me without saying a word or even nodding in agreement. I was starting to feel frustrated, though I didn't know if it was because she wasn't cooperating as seamlessly as I would have liked or if it was because of the situation in its entirety. Either way, my temper was flaring, and I knew that would only make succeeding at rescuing the A'li-uud more difficult, so I took a deep breath, released it, and took another. Then, I got to my feet.

"We need the keys," I said.

"Yeah," she agreed, standing up too. "But where would they be? Who would have them?"

I steeled myself and responded, "Let's start with Griggs."

***

We crept through the ship so quietly and carefully I actually alarmed myself when I heard my own footsteps. The two men had joined us, *which I was exceptionally grateful for,* and we were stalking the corridors two-by-two. I had decided that our best chance of finding Griggs without running into too many other crewmembers would be to start by looking at the rear of the ship near the brig and the loading bay. It stood to reason that the Chief Security Officer would linger in those parts.

    My breath hooked in my throat when a short, skinny woman rounded the corner and came face-to-face with us. She looked as stern as a private school teacher, but her face split into a smile as she saw us. Rather than stopping and speaking, she merely inclined her head in greeting and continued walking past us. Relief burst from my pores, and I hoped she had heard we were onboard and thought nothing of our wandering.

We reached the crossway that could lead us back to the main part of the ship, to the loading bay, or to the brig. I looked left and right, hoping to see Griggs or hear his coarse voice, but there was no indication of his whereabouts. Panic was overtaking me now, and I knew I needed to make a decision about which way to go. I decided to go straight down the hall which would take us to the brig.

When we entered the room, it was as dim and dank as the brig had been aboard the *Paragon*. There were six cells lining both sides of an aisle, as I'd predicted, and in eight of the cells were our A'li-uud crewmates. Ca-es'a was in the cell nearest to the door on the left.

"Oh my God," I whispered, rushing to him, wrapping my hands around the bars to peer in at him. "Are you okay?"

"I am fine," he muttered bitterly. "My concern is for you."

"They won't let us go back to Albaterra. The captain wants to have you killed and to bring us back to Earth," I explained in a rush.

Ca-es'a made an angry noise in his throat. In the poor lighting of the room, his nearly black skin looked even darker, but I could see his white eyes narrowing into aggressive slits. "I do not wish to kill humans, Tabitha, but I will if I am forced."

"I know," I said, looking at him with understanding. "I will, too."

I turned around to look at the others with me, and I saw Leanne's eyes skimming the cells. There was an expression of satisfaction on her face, and I realized she found the situation some kind of justice for her predicament over the last couple of months. While I couldn't blame her, it angered me.

"Could you do something?" I snapped quietly. "Find the keys!"

"The keys are with the hairy man," Ca-es'a said. I looked back at him with wide eyes. "I saw one of the humans give them to him after locking us in here. I did not hear his name."

"Griggs," I murmured.

Without warning, Ca-es'a pressed his face up against the bars and looked at me intently. "Tabitha, I do not want you to put yourself in danger. You are the only thing that matters to Rex, and he entrusted me with your safety. I cannot do much from in here, but I can insist you do not endanger yourself."

"I'm not going to let them kill you," I whispered fiercely. "It's not Rex's decision what I choose to do, and I choose to save you."

A strange smile lifted the corners of Ca-es'a's lips, and, before I could inquire about the cause, he said a little proudly, "You would make a strong A'li-uud warrior, Tabitha Bartel."

I couldn't help but smile back, and I pressed my fingers to his. "I will get you out of here," I vowed. Then, before he could try to convince me otherwise, I turned to my human sidekicks. "We have to find Griggs."

"I don't think that'll be a problem," Leanne said, speaking at full volume.

My eyes flicked to the door, and I saw Griggs in the threshold. Rather than the emotionless mask he had worn in the command center, his face was contorted with rage. He lunged forward and seized one of my two men around the middle. Pulling him up against his body, Griggs lifted a pistol and pointed it at the man's head.

"Come with me," he growled. "Any funny business and I will paint these walls with his blood."

My heart sank into my stomach. I glanced back at Ca-es'a, and he looked angrier than I had ever seen him. Griggs made a strange, animalistic snarling sound and jerked his head backward, motioning for us to leave the room and go with him. I left first, followed by Leanne and the other man, and Griggs slammed the door to the brig closed with his foot.

"Move," he ordered.

I started walking, my entire body rapidly growing numb with fear for the A'li-uud and for us. He marched us to the command center, all the while keeping the gun pointed at my crewmate's temple. When we entered, Captain Powell looked up, and the expression of unrestrained delight shimmering over his face sickened me.

"Well, well, well!" He crowed. If he'd been a child, I would have expected him to jump up and down while clapping excitedly. "We've got a group of vigilantes in our hands, don't we?"

"They were in the brig with the aliens," Griggs informed him. "I thought I ought to bring them straight to you."

"Thank you very much, Officer Griggs," Powell said appreciatively. "You can let that one go. I don't think they're going to do anything stupid now."

Griggs released his captive, shoving him forward so hard that the man fell to his hands and knees. He scrambled up at once, dusting himself off, and shot Griggs a look so furious it would have shriveled any other man. Griggs, however, simply looked back at him carelessly.

"See that the brig is locked, Officer," Captain Powell commanded. Griggs nodded and departed, leaving us with only the *Epitome* crew in the command center. Powell turned his attention to me. "You're even more foolish than I'd thought, Miss Bartel. Here we are, kind enough to allow you on our ship and rescue you from the evildoings of those creatures, and your first act is to betray us?"

"You're not rescuing me from anything," I snapped. I was no longer frightened of Powell—*intimidated, yes, but not frightened*—and I didn't force myself to hide my rage. "You're the evildoer here, not them."

"How touching," he replied dryly.

"Release the A'li-uud, give us our ship, and let us go," I said unwaveringly, staring at him just as hard as he was staring at me.

He lifted a finger and pointed to his left breast where the captain's logo was stitched. "You do not give the orders here, Miss Bartel."

"And you have no right to hold us hostage!" I screamed. I had lost all control of myself, and even Leanne's fingers suddenly closing around my wrist did nothing to calm me down and reign myself in.

I yanked my arm away from her, breaking her hold, and glared furiously at Powell.

"I am keeping you safe." His voice had become frozen, engulfed in ice at the accusation of criminal behavior. "My job as captain is to keep you safe, and your job as a member of this fleet is to respect me and behave accordingly."

Everything inside of me was telling me to attack this man. I wanted to leap at him, to tackle him to the ground and pummel him with my fists over and over like Pugna'ta had done to me on the dining room floor of Rex's palace. My fingers itched to close around his throat and slowly reduce his airflow until he was unable to breathe and conceded to let me off the ship so I could return to the love of my life.

I knew, however, that none of those actions would result in my favor, but I had something else in my arsenal that would.

"The captain's job is to take over responsibility for a crew when said crew's captain can no longer do his duty, right?" I asked calculatingly.

"That's correct, Miss Bartel," Powell replied with exaggerated pride.

"Then, you need to land on Albaterra now," I told him. He crooked a brow and tilted his head with curiosity, and I said, "There are *Paragon* survivors who need to be rescued."

Chapter 9

Rex

The tension in the council chamber remained peaked even after Torik had been taken out, and the silence was so thick it was practically suffocating. Vi'den remained standing with his eyes closed, taking deep, labored breaths, and I realized that the trial had been emotionally draining for him. For Vi'den, Torik's crime was as painful and heartbreaking as losing Tabitha would have been for me. He held affection for several individuals, myself included, but his true love was the A'li-uud and everything we stood for. To look in the face of such an atrocious act by one of his own was, perhaps, the most egregious betrayal Vi'den could ever experience. As I watched him, I felt pity and even a hint of guilt flood through me.

Suddenly, grand double doors which were the proper entrance to the chamber burst open, and six A'li-uud warriors raced in. The one in front, wearing heavy metal armor and wielding a sword, approached the circle while the others fell back near the wall.

"Forgive my intrusion, Great Ones," the armored A'li-uud said in a rush, panting so heavily his words meshed together. "I had to tell you at once. A human ship is descending upon Albaterra. It has already entered the atmosphere and is rapidly moving in to land."

Several of the Elders jumped to their feet, Duke and I among them. "Where?" I demanded. "Where is it predicted to land?"

"We do not know, but it entered the atmosphere over Dhal'at and it seems to be heading east."

I whirled around to look at Vi'den. He returned my gaze with an alert, understanding look of his own. Duke was looking at me as well, and Ma'ris had a thoughtful expression on his face. We were the only four who were aware of the plan Tabitha, and I were embarking upon, and, thus, we seemed to be in a wholly different state of mind upon receiving this news than the other Elders, who appeared to be panicked and confused.

"If Tabitha's onboard, they're going to land in Campestria," I said to Vi'den, ignoring the expressions of surprise around me. "Even if she's not, she would have told them to land there anyway."

"Then we need to go to Campestria," Vi'den said firmly. "All of us."

"We don't know what they want, Vi'den," one of the other Elders said urgently. "They could be planning to attack us all. Is it wise to gather all of our Elders in one place?"

Vi'den frowned slightly and said, "Rex and Tabitha have been working together to eliminate any further human casualties. While Rex was journeying around Albaterra to meet with each one of you and plead his case, Tabitha went into space with a crew of humans from her crashed ship and several of Rex's warriors to warn the remaining human ships about the potential danger to befall them at our hand. It is highly unlikely the ship is acting of its own accord to perpetrate violence against us without sufficient weapons and soldiers to fight. We need to meet them as a governmental unit to demonstrate solidarity and present a hand of authoritative cooperation."

There were looks of uncertainty, disagreement, and outright horror passed around, but nobody negated Vi'den's words. He turned back to me.

"Rex, we do not have time to gather armies from our kingdoms and assemble them in Campestria, so you are going to have to call all of your warriors. I do not believe we are looking at a battle, but it would be foolish of us not to be prepared. Take Duke and collect as many of your warriors together as you can, we will soon join you."

Duke and I looked at one another, and he gave me a nod of support.

"I'll see you all shortly," I said to the circle.

When Duke and I stepped outside through the massive double doors, he asked, "Do you believe Tabitha is on the ship?"

"It would be a really strange coincidence if she wasn't," I said, though I sounded much more confident than I felt. He just looked at me, and I knew he didn't believe me, so I sighed and admitted, "I hope she is, but I'm not sure. For all we know, they could be stupid, arrogant humans who heard we had plans to harm them and decided they wanted to throw the first punch."

"Will Tabitha forgive you if we have to kill them?"

I bit down on my lower lip a little harder than I'd intended as he vocalized the very question I had been too afraid to ask myself. "I don't know," I said quietly. "But I can't let that stop me from keeping my people safe."

Duke clapped a hand on my shoulder. I could tell on his face that he agreed with me; I could absolutely not put the A'li-uud in danger for fear of Tabitha's wrath, but there was also genuine sympathy on his stern features for my predicament. We looked at each other, and then we tipped our faces upwards and hopped on the winds.

***

It felt strange to have my warriors lined up in rows behind me without having Ca-es'a at my side or standing in the front. I hoped he was onboard the ship that would soon be landing, but, more than that, I hoped I would be seeing Tabitha in a matter of minutes. It was astounding to realize I had literally seen her off that morning because it felt like it had been days, even weeks. So much had happened in that short time, and I was worried she had dealt with just as many crazy, unpredicted events as I had.

    The sun was low in the sky now, as it was late in the day, nearing nightfall, but my village had never been more alive. Duke and I had recruited every single warrior in the village and even ventured to other smaller camps and communities within Campestria to call those warriors to duty as well. Some of their families had traveled with them to Campestria's capital, where we were gathered. Nearly every citizen of my own village was crowded outside of their homes and around the circular road which served as the meeting point. I had considered sending them back into their houses for their own safety, but I wasn't naïve. I knew that, if things didn't go amicably, they would be at just as much risk in their homes as they would be out in the open, and my people would most likely be more prepared to fight or flee if they weren't surprised by an attack.

None of the other Elders had arrived yet, but the breeze was wafting more insistently over my face than usual, and I knew they were coming. I had a tight knot in my stomach of nerves, not out of anxiety for what could happen when the humans landed but out of fear that Tabitha wasn't onboard, that something had happened to her. I clenched my teeth together tightly and kept my eyes trained on the sky above in an attempt to distract myself from the disquiet gripping my core.

Suddenly, Vi'den appeared in front of me, and Ma'ris materialized immediately after. Duke remained emotionless and still, but I jumped in surprise. Both aged Elders seemed more at ease than they had during Torik's trial.

"Are we the first?" Ma'ris gurgled.

"Yes," I replied.

The villagers surrounding us were eyeing Vi'den and Ma'ris with interest, most likely because of their dress, which was so different than Campestrians were accustomed to. Vi'den's purple and silver robes cascaded down into the dirt and seemed to sway in tune to the melody of the breezes. Ma'ris, on the other hand, was wearing shiny green robes which I was certain were woven from very thin strands of the same seaweed his warriors wore. It made his clothes look as though they were chronically wet, almost like he had just stepped out from the ocean, though there were no droplets falling from him. I could hear the Campestrians murmuring excitedly, and several children pointed.

"I think we have enough warriors," Vi'den said, studying the rows upon rows of A'li-uud lined up behind me with weapons in their hands or strapped to their hips. Between Duke and I, we had gathered one hundred men upward, and Tabitha had told me the *Paragon* was made up of a crew of less than that. I nodded in agreement with Vi'den.

Duke, however, looked doubtful. "We do not know what they have or how many humans are onboard," he said assertively. "I am willing to bring some of my own warriors to join and strengthen our numbers."

"There is no time for your warriors to make the journey from Montemba, I'm afraid," Vi'den said with a shake of his head. "No, this will have to do."

"It is plenty," Ma'ris chimed in.

I looked back to the sky, and, this time, I didn't look away when several more Elders arrived. Vi'den, Ma'ris, and Duke addressed them and informed them of our current status, and, when Kharid flew in, I heard him relating the newest information about the ship.

"It has been spotted over Maquarian waters," he announced in his thick, crimped accent. "It is coming this way. Even if the intent was not to land here, they might reconsider if they see us gathered in such great numbers."

"Then, here we will stay," Vi'den said firmly. I imagined him doing his characteristic head bob as he spoke, but I didn't look away from the heavens to confirm my suspicions.

When the final three Elders arrived, I was finally forced to tear my gaze away from the sky, which was no longer the brilliant turquoise of the day; it had melted into a rather royal color of blue. To my surprise, none of the villagers had returned to their homes out of boredom or anxiety. In fact, it seemed that more had gathered. I spotted my parents with my two young siblings near one of the walls which protected my palace, and our gazes met. Mother looked fearful and clung to my brother's shoulders as though he were about to fly away, and father seemed stoic and matter-of-fact as he held my sister in his arms. *Seeing them sent a spark of peace through me which came to rest in my stomach and eased my fears slightly.*

"Do we have a plan of action upon the arrival of the humans?" Kharid asked suddenly, interrupting the silence that had fallen.

Duke and I looked at one another, and I turned to Vi'den. "Under normal circumstances, we would hold a vote," he said. "In this case, I think it will simply be a matter of discussion."

"I think it ought to depend on what they do when they disembark," said Ma'ris.

"Yes, but we should have plans in place for any course of events that may unfold," Duke noted.

Crossing my arms over my chest, I glanced up at the sky again. The ship was nowhere in sight. "If they are peaceful, we hold our ground and speak with them. We should be open for negotiation if that's what they are seeking. I don't want a confrontation to result in the loss of my warriors if they happen to be onboard," I said calmly.

"We, of course, want to ensure the return of your warriors," Vi'den agreed. "And, as they belong to your tribe, I am comfortable with whatever you feel is best to secure them."

"Assuming the humans are not looking for war, I will attempt to have my warriors returned to me before any other proceedings," I said. "They went to space on my orders, and I owe it to them to do everything in my power to bring them back safely."

"Of course," Ma'ris agreed.

"So, if they are peaceful, we will get the warriors back," Duke said. "What will we do then?"

Vi'den pursed his lips slightly. "We will find out what it is they seek. Perhaps they are merely curious about us, or perhaps they wish to change our minds about destroying them. In any case, we do not attack without provocation."

"They might be here for the others," I said suddenly, an idea occurring to me. My eyes had drifted to the center of the circular road upon which we stood, where the vigibrach tree marked the entrance to the underground dungeon. "We still have the surviving members of the *Paragon* crash in our holding cells just below that tree. If Tabitha has told them there are other survivors, they might be coming to retrieve them."

"If that is the case, we cannot turn them over," Duke interjected at once. All eyes turned to him. "They know about us. Worse, the *Paragon* survivors will return to Earth and tell the story of being bombed by our people and held as hostages for months. That will incite a war between our two races."

"It may not," I contradicted. "They might just want to go home."

"Of course they want to go home," Duke said, rather scornfully. "Do you truly expect they will tell no one of their encounters once they get there?"

I stared at him and didn't answer. I knew he was right. If the ship was landing on Albaterra to free the imprisoned *Paragon* humans and we released them to return to their home planet, knowledge of us would spread like wildfire. It would reach the highest echelon of human authority, and just one survivor would have to tell his story to convince all of Earth that the A'li-uud were cruel, heartless creatures who needed to be stopped. Nevertheless, I was reminded of a conversation I'd had with Tabitha about what to do with her crewmembers. I had insisted it would be impossible for them to live safely on Albaterra because of the risk of vigilante A'li-uud acting out of fear and ignorance, yet it was equally as impossible to return them to Earth for the very reasons I was mulling over now. She had, in horror, asked if that only left the option of killing them, and I hadn't had an answer.

I had an answer now. "We have to let them go," I said with regretful decision. "We can't let them stay here, and we cannot murder them for the sake of solving a problem."

There was obvious disagreement on Duke's face, but Vi'den looked rather admiringly at me, and Ma'ris very clearly thought I was correct. The other Elders were listening intently to our exchange with deeply engrossed expressions on their faces, though they said nothing.

"Fine," Duke finally said. "So, this is our plan if they come peacefully. What do you suggest we do if they come looking for war?"

I wished I could've hesitated. I wished I didn't have to say the words which came out of my mouth so easily as they the air I breathed. Even as I said it, I felt immediate regret. Nevertheless, I knew it had to be done.

"We kill them."

Chapter 10

Tabitha

Seeing the terrain of Campestria blossoming out beneath the *Epitome* through the huge command center window as we descended to the ground was such an emotional upheaval that tears actually sprang into my eyes, and my throat was filled with a lump so big I almost couldn't breathe.

As we had dropped lower and lower, we all realized there were rows upon rows of A'li-uud lined up. I heard Captain Powell scoff and mutter, "All ready to attack, and we're supposed to sympathize with them?" I chose to ignore him, however, and scoured the faces of the A'li-uud until I found the one I was looking for. Standing at the front of the bunch with the other Elders all around him there was Rex, and, as his eyes lifted to the massive window. I was certain he could actually see me and our eyes met. My stomach tumbled with excitement and love, and a thought burst into my mind I never would have expected.

You're home.

The moment the *Epitome* came to a stop, I rushed from the window to the command center door, eager to fly into Rex's arms. Before I reached the threshold, however, Powell threw his arms around my waist and lifted me into the air, my legs flailing like octopus tentacles.

"Not so fast, Miss Bartel," he said in my ear. "I think we're going to need a little leverage."

"He's going to kill you," I hissed furiously, trying to kick his knees and shins.

I could almost feel his amused smile pressing into me from behind, and he asked, "Is this the Rex you've told me so much about?"

Instead of answering, I continued swinging my legs, trying to make contact with any part of him I could to make him release me. I felt my heel connect with his left knee, but he didn't flinch. If anything, his grip became all the tighter.

"I never thought there would come a day a human would fall in love with an alien," he said. His voice was almost a sickening purr. "But we can work with that. What do you think your beloved would do to make sure your pretty little head stayed attached to your body?"

"Get off of me!" I shouted, kicking again with much more vigor and vehemence than before.

"Keep it up, and I'll kill that dark bodyguard you've got," he snarled.

I went limp at once. Ca-es'a was so close to freedom I wasn't going to compromise it by struggling, and I told myself silently Rex would make this all right again as soon as we got off this nightmare of a ship.

"You're smarter than I thought, Miss Bartel," Powell said approvingly. "Shall we go see your boyfriend?"

Leanne, who had been watching with wide, terrified eyes and was calmly held by the bald lieutenant, met my gaze. She looked at me imploringly, begging me to keep my cool, but I looked away from her so she wouldn't see the furious, terrified tears threatening to douse my cheeks.

Captain Powell hauled me through the ship like a sack of potatoes, throwing me over his shoulder, striding with purpose. I knew I was nearly off the *Epitome* when the earthen smell of Campestrian air reached my nostrils, and, just a moment later, Powell descended a ramp with me in tow. The moment I saw the thick, beige grasses beneath his feet, I started twisting, trying to get away.

A roar filled the air, and I recognized the voice at once as Rex's. *I was struck by two bolts instantly; one of lust and love, and the other of terror he would put himself in danger to save me.* I wanted to call out to him, but, before I could,

Powell wrenched me from his shoulder and set me on the ground. He spun me around until I was facing the army of A'li-uud, the Elders, and Rex, who were near enough to make out their faces but far enough I would have to sprint to reach them before Powell could catch up. I felt a cool, sharp something against my throat, and Powell tipped my face upward by the chin so I could only see the heads of the A'li-uud rather than their entire bodies. *I realized he was holding me at knifepoint.*

"We are not here to fight," Powell called out. His voice seemed to disintegrate into the open expanse of prairie lands, but I knew that the A'li-uud had heard him by the distant sounds of clacking and clicking that was their native tongue. Then, quietly to me, he asked, "Do these things speak English?"

"Yes," I muttered back in a voice strained by the fear of accidentally slitting myself with the blade.

"I am Captain Powell of the *Epitome*," he continued loudly. I saw the eyes of the other Elders staring at him, but Rex's eyes were fixed solely on me, unmoving and intense. "We are here to retrieve the survivors of the *Paragon*."

The tall, slender form of Vi'den stepped forward, and Powell tightened the knife against my neck. Rex made a move to leap forward, but Vi'den threw out an arm to stop him. They both stood still in their places and looked at Powell, Rex with fury on his face and Vi'den with tolerance.

"I'll kill her if you come any closer," Powell threatened. "I'll slit her throat, and her blood can water the soil of your godforsaken planet."

"I will rip your head off with my bare hands," Rex barked suddenly.

His voice rang through my ears like the sweetest melody. Even in his angry, panicked, fearful tone, it was the most beautiful sound I had ever heard, and I actually began to weep with the sheer loveliness of it. Powell mistook my tears as fear, however, and I could feel his mouth spread into a grin against my ear.

"You must be Rex," he said. "Miss Bartel has told me all about you."

I heard a growl from Rex's throat which carried across the breeze and lit upon me. I could feel his restraint so clearly in the growl I wondered how he was managing to keep himself from launching at Powell and doing the exact thing he'd threatened.

Shuffling noises behind me made my ears prick, and then I saw Ca-es'a appear on my right in my peripheral vision. There was a human behind him with a gun pressed against the base of Ca-es'a's skull. I was unable to turn my head and look at him, but, out of the corner of my eyes, I could see Ca-es'a wore a stoic expression that masked the kind of rage only a warrior could possess.

"Bring out the humans you're holding hostage!" Powell shouted commandingly to the Elders. "Bring them out, or I will kill her and make this one eat the corpse!"

I heard a flutter of clacking sounds, and Vi'den tightened his grip around Rex. Several warriors left their places in the rows and moved toward the vigibrach tree which stood regally in the center of the dirt road circle. I had lost sight of them before they descended the stairs that led to the underground dungeons. For several long, silent minutes, I could do nothing but stand and look back at Rex as he stared at me, his chest heaving in and out dramatically. *Even beneath the fury that swirled in his eyes, I could see such love it rendered me breathless. I hoped he could see the same reflecting back at him in my gaze.*

Finally, I heard the pattering of many footsteps, and Powell's head turned. As it did, the blade pressed into my skin slightly, and I felt the pain of several layers of skin being sliced. I cried out, and he relaxed his hold a little, but Rex jumped forward.

"Don't!" Powell bellowed, thrusting the blade back against my throat so hard I gagged, and hot, thick blood dribbled down onto my collar. I knew I had been cut open, but I didn't know how bad the wound was, and I had no way to find out.

Rex froze. He had crossed about half of the distance between the A'li-uud and us, and he was in a crouched, cat-like position. I knew he would have been able to kill Powell before Powell would have ever had the chance to slit my throat, but I also knew Rex was too afraid of risking my life to take the chance. He hovered over the grasses like a lion on the hunt, and his eyes were nearly imperceptible as they had narrowed into such thin slits they were mere lines on his blue face. His expression was one so twisted it could no longer be categorized as rage, fury, anger or any other human emotion; he had transcended normal response and had elevated into something only felt by the ethereal.

"Let her go," Rex snarled. The sound was almost unrecognizable.

"Sorry, friend," Captain Powell said unapologetically. "I need something to keep you from doing some freaky alien mind-control thing."

"They can't do *mind control*," I said. My voice was more of a crackling squeak than a full, rounded tone, but the words came out before I could stop them. "They're not witches."

"You don't know—"

Captain Powell's words were cut off suddenly as Rex launched himself forward again. I was sent rolling away as my love's strong, lithe, muscular body tackled Captain Powell to the ground, and I groaned in pain as my arm was crushed beneath me. My concern overrode the sting, however, and I bolted upright. In the grasses rolled Rex and Powell, with Powell's knife-wielding hand lifted over Rex's back. I shouted an intelligible cry and jumped to my feet, racing forward to slam my knees over Powell's arm. As I pinned it to the ground, I wrestled the knife from his hand before skittering away on all fours like a crab. Rex was straddling Powell, and he was pummeling fist after fist into Powell's face in a manner identical to Pugna'ta when she had assaulted me.

In response, all of the *Epitome* crew who had brought forth the A'li-uud captives and had been holding them at gunpoint rushed forward to the brawl, leaving the A'li-uud unattended. Ca-es'a was the first to react in his freedom. With a jump that could have rivaled a kangaroo or a rabbit, he sprang into the air and came down to land on one of the humans' backs. His hands wrapped around the man's throat and squeezed. Within seconds the man's face had gone from pale peach to a purplish-blue which could have rivaled the skin tone of any A'li-uud present.

"No!" I shouted, shooting across the ground to Ca-es'a. I grabbed his ankle and pulled, wrenching him from the man's back. "Don't kill him!"

Ca-es'a didn't even look at me; he just sprang again. This time, he intercepted a gun one of the men had raised and pointed at Rex's scuffling back, and he threw it so far it disappeared before it even hit the ground. The other A'li-uud were in hand-to-hand combat with the other members of the *Epitome*, and then I heard a war cry.

As I turned around, I saw the rows of warriors who had been lined up whooping and stampeding toward the scene of the fight. I watched in horror as human after human dropped to the ground with lacerated throats, missing limbs, and broken necks. In the span of mere minutes, nearly all of the *Epitome* soldiers were on the ground, either dead or gravely injured. Rex was still on top of Powell, beating him within an inch of his life, and I started to sprint toward him to pull him off.

Before I could, Leanne seized my hand and yanked me backward so hard I fell onto my rear.

"You can't!" She cried, helping to pull me to my feet. "You'll get killed just by getting involved!"

"Leanne!" I gasped. I wanted to say more, to insist we had to stop this, to tell her that innocent people were dying because everyone was afraid of the other. I wanted to make her help me get Rex away from Powell before he killed him, too. I couldn't form the words, though. The scene unfolding before me was one of such horror and bloodshed I couldn't form the words—I couldn't even think them—and all I could do was grip her hand tightly as tears rained from my eyes.

"Enough."

The voice was not a shout or a roar, but it boomed across the endless prairie as though it had come through a loudspeaker. I knew it at once it was Vi'den, and I felt such a flood of relief for his authority and presence I actually dropped back to my knees, nearly tugging Leanne down with me.

As though controlled like puppets, the A'li-uud ceased their fighting immediately. The few humans who remained standing, including the bald lieutenant, looked unsure as to if they should use the opportunity to slay the aliens nearest them or if they should listen to the command. All heads turned toward Vi'den. He hadn't moved from his spot where the rows of A'li-uud had originated, but he spoke so boldly it sounded as though he were mere feet away.

"There will be no more senseless bloodshed," he said. His white eyes were flashing fiercely, and I couldn't tell if he was angry or just insistent. "We are fighting for the same thing. You have our people, and we have yours. The only solution is to make an exchange."

The bald lieutenant, Lieutenant Maylor, looked down at his captain, who was on the ground beneath Rex's body with a face so covered in blood he was unrecognizable. He made a strange, inhuman gurgling noise, and the lieutenant stiffened. He looked back up to Vi'den, and something in his face had changed. He had taken charge.

"Agreed," he said.

"Please bring forth the survivors," Vi'den announced to the nearest Elder, who had skin almost as dark as Ca-es'a and wore a hood of strange fabric over his head. The Elder nodded and made a motion with his hand. My *Paragon* crewmates were released from their shackles one by one until they were all released, and they stood in place with uncertain looks on their faces. Vi'den's eyes slid over each one. "You are free to join your kind."

The captain was the first to step forward, and he moved almost on tiptoe as though he was afraid he would step on a bomb. I nodded to him encouragingly, and his stance relaxed as he continued forward to the ship. The others followed quickly behind him, scurrying like mice. Leanne's hand was in mine, gripping so tightly sweat formed between our skin. I could feel her wanting to go to the others and reassure them, but I squeezed a little harder to impress upon the importance of her remaining beside me for the moment.

Lieutenant Maylor greeted the captain with a clap on the back, and then he said to Vi'den, "You can have yours."

Vi'den inclined his head. "Warriors, please return to your positions," he said. The warriors retreated at once, filing back into their rows, and the remaining A'li-uud from my crew went with them. Only Ca-es'a remained behind, standing next to Rex, who was still on top of Powell with a fist retracted in the air, ready to strike again. Ca-es'a pressed a hand to Rex's neck and said something in the native language.

In English, Rex snapped, "Not until I kill him." Then, his fist thrust forward again and crushed against Powell's nose.

Chapter 11

Rex

I thought my fight with Torik would be the only time I would ever wish to senselessly kill another. I honestly believed it would never again be a desire for me to take a life.

I was wrong.

When I'd seen Tabitha brought out from that ship over the human's shoulder and then seen him place a knife to her throat like she was a hicorn about to be dinner, something inside of me had erupted with such heat and hatred, I'd lost all sense of who I was. I no longer recognized my surroundings or those beside me. The knowledge that my parents, my siblings, my villagers, my warriors, and my Elder brotherhood were all around watching me had absolutely no meaning. I didn't care how many witnesses were present to see me destroy the human who was threatening the life of the woman I loved.

    The first contact my knuckles made with his face was like a spiritual release. I could feel every ounce of rage pouring from my hands into his jaw, his cheek, his nose, and when the red stream of blood spilled from the corner of his mouth, I was riddled with the glory of redemption. I struck him again, and then again, and then again, over and over until I lost complete control of myself and watched my fists flying back and forth almost like I was a third party looking on. I could actually see myself attacking him in my mind's eye. *There was the Rex that was atop him, barreling rage into the human's head, and there was the Rex standing off to the side, watching as the pale skin quickly became ruddy and stained with the bloody evidence of the assault.*

It was at that moment that I knew Tabitha was my world. I knew I loved her; I even knew I would have done anything for her. This was the first time, however, that I knew with every fiber of my being she was the sun around which I orbited. Without her, there was nothing; no life, no love, and no purpose. To have seen her a mere strike away from death was like watching a black hole swallowing up Albaterra and rendering everything into non-existence. Not only would I have done anything in my power to save her, but I would have slain myself, skinned my body alive and plucked every muscle from my form, to ensure her safety. Tabitha had become my whole being.

    I didn't know why I stopped when Vi'den gave his command. It shouldn't have mattered.

Seeing the human still and limp beneath me, his features unrecognizable for the sheer pool of blood that had blossomed on his face had not satisfied my bloodlust. In fact, it made me all the more eager to wrench the life from his soul and send him into the oblivion of death. Hearing Vi'den, however, pulled me out of my hateful trance and brought me back to reality.

As the hostages were exchanged and Ca-es'a laid a hand upon my neck, I felt frighteningly empty. It was as though Tabitha had been killed after all and I had nothing left.

"Come, Wise One," Ca-es'a murmured softly. "All is well."

I looked up at him, twisting my neck to see him properly. His face was one riddled with concern, either for my sanity or for the consequences of my actions. I then twisted my neck the other way, my eyes flicking from one face to another until I saw Tabitha. She was on her knees, her hand clutching Leanne's, and her face was streaked with the tears she cried when she was emotional. *Her tears had always fascinated me; the first time she had cried, I had been perplexed by the strange moisture dribbling down her face.* Now, though, I understood she cried when her emotions were so strong she just couldn't hold them in, and to see her in such a state sent me to the heights of protectiveness.

"Not until I kill him," I said to Ca-es'a. Then, I sank my fist into the human's face again.

Ca-es'a's hand swung down and circled around my arm, and he yanked with all his might. I was pulled off of the man entirely, falling onto the grasses beneath us on my back, and I jumped to my feet within the second. Ca-es'a looked at me with a mixed expression, partially stern and partially frightened. *He had never seen me in such a fit before, and, frankly, I had never felt such an intense rush of emotion before, either.*

"You have to stop!" He cried. He was speaking our native language, and I could see the humans around looking at us in confusion out of my peripheral vision. "This is not our way!"

"Stand down, Ca-es'a," I hissed, also speaking the native tongue.

I moved to dive back on top of the human again, but Vi'den spoke in such a terrifying voice I froze mid-jump.

"Rexstrenu'us, you will cease at once."

My fist was still lifted into the air, poised next to my ear to sail into what was left of the captain's nose, and my knees were bent in a crouching spring. I turned slowly, my arm lowering to my side, and looked at Vi'den.

"He was going to kill Tabitha," I said. We were speaking English again, and the humans seemed relieved to understand the exchange.

"But he did not," Vi'den replied rather softly. I didn't even know if his voice carried over the breeze to ears that were not A'li-uud, but I didn't care. "We do not kill nonsensically."

"He must pay for his crime," I said as the anger finally started to deflate within me.

Vi'den stared at me with such intensity I could feel his gaze burning on my skin. "It is more important that you offer support to Tabitha. She needs you now."

I turned my head to look at Tabitha. She was still kneeling, still clutching Leanne's hand, and it looked as though every bit of strength she had ever possessed was the only thing keeping her from imploding into a million little pieces. The tear stains on her cheeks shone like aspex sparkles in the setting sunlight. I let myself look to Leanne, and something in her eyes told me what to do.

In an instant, I crossed the space between myself and Tabitha. I dropped to my knees and took Tabitha in my arms, pulling her against me so tightly her body seemed to become one with mine.

The moment our skin touched, she burst. Sobs poured from her like water from a stream, billowing outward, filling me with her sorrow. I clutched her head, tangling my fingers in her hair and holding her head against my chest as her tears slithered over the muscled curves and angles of my bare chest.

"I'm sorry," I whispered to her. "I'm so sorry."

"I was so scared," she whispered back. I could feel her lips moving against me with each word.

"It's all right. It's all fine now," I reassured, stroking my fingers through her hair and brushing the fingers of my other hand down her back.

Silence filled my prairie kingdom as I held her, rocking slightly from side to side until her weeping faded into sniffles, which then faded into silence. She turned her face up to me, and I crushed my lips against hers with such ferocity that, had we not been surrounded by every A'li-uud in my village and others, I would have taken her right there. The blood at her throat was beginning to coagulate and dry, leaving streaks much like her tears on her collarbone, though they were streaks of a dull red hue. I tilted her head up a little further to examine the wound.

"Does it hurt?" I murmured, pressing a fingertip to the very edge.

"It's fine," she whimpered. She dropped her chin and kissed me again, and then I helped her to her feet.

"The Elders must convene," Vi'den announced. He was looking at the human with the bald head who had taken control when I'd rendered the captain useless. "I ask that you wait."

The bald man considered this before grudgingly saying, "Fine."

Vi'den looked at me, and I knew he was brandishing me over. I hooked an arm around Tabitha's waist and brought her with me, leaving Leanne standing alone near the other humans. At first, Vi'den looked as though he wanted to tell me to leave Tabitha behind and come alone, but he seemed to reconsider when he saw the look on my face. Once we were near enough to form a small circle with the other Elders, Vi'den spoke.

"I do not believe we have any reason to prevent their leaving," he said. "All confrontation has simply been in defense of ourselves. There has been no malicious intent."

"If we let them go, they will go back to Earth with knowledge of us," Kharid pointed out.

"That is unacceptable," Duke said a little aggressively.

Tabitha was curled into my body, the side of her face pressed against my chest and her eyes turned down to the ground. I didn't know if she was listening, or if she even cared about the conversation, but I was feeling more at peace having her against me than I had since she'd left that morning. I didn't feel a need to insist she contributes her opinion.

"We don't have a choice." I didn't mean to say it, but I couldn't help it. "It has come to the time when humans will learn of our existence, and the only thing we can do is accept it. We're not going to kill them just to avoid future problems."

"You say that while you're covered in the captain's blood," Duke replied. There was a very small smile on his face, a rare occurrence for him but not an altogether unwelcome one.

"I know," I said, nodding with slight shame. "But they wouldn't be safe living here, and I'm sure they wouldn't want to anyway. They have families and friends back on Earth. We need to let them go."

"What are we to do then?" Ma'ris burbled. "Do we prepare for a war we are not certain is to come?"

"It doesn't matter," I said back sharply. "There is no other choice."

Vi'den looked downward at my chest, and I realized he was looking at Tabitha. "Tabitha, what say you?"

She turned her head upward, and the expression on her face was clearly surprised at even being asked to weigh in on an Elder issue. Then, in a small voice, she murmured, "Let them go."

I cradled her head in my hand and looked around at the other Elders. "Anyone else?" I asked a little confrontationally.

There was silence, and Vi'den nodded. "So it is."

We all turned back toward the humans, and Vi'den, Tabitha, and I walked back to them. The bald man stood a little taller as we approached, as though he was expecting another fight to break out. "Well?" He asked.

"You are welcome to take the *Paragon* survivors," Vi'den said. He spoke rather kindly, more than I would have. "We wish you a safe trip back to Earth."

The man looked startled by this turn of events and glanced from my face to Vi'den's and back again. He addressed me as he asked, "That's it? You're not going to try to kill us or blow us out of the sky?"

"That's not what we are," I replied rather sharply. "We are not a conquering people. We only wish to live in respect and peace."

He frowned slightly, and I could tell he was wondering if my statement was a jab at him or his race. He wouldn't have been wrong on either count, but, after a moment, he seemed to dismiss any additional consideration and nodded. "Okay. We'll need a few minutes to get everyone settled onboard and reestablish command. You did a good number on my captain."

I just stared at him unblinkingly, and he stared back for a brief moment before he turned around and began barking orders to the other humans. Leanne scurried over to us and pulled Tabitha away from me to hug her.

"I hate to say it," I heard her murmur, "but I didn't think it would turn out like this."

"Neither did I," Tabitha admitted.

As they hugged and talked quietly amongst themselves, I turned to Vi'den and spoke in the native A'li-uud language. "Do you think we're being wise letting them go? We've observed humanity long enough to know that, once word gets back to their superiors, they will come for us, either to destroy us or to study us."

"I do not know," Vi'den answered honestly. He looked thoughtful and not at all frightened or concerned. "I believe we will be seeing humans again in the relatively near future, but I cannot say if it will be on their whim or ours."

"You intend to send A'li-uud to Earth?"

"I intend to explore the idea," he said. "It will be a topic for the Forum, to be sure. Would you not desire to visit Tabitha?"

Suddenly, my heart plummeted into my stomach. It hadn't even occurred to me that she would be amongst those humans who were returning to Earth, that she wouldn't remain behind. I could literally have been spending the last minutes of her time on Albaterra discussing the future of the A'li-uud with Vi'den rather than with her.

Turning slowly, I looked at her. She and Leanne had broken apart, but they were still deep in conversation. Without answering Vi'den, I started to walk over to her, and, when I reached her, I took her hands. She looked at me in surprise, not having realized I'd walked up behind her.

"What's wrong?" She asked the moment her eyes fell on my face.

Something behind my eyes burned, and I wondered if this was what she felt when she cried.

I opened my mouth to tell her I loved her, that I'd miss her, but I couldn't say the words. Instead, I croaked desperately, "Stay with me."

Chapter 12

Tabitha

"What?"

I wasn't sure I had heard him correctly, and I immediately assumed the dramatic tumult of events from the course of the day had rattled me to the point of incomprehension.

"Stay with me," he repeated, and I knew I hadn't misheard him after all.

I blinked, trying to process his words. "What do you mean?"

"Don't go back to Earth. Stay here with me on Albaterra," he pleaded. His eyes were wider than I had ever seen them, and he looked so desperate it was as if he was begging for his life. "Live in my palace with me. I'll give you everything you want. Just, please, don't go."

"I-I don't—" My mouth opened and closed like a fish underwater as I searched desperately for some way to reply. "I don't know if I can."

"Of course you can," he said insistently, squeezing my hands even more tightly. His eyes were plunging into mine, burrowing within, seeking my soul.

Every bit of myself was screaming to accept the offer at once. I wanted to shriek my agreement, throw my arms around him, and kiss him with more passion than I'd ever possessed. It was as if he was a magnet and I was a chunk of metal being pulled to him. Yet, I couldn't say the words that kept running through my mind. All I could do was shake my head wordlessly.

"I love you," he whispered. His face was slowly changing, becoming sadder and sadder until he looked utterly broken, and I realized he thought I was rejecting him. The realization snapped me back into control of myself, and I immediately regained the ability to talk.

"Of course I'll stay," I said in a whoosh of breath. "I love you too. I don't want to be without you."

His face lit up so brightly it could have been pitch-dark out, and I would've been able to see clearly. He swooped forward, and then our lips were pressed together so tightly that there wasn't a bit of air between. My tongue intertwined with his, rolling and twisting and dancing, and I relished his flavor like it was the last thing I would ever taste. *Every single bit of me felt lighter than it ever had.*

I heard a gentle cough behind me, and Rex and I broke apart. Looking over my shoulder, I saw Leanne standing a short distance away, looking at us awkwardly. I planted another kiss on Rex's mouth, much briefer this time, and bounded over to her.

"Rex asked me to stay on Albaterra," I told her joyously.

"I heard," she replied. There was a smile on her face, but I could easily see sorrow beneath the grin, and I furrowed my brow.

"What's wrong?" I asked, suddenly concerned.

She shook her head, still smiling and still sorrowful. "I'm just going to miss you," she admitted, reaching forward to squeeze my hand in hers. "We'll probably never see each other again."

The thought hadn't occurred to me, and my heart sank as I realized that what she said was true. I frowned and shook my head. "No, why don't you stay, too? Rex is an Elder, he can get you a great place to stay, or you could even stay at the palace with us. It's big enough—"

"Tabitha," she interrupted, leaning toward me earnestly. She gave me a knowing look. "You know that's not going to happen."

"But why not?" I persisted. "Really, it's so gorgeous here, and—"

"Honey." She brushed a strand of my hair behind my ear, and I saw tears forming in her eyes. "I can't stay here. I've got too much Armani and Louis Vuitton and Chanel to wear; I'm not one for the skins and straw types of fashions." We both laughed tearfully, and I nodded reluctantly.

"I know," I said, brushing my own eyes. "I know. But I had to try."

She laughed again and pulled me against her. I hugged her with all my might, realizing this could very well have been the last time I would ever hug my best friend. She kissed my cheek affectionately, and then we stepped back.

"I'm going to miss you," she said mournfully.

"Me too," I replied. I was only one more word away from blubbering, so I tried to make a joke. "It's not like we'll be able to email."

We both broke then, sobs pouring forth from us with absolutely no restraint, and we threw our arms around one another once more. I heard Rex's footsteps behind me, and I felt his hand on my shoulder, so I pulled away from Leanne and wiped my palm over my face to clear it of the tears misting my vision. I looked at Rex.

"They're ready," he murmured apologetically. "At least, they need everyone on board."

"Okay," I whispered. Leanne and I looked at each other again and hugged one final time.

"I love you," she murmured in my ear.

"I love you too," I said, squeezing her tightly. "So much."

As she climbed the ramp into the ship, she looked back once and met my gaze. I lifted my hand in a wave, an action she mirrored, and then she was gone. Once her back disappeared into the *Epitome*, I whirled around and threw myself into Rex's arms, sobbing stormily. I already missed

Leanne desperately, and I cried partially for that, but my tears were mainly from the sheer overwhelming emotions of the day finally finding their release.

Finally, Rex took my face in his hands and tilted it up to look at him. "I'm sorry," he said. He truly looked like it. "I know you'll miss her."

"Yes, I will," I replied honestly. Then, allowing a smile to break through my misery, I said, "But I'm never going to have to miss you."

He chuckled and brushed the tip of his nose against mine. "No, you won't. You're going to be around me so much you'll get sick of me."

I giggled and shook my head. "Impossible."

***

His body was on top of mine, his blue skin hot and smooth and taut. I shivered as his fingertips skimmed the curve of my hip, traveling down the length of my thigh before swooping back up along my inner leg, seeking my most intimate of areas. His touch was confident and capable, but his expression reminded me he was anxious about doing something wrong. We had only been together once before, after all.

"Go ahead," I urged him softly, pressing my lips to his chin in a delicate kiss. "Please."

His palm cupped my womanhood, and his thumb found the sensitive little button which sent me into writhing spasms the moment he pressed down on it. He pulsed his digit in consistent throbs, and he quirked a questioning brow at me.

"Circles," I gasped.

He obliged at once, rubbing his thumb in a series of smooth, seamless circles over the nerve-laden surface. My hips bucked upward, but he pushed them down with his other hand. Even in his uncertainty about how to be with a human, he was still the dominant, commanding leader I had fallen in love with, and it only served to spike my arousal to new heights. I bit down on my lip, looking up at him through my lashes, and his gaze became shadowed and husky.

"Don't look at me like that," he growled.

I blinked, surprised, and panted between sharp breaths of stimulation, "Why?"

"Because I won't be able to restrain myself," he said, dropping his head to my shoulder, grazing my skin with his teeth.

The growl in his tone as he said the words sent a flash of heat to the apex of my thighs, and I moaned. "Then take me," I begged.

I didn't have to ask him twice. He pushed himself up onto his knees, circled his length with his hand, and guided it to my opening. The moment he made contact, however, he paused. I reached down and took his member in my own hand, scooting my rear down the bed a little to encourage him to enter me further. He inhaled in one quick breath, and I plunged him into me.

Every inch of my body seemed to explode with delight as he filled me with his entire self. He threw his head back with his own sensations of euphoria. I could feel his hips sliding forward very slightly before he'd jerk them back, and I realized he was practicing unexpected and rather unwelcome restraint.

"Take me!" I cried again.

He suddenly hooked his hands on either side of my waist and flipped us both over until he was on his back and I was straddling him on top. I pressed my palms to his chest to balance myself, and then I began rocking my body back and forth while lifting myself up and down on my knees. Rex groaned loudly, jerking his head back into the pillows and focusing his ghostly eyes on my figure, watching the sway and bounce of my breasts with each movement. I could feel his gaze as intensely as if it was his fingers, and it turned me on so much more that I started bouncing twice as fast.

Rex's fingers were still clenching my waist in the same place they had to roll us over, and he started to use the leverage to help lift me up and bring me back down atop him. Faster and faster, our bodies moved in synchronization, taking each other, becoming one. I was breathing in short, quick gasps, and his breath sounded just as coarse and shaky as my own. *All we knew was each other, all we felt was each other, and all we cared about was each other.*

"I love you," he purred breathlessly.

"I love you too," I cried back. Then, I broke apart.

The dark bedroom unraveled around me, disintegrating into nothing but cloudy powder and flame. *The only thing I could see was the whiteness of Rex's eyes; nothing else existed.* My entire body, from the very tips of my fingers to the smallest toes on my feet, had come alive and danced with powerful, gripping pleasure. The climax was so intense I truly believed in the midst of it that I had died and gone to Heaven. Beneath me, Rex groaned, and I felt him start to shudder beneath me. My legs, one on either side of him, were clutching his body so tightly I actually trembled right along with him as he peaked. His rough cries filled my ears. My mind and my being, and his pleasure became mine.

    When we slowed to a stop, I collapsed on top of him, our chests pressing against each other and our breath mingling together. He brought his lips to my forehead, kissing me sweetly and lovingly. His skin, even warmer than usual, was as comforting as an electric blanket on a cool autumn night, and I could hear his heart thudding against my ear. *That heart thudded for me, just as mine thudded for him. Our love had survived and brought us out on the other side stronger than ever.*

I was the human girl who had fallen in love with an alien, and I would never have had it any other way.

The End

Thank you for reading Albaterra Invasion! I am sure you like it! Please post your honest review on Amazon If it is possible! It will be helpful and encouraging for me.

Albaterra Abduction is coming soon!

Stay Tuned and connect with me on my platforms

Printed in Great Britain
by Amazon